FROM TEXT TO TXTING

FROM TEXT TO

TXTING

New Media in the Classroom

Edited by Paul Budra & Clint Burnham

INDIANA UNIVERSITY PRESS

Bloomington & Indianapolis

This book is a publication of

Indiana University Press
601 North Morton Street
Bloomington, Indiana 47404-3797 USA

www.iupress.indiana.edu

Telephone orders 800-842-6796
Fax orders 812-855-7931

MANUFACTURED IN THE
UNITED STATES OF AMERICA

Library of Congress
Cataloging-in-Publication Data

From text to txting : new media
in the classroom / edited by Paul
Budra and Clint Burnham.
    p. cm.
    Includes index.
    ISBN 978-0-253-00310-2 (cl : alk.
paper) – ISBN 978-0-253-00578-6 (pb :
alk. paper) – ISBN 978-0-253-00720-9
(eb) 1. Educational technology – Social
aspects. 2. Education – Effect of
technological innovations on. 3. Popular
culture – Effect of technological
innovations on. 4. Digital media. 5.
Social media. I. Budra, Paul Vincent,
[date] II. Burnham, Clint, [date]
    LB1028.3.F77 2012
    371.33 – dc23   2012004593

1 2 3 4 5   17 16 15 14 13 12

For my mother, Gay Budra
P. B.

For my father, Lee Burnham
C. B.

Contents

Acknowledgments

We would like to thank Simon Fraser University and the Office of Research Services for providing financial support for this project in the form of a University Publications Fund Grant and a President's Research Start-Up Grant. The intellectual generosity of our colleagues in SFU's English Department was an inspiration, while the commitment of the dean of arts and social sciences to excellence in university teaching was a potent reminder that any theoretical practice faces its most important test in the classroom. Thanks to all of them. Finally, we would like to thank our contributors for their insight, creativity, and patience.

Introduction

PAUL BUDRA AND CLINT BURNHAM

This book is a response to two changes in humanities education since the 1980s: on the one hand, there has been an explosion of popular, paraliterary, and digital cultural forms, which have an increasing grip on our students; on the other hand (but not entirely unrelated), there is a need for humanities departments to change their tools for remediation in the face of demographic and textual sea changes.[1] In an age when the word "text" is increasingly used as a metaphor (the text of the ----), when "read" can mean any interpretive act (a reading of a photograph), when screens have replaced books, emoticons have reintroduced the pictograph, and students are infinitely more familiar with the storylines of video games than the plots of Shakespeare's plays, humanities departments risk becoming (even further) marginalized in the academy unless they retool. Academic literary critics who do not engage with the profound shifts in the delivery of narrative, verse, and argument stand on the cusp of becoming curators of an outdated print culture, antiquarians of the book. The contributors to *this* book believe that literary critics should be doing just the opposite: with our knowledge of literary history and form, our skills of close reading and cultural contextualization, literary critics should be interpreting, assessing, and explaining the effects that the remediation of print is having *now* to a populace that, for the most part, simply accepts these innovations as technological fashion. The chapters in this book, then, seek to address the question of the value of the skills that literary studies promote in an age when more people read "tweets" than essays and text messages than newspapers. In this introduction we would like to accomplish two tasks, the first of which is to argue that literary studies has to recognize the historic mutability of its object(s). These texts have swung in and out of historical fashion (and fascination) and they have come to be seen, increasingly, as signifying practices. Second, we argue that such studies today should take their cue from the abundance of critical methods to be found both in literary history and in parallel or emergent disciplines. We can, and should, engage with the literary-critical practices to be found in theory, in popular discourse, and in dialogue with the historical situation of our classrooms and students. This is not to say that there are not difficulties, and we address these challenges too.

The reluctance of some literary critics to make this engagement is partly driven by a misunderstanding of what constitutes the subject of their study. Both Roland Barthes and Raymond Williams have argued for the comparative recentness of "literature" as a category of imaginative writing.[2] The etymology of the term seems to support their claim: the English word "literature" did not appear until late in the fourteenth century and then it meant an "acquaintance with 'letters' or books" (OED), in short, knowledge of written culture, a sort of secondary literacy. The word does not take on the meaning "[l]iterary work or production; the activity or profession of a man of letters; the realm of letters" until the late eighteenth century. As for the most common definition now, "[l]iterary productions as a whole; the body of writings produced in a particular country or period, or in the world in general," that did not appear until a decade or so into the nineteenth century. This understanding of the literary and the academic field of study it generated seems to have given literature scholars a blinkered notion of the scope of their subject: literary studies started sometime in the late eighteenth century in response to the proliferation of texts and the bourgeois phenomenon of recreational reading and so it is defined by text and print. Period.

But Barthes and, especially, Williams were making polemical points with their radical historicization of the term. And while they are certainly right about the proliferation of the text due to print technology, they are demonstrably wrong in the assertion of the newness of the literary as a conceptual category because they ignore the classical roots of the term: "*Littera* means letter, and *litteratura* in Latin was a translation of the Greek word *grammatiké,* the knowledge of reading and writing, as Quintilian tells us in his *Institutiones*" (Wellek 16). Classical writers made fine distinctions within this broad meaning: "In Cicero . . . we find the terms *Graecase literae, historia litteris nobis,* and *stadium litterarum.* The term *litteratura* is used by him in the sense of erudition, literary culture, when he speaks of Caesar having *littera-tura* in a list of qualities" (Wellek 17). And by the second century CE the term was being used to designate a specific body of writing—holy writ—to distinguish it from other and pagan writing.[3]

We do not need the evidence of patristic distinctions, however, to recognize the tenuousness of Barthes's and Williams's claim, for "the recency of 'literature' . . . does not prove the absence of a unitary term for the central genres earlier" (Fowler 9). Too, value rankings are not historically stable: yesterday's literary trash has a way of slipping into today's canon. Ben Jonson was ridiculed in 1616 for presuming to publish his plays in a folio as though they were real literature (that is, poetry) rather than popular entertainment. Novels were considered misleading fictions in the seventeenth century and were dismissed as an "effeminate" entertainment. Comic books were considered not only childish trash, but so morally dangerous that they were the subject of a U.S. Senate subcommittee in 1954 at which psychiatrist and anti-comics crusader Fredric Wertham declared, "Hitler was a beginner compared to the comic-book industry."[4] But early modern English drama is now recognized as one of the great literary accomplishments of world history; the novel is perhaps the most ubiquitous literary experience in the world; and in 1992 a comic book won a special Pulitzer Prize. What happened?

One of three scenarios. The first, and most common, is that a marginalized category of writing produced something so good that critics and the public made it an exception. Art Spiegelman's *Maus* was a comic book, but a deeply complex comic book about the most serious subject in modern history: the Holocaust. It won a literary award. It became, de facto, literature. Similarly, science fiction, long relegated to pulp magazines and teenage boys' closets, was used by "serious" writers such as George Orwell and Aldous Huxley to produce novels that could not be dismissed on the basis of their category. The second is that a critic or school of critics mounted a defense of a marginalized form and successfully rehabilitated it. The legitimization of the novel is, in large part, due to the efforts of French critic Pierre-Daniel Huet. In the late seventeenth century he defended what he called "Romances" on both pedagogical and moral grounds: "Nothing so much refines and polishes Wit; conduces so much to the Forming and Advancing it to the Approbation of the World, as the Reading of Romances. These are the Dumb Tutors, which succeed those of the College, and teach us how to Live and Speak by a more Persuasive and Instructive Method than their's [sic]" (qtd. in Williams, Novel and Romance 40–41). The third is a historical reconsideration of a form. Ben Jonson may have been ridiculed for treating his plays as though they were poems, but during the Restoration his works and, especially, those of his contemporary Shakespeare were dusted off for the newly reopened theaters. They were staged, edited, and later disseminated throughout the British Empire as proof of England's parallel imperium of letters.

This third possibility need not be so dramatically geopolitical. Shifts in literary theory can resurrect and reinvigorate both dubious literary categories and specific texts. Gothic literature, especially in lurid articulations such as Matthew Gregory Lewis's Ambrosio, or, The Monk, was long dismissed as a sort of morbid pornography for wan and socially inept teenagers. Late twentieth-century criticism, however, which fetishized the transgressive, fixated on representations of sexuality, and deconstructed notions of the self, adopted the Gothic as its own mad scientist's laboratory of cultural exegesis.[5] Similarly, children's literature was revealed to be an extraordinarily complex cultural product, and graduate students began writing papers on the subversive Mr. Toad. Individual books that had been dismissed for such small problems as clichéd writing, flat characterization, and laughable plots were redeemed in university lecture halls by witty young professors who bent the texts to their political, historical, cultural, and sexual agendas. And so David Lodge's fictional Robyn Penrose ("A character who, rather awkwardly . . . doesn't herself believe in the concept of character"; 21) lectures on the industrial landscapes described in nineteenth-century novels, using them to underline the fact that "industrial capitalization is phallocentric" (49). Bad literature proved good fodder for cultural analysis. And as the books were ordered en masse for mega-classes of freshmen, publishers took note. Yesterday's dime store novel was Penguinified and moved to that exclusive shelf in the mall's bookstore marked "Literature."

It is this professionalization of literary studies in the academy—not literature itself, not taxonomies, not value judgments, not shifts in the appreciation of a specific literary genre—that is relatively new. The "English School" at Oxford was not founded until 1894, and then over objections that the study of such an idle subject would prove "a miserably inadequate training, however well taught" (qtd. in Palmer 111). The original curriculum of that school contained no literature written after 1800, and fully half of its content predated Shakespeare. The approaches taken to the literature were largely linguistic and philological.

It was not until well into the twentieth century that English departments came to dominate arts faculties, and that domination was short-lived. While an English degree might have been sufficient credentialing for entry into industry and many professions up until the 1960s, the next decade saw a rise in managerial science and a broad shift toward a technology-driven academy that suddenly made English majors the butt of cruel, although perhaps accurate, jokes on many a campus. As John Guillory and Paul Delany have pointed out, it was at this exact moment of incipient institutional marginality that arts departments in universities became political. Scholars in these departments used the tools provided by French theory to dissect the cultural artifacts in their canon—to dissect the whole idea of canonicity—in order to demonstrate the dynamics of power, repression, and subversion within the epistemes that produced them. Some thirty or more years after the politicization of English studies, literature professors still, for the most part, cling to the historicized definition of the literary offered by Barthes and Williams. Yes, they teach books by "marginal" and postcolonial writers, and yes, they apply their skills to some forms of popular culture (usually film), but mainly they are still thinking in the terms set by the print culture of modernity. But as this short overview of what constitutes the literary has demonstrated, the rise of print culture, for all its significance, was simply a change, not a beginning. The genealogy of literature predates the printing press (and even the manuscript), and if the printed word is ever made extinct by digital screens, literature will survive that transition too. The question is: Will literary studies survive, or will it continue to fight a rearguard battle, demanding that the sciences listen to its special kind of knowledge while offering radical readings of Elizabeth Browning poems to a world that does most of its reading on cell phones?

We should also think about the concept of literature, about whether literature is a matter of text or practice. This question has been opened by a number of critics over the past century; three arguments that are worth reviewing are those of Terry Eagleton, Raymond Williams, and Jean-Paul Sartre. Eagleton's foray into the issue comes in his bestselling *Literary Theory*, a text whose genre (an introduction for undergraduates) should not keep us from ceding its heuristic value. What is literature, Eagleton asks: is it the canon, or is it a matter of formal devices? Or is it more contextual, a matter of the academy (literature is what gets taught, Barthes once declared), a matter of practice, in the sense that *how we read* changes a "text" into "literature"? In any case, we can think of examples that disprove any one set of criteria. Advertisements often employ poetic figures; one generation's or nation's classic may soon be forgotten or ignored. Here we might think of Zora Neale Hurston's neglect and then rediscovery, or how Max Beerbohm's fictional poet Enoch Soames sold his soul to the devil so he could go one hundred years into the future and see how posterity had assessed his presumed-to-be-immortal works; the only reference to himself he could find in the British Museum's library was as a character in a Max Beerbohm story.

In one of the set pieces that always make Eagleton a fun read, he describes a drunk in a London tube station blearily reading the sign "Dogs must be carried on the escalator." "How true!" the inebriate declares, thereby finding a "universal" theme in the signage. And we can extend Eagleton's defamiliarization of what literature is: is it a matter of just another commodity? (Like milk in a grocery store, literature is always on the back wall: it's good for you.) Too elastic a criterion is as useless as one that is too rigid. Can *anything* be literature? Or should literature be provisionally defined as depending upon both formal historical criteria *and* reading practices? If a student (or teacher) reads a José Saramago novel just to have finished it before class, such instrumental consumption is probably not a literary practice, but this does not preclude *Blindness's* literary value.

Which is to say that there is a certain constitutive indeterminacy of the literary as a category or value. Raymond Williams, in *Marxism and Literature* (1977) and *Keywords* (1976), has traced the historical ways in which literature has morphed from meaning literacy (in the early modern period) and many forms of writing until, with the Romantics, it came to signify imaginative genres: poetry, then drama, and finally the novel. And Sartre in *What Is Literature?* finds especially in the African American writer Richard Wright the important notion of audience; Wright's is divided between white radicals and the black bourgeoisie: "Wright, a writer for a split public, has been able both to maintain and go beyond this split. He has made it the pretext for a work of art" (74). Sartre argues that this bifurcation in Wright's audience is what has made his writing into great literature: writing neither for his brothers, nor, in a didactic mode, for sympathetic whites, his work became literary because of its historical reception.

The role of the audience – of reception – in both Eagleton and Sartre, then, meets the historical and conceptual changeability of what constitutes literature. Thus we could say that "literature" is overdetermined as a category: by the production forces of publishers and booksellers; by the critical work of journalists and academics; by the classroom, be it secondary or postsecondary; by other institutions like Oprah's book club and the myriad of informal ones; and by the author and the aesthetic tendencies of his or her age.

Key, then, to understanding such paraliterary forms as text messages or comic books is conceiving of literature as a matter of practice, of process, of forms of reading. Which is to say, forms of reading that bring to the text a unique set of critical methodologies, setting apart what we, as literary critics, do from such cognate disciplines as philosophy, sociology, history, or communications. Now the problem with declaring that our methods trump those in other disciplines is of course that literary-critical scholarship has, since the 1980s in the Anglo American academy, drawn extensively from those same disciplines – or at least we have seen a similar vogue for the semiotic, the deconstructive, and the institutional critique.

Let's own these methods. Let us make the claim that it is in literary studies that such methods are uniquely harnessed to an attention to the text as a form of expression. This is not always true, and perhaps there are historians who read Cormac McCarthy not just for his take on the Texas border country, but also in terms of his intervention into the genre of the western.[6] But that distinction (between the referential history and the genre history) is a good one, and a useful way of thinking about how we can read the new and popular forms *as literature.* Reading new and popular forms as literature, then, means more than just talking about video games in terms of cognitive skills development (Johnson) or talking about hip-hop for its sociological implications for black American youth (Quinn).

So what are these methods? Here we need not list, catalog-like, the theoretical pursuits that have clogged the lit prof's inbox over the past quarter-century: the isms, the posts, the -otics and the -ologies studies. Instead, let's think of the distinction between intrinsic and extrinsic interpretation – or, better yet, let's start with interpretation. We would argue that what constitutes literary criticism is the interpretive act. This is the act of accounting for intrinsic, or formal, aspects of a text as well as, indeed in relation to, its extrinsic, or contextual, situation. If the great insight but also weakness of various forms of close readings (from New Criticism to deconstruction) is their exclusive focus on the former, on the intrinsic, then the same double liability of the great political readings (from New Historicism to the posts and cultural studies) has been to fetishize the latter, the extrinsic, and hence the blending of English literary studies into the broad category of "cultural studies" and its often less than deft application of the theoretical tools developed in philosophy, history, linguistics, and the social sciences.

Furthermore, by articulating the formal and the historical, we must also inquire into the status of our object, our text: literature. We cannot but conclude that if historical conditions dictate an enlarging of the canon, of what is "literature," then formal inquiry demands a critical accounting for that new content. Aristotle distinguished the poet Homer from the physiologist Empedocles not simply on the basis of form – both authors wrote in verse – but on the content of that form. Perhaps 99 percent of the text messages being sent on cell phones are of the "C U L8R" variety, conveying practical information in the shortest and most inelegant way possible, but some of the most popular novels produced in Japan in the twenty-first century were composed and originally transmitted on cell phones.[7]

While critiques of the single-author model of literary creation are nothing new—neither in the twentieth century (from the New Critics' "intentional fallacy" to Barthes's "death of the author" and Foucault's "what is an author?"), nor in the pre-Romantic theories of originality and classical pastiche—new technologies and popular forms have certainly accelerated the demise of that model. And this is as it should be. Indeed, looking at other cultural forms, such as visual art, we can see that practitioners and critics have also been toying with other theories. German art critic Boris Groys, for example, argued in 2008:

> The traditional, sovereign authorship of an individual artist has de facto disappeared. . . . When confronting an art exhibition, we are dealing with multiple authorship. . . . Consequently, authorial praxis as it functions in the context of art today is increasingly like that of film, music, and theater. . . . The long list of participants that appears at the end of a film, as the viewers gradually begin to leave their seats and make their way to the exit, manifests the fate of authorship in our age, something the art system cannot escape. (96–97)

Nor, dare we say, the literary system. It is worth noting two features of Groys's argument: on the one hand, he is dealing with an "art system" that has, since Marcel Duchamp (or Andy Warhol), seen radical revisions of originality and creation. The concept of the ready-made (be it a urinal or a box of soap) has meant for some time that artistic practice is concerned as much with selection as it is with creation. And while literary provocateurs do emulate some of these principles (e.g., the Oulipo movement in 1960s Europe,[8] or the "pataphysicians" of the North American avant-garde),[9] much of what is considered to be "literature" today is still produced and theorized under the rubric of the single author. So our motivation for proposing we move beyond such a theory is due not so much to changing literary practices per se, but to our notion of expanding the definition of literature to new technological or popular forms.

But, on the other hand, Groys makes some astute points about how to think about both the author and the work: the first is multiple in the sense that it may include curators, critics, the architects of exhibition spaces (even "the choice of the architect by the committees responsible"; 97); the second is multiple or post-monolithic in that it may include unexhibited work, proposals for work, drafts, or sketches—which is to say that the work is an archive, an infinitely expandable archive. The screenplay is thus part of the archive of a film; and ephemeral or digital forms, too, suggest an ever-expanding notion of what constitutes the literary object or work.

And there is also an irony here, as any reader of film criticism (or, more recently, comics criticism) will be aware. At the same time that the structuralists and poststructuralists in the 1960s and '70s were demolishing the edifice of the author, film critics in France (the *Cahiers du Cinéma* group) and elsewhere (Andrew Sarris) were elevating that same model via the theory of the auteur.[10] Too, this theory of the film auteur has found adherents in the work of Douglas Wolk and others in the field of comics criticism, where especially the "literary" graphic novel has been identified as the creation of a single author. Thus Wolk declares that the "creator of a comic – the person who applies pen to drawing board . . . – is its author, and comics produced under the sole or chief creative control of a single person are more likely to be good . . . than comics produced under the aegis of an editor who hires them all individually" (31).

But while the production of even the canonized graphic novels varies from single author (Art Spiegelman's *Maus*) to collaborations (Harvey Pekar's *American Splendor* series utilizes various artists for Pekar's narratives; Alan Moore collaborates with different artists for such projects as *Watchmen*), the commercial or mainstream comics world has for decades seen a film studio–like division of labor: artists, colorists, pencillers, etc. And while a published film screenplay is often identified with the film's screenwriter, one scholar of the screenplay has posited that "in both the popular marketplace and the academy, the published screenplay positions itself within and complicates such cultural categories as canon, author, authority, and property" (Mota 217).

These contradictions seem to be par for the course: if film critics in the 1960s sought to elevate the director as the auteur as a way of borrowing cultural credibility from literature, and if video game studios now call themselves publishers and advertise the "creator" of a game on the packaging, such strategies should not be seen simply as a matter of Freudian disavowal: the denial of a collective effort and the fetishization of the creative individual. Rather, the oscillation between collective and singular models is symptomatic of radical uncertainty in the critical apparatus itself. It is into this uncertain space that this collection of essays inserts itself: as an intervention into the critical reception of new, paraliterary forms.

This would seem to be a particularly apt moment in which to attempt such a critical turn, for not only have the new technologies confused the long-standing author-press-reader literary triptych, but the early twenty-first century has witnessed a new stage in the complication of the high culture–low culture divide. We have already touched on this long-standing duality in our brief discussion of the historical fates of some originally marginal genres and individual texts, but we should take a moment to briefly trace its origins. What is often neglected in overviews of the high culture–low culture debate is how it has been historically defined by affect. Think of Philip Sidney's dismissal of professional writers as "base servile wits" or Theodor Adorno's discussion of classical music and its contemplative audience versus popular music and its inattentive audience ("Popular" 40–42). Near the start of the Enlightenment, Descartes began "the gradual epistemic process toward abstractions that overtakes early modern discourses of body and mind" (Paster 246), which would essentialize this division between emotion and reason. The logical conclusion of its implications form the basis for Kant's theory of art: "The word *aesthetics*, ironically, derives from Greek terms, such as *aisthesis*, that refer to feelings. But Immanuel Kant, in his formative, highly influential treatise on aesthetics, *Critique of Judgement* (1790), announced that the taste for emotion fed by 'mercenary' or commercial art is 'always barbaric'" (Nehring xi). Or as Pierre Bourdieu explains it in his sociology of taste, Kant's "negation of enjoyment–inferior, coarse, vulgar, mercenary, venal, servile, in a word, natural–implies affirmation of the sublimity of those who can be satisfied with sublimated, refined, distinguished, disinterested, gratuitous, free pleasures" (491). Adorno is more succinct: "the very idea that enjoyment is of the essence of art deserves to be thrown overboard" (*Aesthetic* 22). In such formulations, people who take pleasure in affect-stirring popular culture are vulgar and unenlightened. As Bourdieu has demonstrated, "Intellectuals could be said to believe in the representation–literature, theatre, painting–more than in the things represented, whereas the people chiefly expect representations and the conventions which govern them to allow them to believe 'naively' in the things represented" (5). And herein the high-low culture divide has rested for centuries.

The divide has begun to break down, or at least transform. In the academy, this is largely due to the long-felt influence of Roland Barthes's *Mythologies*. Barthes, in that series of masterful essays, analyzed contemporary French culture: mass culture, material culture, the vulgar, and the marginalized. In it he read the semiology of control and tradition, exploding the conflation of, as he put it, "Nature and History" (11). Mass and material cultures were demonstrated to be more representative of a cultural moment than the canonical works of art favored by the upwardly mobile. And so low and mass cultures offer more culturally revealing "texts" than the canon of great works traditionally promoted by the academy as the epitome of a culture's self-knowledge and expression. Those courses in popular and children's literature mentioned earlier exploded on campuses, and some knowledge of semiotics became de rigueur for cutting-edge intellectuals in the late 1970s. But while the academy now allowed that low cultural forms were sociologically or politically significant, the advent of television studies and scholarly books on Madonna did not completely demolish the high-low divide. In fact, in some ways it was reasserted through the political analyses that the critics performed: "A rather curious disjunction has appeared between an élite to whom are assigned ideas and ideologies, and the rest of the population who are to be studied more anthropologically, as the possessors of less self-conscious mentalities" (Bryson 20). Popular, low culture could be deconstructed, but it could not be consumed without irony by anyone with a graduate degree. The theory dodgers who were swept up in the affective manipulations of *Titanic* were viewed with withering pity.

There is some evidence that a further, and perhaps final, breakdown of the high-low dichotomy is occurring. For one thing, the demographic shift in the academy that has followed the retirement of the professors hired to educate the baby boomers means there is now a generation of professional scholars who were raised on cable television, post-punk rock, and the internet. The culture of this intellectual class *is* mass culture. We were not alive when rock music was considered a passing fad or the right sort of people went to the opera. We have been raised in an era in which "some cultural choices from different classes are *converging*, making the classes more similar in their choices than in the past" (Gans 10). This generation has also seen increasingly multicultural urban centers and the expansion of the technologies of cultural transmission. And while it may be that the hoary debate of what defines high and low culture is increasingly irrelevant in a world in which television offers narratives of novelistic complexity and the professoriat lines up for movies based on Marvel comic books, there is one area of cultural production in which it is still largely at play: "serious" literature. Who reads Paul Auster on the bus besides students cramming for their postmodern lit exam? Who opens *Paradise Lost* in the bathtub? Who browses through Ezra Pound's *Cantos* in front of the fireplace? Such works are kept alive by scholarly industry and it is difficult to believe they would long survive the closing of the academy. While popular and children's novels have infiltrated university English classes, there is little evidence that intellectually demanding or formally challenging writing is gaining mass appeal outside of them. And so a hierarchy remains.

If this historical instability of the high culture–low culture divide were not enough to give us pause, critical arguments since the 1960s have demonstrated the necessity of questioning the divide's heuristic use for critical questions of value. Thus the novelist Tom McCarthy's book *Tintin and the Secret of Literature* can be usefully compared to Steve Johnson's more cognitive-instrumental *Everything Bad Is Good for You*. Interestingly, McCarthy's text is a rebuke to Eagleton's notion that literary reading – or practice – performatively creates the category of literature (as in the drunk reading the subway sign). That is, McCarthy engages in a deep poststructuralist reading of the Tintin comics, but without conferring upon the comics any literary value or ontology: "should we now claim, posthumously, on Hergé's behalf, that in fact he *was* a writer, and a great one?" he asks. "My short answer to this question is no. . . . To confuse comics with literature would be a mistake" (32).

What McCarthy neglects in his otherwise stupendous book is how arguments about whether some delinquent form is part of literature (or art, or serious music, etc.) depend upon a fairly stable or traditional definition of the literary.[11] Steve Johnson starts off *Everything Bad Is Good for You* in some ways agreeing with McCarthy: "I do not believe that most of today's pop culture is made up of masterpieces that will some-day be taught alongside Joyce and Chaucer in college survey courses" (11). (Note that the same could be said of most literary fiction published today.) However, Johnson's caveat is because it is not to high culture one should now go if one desires authority: rather, it is to science, prag-matism, and the cognitive sciences. Very early in his book he seeks to separate his approach from cultural studies: "It is closer, in a sense, to physics than to poetry" (10). Johnson argues, then, that cognitive forces work in concert with the market and its technological delivery systems: *Grand Theft Auto* is important, or sells well, because its very complexity demands increasing attention from viewers/players.[12] Johnson's most compelling argument lies around complexity. He especially is able to show how U.S. television programs have dramatically developed since the 1950s, from the mono-plotted *Dragnet* to the more adventurous *Hill Street Blues* of the 1980s and the early twenty-first-century's *Sopranos* and *24*. This complexity, he argues, is due in no small part to the twin engines of fan obsessions (via internet chat rooms and blogs) and the technology of not just reproduction but repetition (repeated screen-ings via cable, DVD sales). Thus more detail, plot twists, and subtle characterizations can be built in with the (realistic) expectation that viewers will catch on and elucidate each other. In effect, the television fan world is one big graduate seminar.

These arguments, then, signal what are for us two connected forces behind the present collection: first, the necessity to talk about popular forms in relation to high culture; and second, the ways in which such new forms come about through a messy convergence of the economic and the formal. The distinction between high and low culture is not one of value, and if we are not to cede critical territory to blogs and DVD extras, we should leap into the fray. Whatever the theoretical and historical arguments for the inclusion or exclusion of new forms from the category of literature, the testing ground for the application of those arguments will probably be the classroom. Theorists may speculate all they want about the ontological status of a text that has, say, an ephemeral existence on cell phones, but until students can be convinced that those text messages are potentially something more than mere expediencies for their social lives, who will believe it? More important though, the opposite might also be true. That is, if the new forms produce texts that prove to be teachable, this could be an a posteriori argument for their literariness.

There are challenges to bringing some of these new forms into the laboratory that is a university or college English class. Some of the forms are ephemeral: the narrative generated in a role-playing game disappears once that game is over and, while it exists, it is only available to the game's participants. Other forms have complex relationships with other, nonliterary cultural products: a screenplay is, in the majority of cases, a "score" for a movie. Still others may require forms of critical knowledge that are outside the training of most literary critics: graphic novels and many websites rely on visual codes as much as they do on language and narrative. The demographics of the academy may also prove to be a problem. Marc Prensky has distinguished between digital natives – young people who have grown up with new technologies – and digital immigrants: older people who have had to learn those technologies. Prensky has called the discontinuity between these two parts of the population a "singularity." He cites statistics that any professor of literature should memorize before approaching a large class of freshmen students: "Today's average college grads have spent less than 5,000 hours of their lives reading, but over 10,000 hours playing video games." Reading accounts for 16.1 percent of the time that college students spend communicating in any one day. Of that 16.1 percent, 37 percent is spent reading on the internet or text messaging.[13] While older media-savvy instructors can certainly learn about the new technologies, we will always be immigrants, never fully integrating the new technologies into our lives as those who grew up with them have – until, of course, the digital natives themselves become instructors.

But because something may be difficult is no reason it should not be attempted. If the literary experience shifts into new forms, it behooves the literary critic to shift also or risk becoming the guardian of an increasingly dated model of the literary, a model that may eventually become arcane, perhaps comically so. To the student twenty years from now, the single author–press–reader model of literary production may make as much sense as phrenology does to us. And instructors need not go blindly into this new digital continent; they have a great resource in their students themselves. The digital natives can teach the immigrants about their culture.

What users of new digital and popular texts can teach us is precisely how to read those texts; how reading takes place; and how reading practices and conceptions of texts can be, in turn, enriched by our own critical skill set. As a first demonstration – by way of analogy – let us return to Roland Barthes's analysis of popular culture and, in particular, two different takes on the Tour de France. The first, originally published in 1955, displays Barthes's hauteur, including in its title: "The Tour de France as Epic." Here Barthes finds classical literary resonance at every turn: "The Tour's geography, too, is entirely subject to the epic necessity of ordeal. Elements and terrain are personified, for it is against them that man measures himself, and as in every epic it is important that the struggle should match equal measures: man is therefore naturalized, Nature humanized" (81). This passage could be an object lesson in how *not* to read popular culture – imposing on a sporting event the themes and structure of high art. But in a script Barthes wrote for a Canadian film (*Le Sport et les Hommes / What Is Sport?*) in 1960, the reading of the Tour is subtly different: "the Frenchman is not much of a geographer: his geography is not that of books, it is that of the Tour; each year, by means of the Tour, he knows the length of his coasts and the height of his mountains. Each year he recomposes the material unity of his country, each year he tallies his frontiers and his products" (29). In this second reading, Barthes points to the *practice* by which the French sports fan uses the Tour as a form of knowledge, as a reservoir of geographic information. And it is this response to the actual uses and practices engendered by new cultural forms that we see as key to our endeavor here. Whether it is the practice of checking one's status updates on Facebook, immersing oneself in a video game for hours on end, or engaging in the cognitive finesse necessary to follow Flash animation, that practice must be what we criticize.

There are other important benefits to be gained from expanding the canon of what is taught in the classroom. These include, most dramatically, reaching students who may be disaffected with (what they think is) literary culture and, simultaneously, passing on to students skills that will enable them to better navigate – critically – their popular-digital context. It may seem obvious that if you talk in an intelligent way about a Tupac Shakur lyric you may reach those mythical kids at the back of the lecture hall, with their Timberland-clad feet on the desk in front of them and their L.A. Raiders ballcaps carefully skewed sideways.[14] And using such texts as Shakur's "How Long Will They Mourn Me" (from his 1994 album, *Thug Life, Vol. 1*) shows students that we in the professoriat take "their" culture as seriously as we are asking them to take "ours." Too, talking about Shakur in connection with Martin Luther King Jr. and the concept of theodicy – or a Miltonic justifying of the ways of God to man – with the aid of Michael Eric Dyson's *I May Not Get There with You: The True Martin Luther King, Jr.* (2000) engages with the popular in a way that has pedagogical, as well as political, payback.

This example leads to a third principle of teaching the new canon: it is important to impress upon students that just because we are talking about comic books or blogs, they should not think this class will be an easy credit. That is, we will bring the full arsenal of critical, historical, and theoretical interpretations to bear upon the cultural object. This is not a matter of dumbing anything down. The ease with which a student *thinks* he or she can breeze through *Maus* or surf the *Stuff White People Like* blog is comparable, perhaps, to the clever English student deciding to study short stories or lyric poetry rather than Victorian novels or medieval epics, thinking they will be easier. And taking popular culture seriously also does the necessary work of turning elitist students on to texts they might otherwise scorn. Alerting students to the Freudian relation of Artie to his father in *Maus* or the Bourdieu-esque notion of cultural capital that is unpacked in *Stuff White People Like*, then, is a dialectical paideutic that can win over both the slackers and the keeners. Again, as with the readings of Tupac (Dyson's historicizing method) or the Tour de France (Barthes's consideration of the fan), we can and should demonstrate that just as we are talking about texts, not just literature, our argument is that these practices have as much to gain from literary training as our training has to gain from these new practices.

To reiterate: there are challenges to teaching and engaging with nontraditional literary forms. Two glaring ones have to do with the new material conditions in which these texts come to us (mentioned above in relation to role-playing games), and the necessity to develop new critical skills. Ephemerality, as in role-playing games but also text messages, means determining new forms of documentation, perhaps borrowing from the social sciences. In addition, the relation between a screenplay and a film (and the film's soundtrack, and its afterlife as a DVD complete with deleted scenes, documentary, and commentary) means rethinking what precisely the cultural object is. Comics and graphic novels often start their cultural lives as pamphlets (Chester Brown's *Riel*). And so Bart Beatty begins his study of European comics in the 1990s with a comparison between a bestselling collection, Zep's *Tchô, monde cruel,* and a small press art comic, Nadia Raviscioni's *Odette et l'eau,* arguing that the two are examples of conflicting models of cultural production (6). Video games cannot be "read" quickly or dipped into for quotation or close reading: they must be played from beginning to end and some of them, such as *Call of Duty,* can be played in so many ways they do not have to end. Which is to argue, we think, that the very challenge of new or ephemeral or virtual manifestations of cultural products can be the basis for new ways of thinking about what constitutes the text and how that text relates to (or is part of) the audience.

We also may need to update our skill set. There are ways of doing this—as noted above in the discussion of digital natives—that do not mean either a continual upgrade as our computers' software seems to undergo, or relinquishing classroom authority to the digitally savvy. Students fact-checking their instructor's lecture on Wikipedia is probably not a good idea, and not only because of the dubious quality of many of the entries. But students dropping a link to a YouTube video on a course blog can be a way of opening up the information flow, of using "crowd sourcing" as a way of making that information flow less one-way and more like how we'd prefer participation and discussion to happen anyway.

But, again, and in closing this introduction, the question of learning new forms and skills may be less dire than it appears. Presumably this book addresses three generations of scholars. First, there are those in the sunset years (say, over age fifty-five, the tail end of the boomers) who are eager to bring new texts into the classroom; here one's enthusiasm and experience (and, often, digital-native children) will go a long way to meeting the challenge of acquiring new skills. Then, there is the mid-career professoriat, the Gen X instructors who, because of the horrible academic job market in the 1990s, were forced to rely on a variety of teaching and non-academic placements before gaining secure employment: here, economic necessity has endowed such instructors with many of the same skills that are useful in teaching an expanded canon. Finally, the graduate students and entry-level instructors will often come equipped with the digital, or popular-cultural, skills that are necessary for teaching the new canon.

NOTES

1. In a context more specific to literary studies, William B. Warner and Clifford Siskin argue that the "challenge for English departments . . . is to transform ourselves to meet the historical challenge of remediation. Our relevance to universities and to society at large depends on a retooling that mixes some established means of mediation with new tools–and that then deploys both across the newly altered and expanded range of literary activity" (105).

2. See Barthes, *Essais critiques* 125; Williams, *Marxism* 47 and *Keywords* 184–187.

3. See Wellek 17ff.

4. Quoted in Nyberg 63.

5. The respectability of such scholarly work was attested in 1991 by the establishment of the International Gothic Association.

6. More generously, Hillary Chute notes that "one of the best essays on *Maus* is in *Oral History Review*" (457).

7. "'Love Sky,' a debut novel by a young woman named Mika, was read by 20 million people on cellphones or on computers . . . where it was first uploaded" (Onishi 2). See the website *Textnovel* (www.textnovel.com) for a collection of such works, some in progress.

8. See Motte.

9. See *Canadian Pataphysics*; Bök.

10. Among both critics and filmmakers, it should be noted. In a 1972 book-length interview, French director Jean-Pierre Melville noted, "I sometimes read . . . 'Melville is being Bressonian.' I'm sorry but it's Bresson who has always been Melvillean. . . . Look at [Bresson's] *Le Journal d'un Curé de Campagne* . . . and you will see that it's Melville" (qtd. in Nogueira 27).

11. Thus a frequent argument in the comics criticism canon is to deal with the Classic Comics series and other comic-izations of high literature (see, for instance, Versaci, esp. 182–212).

12. This aligning of the market with a cultural genre is perhaps symptomatic of cultural studies in post-Fordism; see, for example, Eithne Quinn, who argues that in "the mixed-up, no-guarantees world of neoliberal America . . . gangsta rap was energized politically by the rejection of collective protest strategies and the embrace of a ruthless drive for profit" (16).

13. See Emanuel et al., esp. 22.

14. Or at least you would have in 2005; today, you might need to reference Jay-Z's *Decoded*.

REFERENCES

Adorno, Theodor W. *Aesthetic Theory.*
Ed. and trans. Robert Hullot-Kentor.
Minneapolis: University of Minne-
sota Press, 1997.

——. "On Popular Music." *Studies
in Philosophy and Social Science* 9
(1941): 17–48.

Aristotle. *Aristotle's Politics and Poetics.*
Trans. Benjamin Jowett and Thomas
Twining. New York: Viking, 1976.

Barthes, Roland. *Essais critiques.* Paris:
Seuil, 1964.

——. *Mythologies.* Ed. and trans.
Annette Lavers. London: Jonathan
Cape, 1972.

——. "The Tour de France as Epic." In
*The Eiffel Tower and Other Mytholo-
gies.* Trans. Richard Howard. New
York: Hill and Wang, 1984. 79–90.

——. *What Is Sport?* Trans. Richard
Howard. New Haven, CT: Yale University Press, 2007.

Beatty, Bart. *Unpopular Culture: Transforming the European Comic Book
in the 1990s.* Toronto: University of
Toronto Press, 2007.

Bök, Christian. *Pataphysics: The Poetics
of an Imaginary Science.* Evanston,
IL: Northwestern University Press,
2001.

Bourdieu, Pierre. *Distinction: A Social
Critique of the Judgment of Taste.*
Trans. Richard Nice. London: Rout-
ledge & Kegan Paul, 1984.

Bryson, Anna. *From Courtesy to Civility:
Changing Codes of Conduct in Early
Modern England.* Oxford: Clarendon,
1998.

Canadian Pataphysics. Ed. Toronto
Research Group. *Open Letter* 4.6–7
(Winter 1981).

Chute, Hillary. "Comics as Literature?
Reading Graphic Narrative." *PMLA*
123.2 (Mar. 2008): 452–465.

Delany, Paul. "The University in Pieces:
Bill Readings and the Fate of the
Humanities." In *Profession 2000.* Ed.
Phyllis Franklin. New York: MLA,
2000. 89–96.

Dyson, Michael Eric. *I May Not Get
There with You: The True Martin
Luther King, Jr.* New York: Free Press,
2000.

Eagleton, Terry. *Literary Theory: An
Introduction.* 2nd ed. Minneapolis:
University of Minnesota Press, 1996.

Edwards, Robert R. "Medieval Literary
Careers: The Theban Track." In *Eu-
ropean Literary Careers: The Author
from Antiquity to the Renaissance.*
Ed. Patrick Cheney and Frederick
A. de Armas. Toronto: University of
Toronto Press, 2002. 104–128.

Emanuel, Richard, et al. "How College
Students Spend Their Time Com-
municating." *International Journal of
Listening* 22 (2008): 13–28.

Fowler, Alastair. *Kinds of Literature: An
Introduction to the Theory of Genres
and Modes.* Cambridge, MA: Harvard University Press, 1982.

Gans, Herbert J. *Popular Culture and
High Culture: An Analysis of the
Evaluation of Taste.* Rev. ed. New
York: Basic, 1999.

Groys, Boris. "Multiple Authorship." In
his *Art Power.* Cambridge, MA: MIT
Press, 2008. 93–100.

Guillory, John. "Preprofessionalism:
What Graduate Students Want." In
Profession 1996. Ed. Phyllis Franklin.
New York: MLA, 1996. 91–99.

Johnson, Steve. *Everything Bad Is Good
for You: How Today's Popular Culture
Is Actually Making Us Smarter.* New
York: Riverhead, 2005.

Kelly, Henry Ansgar. *Ideas and Forms of
Tragedy from Aristotle to the Middle*

Ages. Cambridge: Cambridge University Press, 1993.

La Farge, Paul. Rev. of *Tintin and the Secret of Literature*. *Bookforum* (June–July–Aug. 2008). Web. Accessed 13 Nov. 2009.

Lodge, David. *Nice Work: A Novel*. London: Secker & Warburg, 1988.

McCarthy, Tom. *Tintin and the Secret of Literature*. London: Granta, 2006.

Mota, Miguel. "Derek Jarman's *Caravaggio:* The Screenplay as Book." *Criticism* 47.2 (2005): 215–231.

Motte, Warren F., Jr., ed. and trans. *Oulipo: A Primer of Potential Literature*. Normal, IL: Dalkey Archive Press, 1998.

Nehring, Neil. *Popular Music, Gender, and Postmodernism: Anger Is an Energy*. Thousand Oaks, CA: Sage, 1997.

Nogueira, Rui. *Melville on Melville*. New York: Viking, 1972.

Nyberg, Amy Kriste. *Seal of Approval: The History of the Comics Code*. Jackson: University Press of Mississippi, 1998.

Onishi, Norimitsu. "Thumbs Race as Japan's Best Sellers Go Cellular." *New York Times Electronic Edition* (20 Jan. 2008). Web. Accessed 19 Sept. 2008.

Palmer, D. J. *The Rise of English Studies*. Oxford: Oxford University Press, 1965.

Paster, Gail Kern. *Humoring the Body: Emotions and the Shakespearean Stage*. Chicago: University of Chicago Press, 2004.

Prensky, M. "Digital Natives, Digital Immigrants." *On the Horizon* (Oct. 2001). Web. Accessed 26 Sept. 2008.

Quinn, Eithne. *Nothin' but a "G" Thang: The Culture and Commerce of Gangsta Rap*. New York: Columbia University Press, 2005.

Sartre, Jean-Paul. *What Is Literature?* Trans. Bernard Frechtman. New York: Harper, 1965.

Sidney, Philip. *A Defence of Poetry*. Ed. J. A. Van Dorsten. Oxford: Oxford University Press, 1966.

Spenser, Edmund. *The Faerie Queene*. Ed. A. C. Hamilton. New York: Longman, 2001.

Tapscott, Don, and Anthony D. Williams. *Wikinomics: How Mass Collaboration Changes Everything*. 2nd ed. New York: Portfolio, 2008.

Versaci, Rocco. *This Book Contains Graphic Language: Comics as Literature*. New York: Continuum, 2007.

Warner, William B., and Clifford Siskin. "Stopping Cultural Studies." *Profession 2008* (2008): 94–107.

Wellek, René. "What Is Literature?" In *What Is Literature?* Ed. Paul Hernadi. Bloomington: Indiana University Press, 1978.

Williams, Ioan. *Novel and Romance 1700–1800: A Documentary Record*. London: Routledge and Kegan Paul, 1970.

Williams, Raymond. 1976. *Keywords: A Vocabulary of Culture and Society*. London: Fonta, 1988.

———. 1977. *Marxism and Literature*. New York: Oxford University Press, 1988.

Wolk, Douglas. *Reading Comics: How Graphic Novels Work and What They Mean*. Cambridge: Da Capo, 2007.

1   Roll a D20 and the Author Dies

PAUL BUDRA

Some years ago a friend of mine would drive downtown every Sunday afternoon to play *Dungeons and Dragons.* The "dungeonmaster," the person running the game, was a professor of literature at a prestigious university. All the other players had at least one graduate degree, and several were doctors of law or literature. They would spend up to six hours at a time pretending to be elves, half-elves, gnomes, halflings, or exotic humans negotiating the complicated fantasy world that the dungeonmaster described. My friend played a "dark" elf, a character who, though both a warrior and a magic user, was shunned by the society in which she was raised and so fled to the woods to commune with animals. My friend is an animal lover in real life, and the characters the other participants played were often reflections of their own personalities or professions: for instance, the characters played by lawyers almost never chose to battle monsters; they would attempt to negotiate with them. All the players became deeply involved with their characters. It was not uncommon for a player to leave the game sobbing if her character "died" during the game. And sometimes it was difficult to return to reality when the game was over for the day. At the conclusion of one of these sessions, the band of characters that the participants were playing "found" a treasure of gold and exotic jewels, a pleasing conclusion to an imaginary adventure. But after the session had dispersed for the day, one of the players got in her car and thought to herself, "Thank God. Now I can pay the phone bill."

My friend's adventure with, and in, *Dungeons and Dragons* sheds light on a gaming subculture that is rarely discussed and yet has a pedigree that is over a hundred years old. "In 1811, Herr von Reiswitz and his son, a Prussian artillery officer, modified a version of a game called *War Chess*, which had been created some thirty years before. . . . Herr von Reiswitz conceived the new version of the war-strategy game, christened *Kreigsspiel*, as an aid to educate young Prussian military officers" (Mackay 13). This game used counters to represent troop formations. The counters were moved on a miniature battlefield and the outcome of a battle was settled through the rolling of dice and the adjudication of an impartial referee. In the early twentieth century, H. G. Wells adapted this concept in his game book *Little Wars*. By the mid-twentieth century, many complex, commercially produced war games, most played on elaborate cardboard terrain maps, were available. In 1971 E. Gary Gygax produced a war game called *Chainmail* that capitalized on the popularity of J. R. R. Tolkien's *Lord of the Rings* trilogy by including nonhuman combatant characters—dwarves, elves, monsters, etc.—in such a war game. Shortly after, Gygax teamed up with Dave Arneson, a game designer who proposed having game players take on the roles of individual combatants—characters—rather than troops. Their collaboration resulted in *Dungeons and Dragons*, the first of the "tabletop role-playing games," so designated to differentiate them from video role-playing games.

Unlike most games, *Dungeons and Dragons* is collaborative rather than competitive. The group that sits down to play works together to create a story for the characters they perform. Daniel Mackay has called the game "an *episodic* and *participatory* creation *system* that includes a set of quantified *rules* that assist a group of *players* and a *gamemaster* in determining how their fictional *characters*' spontaneous interactions are resolved" (4–5). Those interactions create the story. The gamemaster not only adjudicates the rules of the game, but also performs minor characters and fills in any necessary description. An individual role-playing game can continue literally for years: "players can continue to play the same character through many role-playing game sessions. These many sessions, when considered together, form a continuous, often complex narrative concerning a stable cast of characters in a consistent, interactive, fictional environment controlled and created by the gamemaster" (Mackay 7).

The logic of the game world and characters is determined by rule-books and mathematical formulas applied to complex dice rolls. While the original *Dungeons and Dragons* rulebooks enabled the gamemaster to create a fantasy world that resembled that in Tolkien's *Lord of the Rings*, many role-playing games set in other fictional worlds have appeared since the 1970s. There are games set in the *Star Wars* universe and that of *Buffy the Vampire Slayer*. The game *Call of Cthulhu* is based on the horror fiction of American writer H. P. Lovecraft while the game *Cyberpunk* draws on the science fiction imaginings of William Gibson and Bruce Sterling. Not only are the imaginary environments of each game different, each game has its own rules for the creation of the characters that the players perform. Most follow the basic *Dungeons and Dragons* formula and describe the characters through a set of characteristics: strength, wisdom, charisma, agility, etc. Each of these categories is given a numeric value that influences game play. So, a character with a high strength number will have an advantage when he "performs" certain strength-related deeds in the fictional environment. In addition to these basic characteristics, characters can have specific skills (say, lock picking) and be capable of performing certain feats ("battle frenzy," perhaps). As the game progresses, characters also (in most games) acquire "experience points." These points accrue and allow the character to evolve, gaining new skills or increasing the numeric advantage of a characteristic. But there are many other systems, including one called the generic universal role-playing system (GURPS) that is designed to be compatible with any gaming environment.

What little scholarly work that has been done on role-playing games has tended to be sociological. Gary Alan Fine has studied role-playing games as a "contemporary urban leisure subculture" (1) in which the gamers create alternate, usually fantastic, imaginary cultural systems. The majority of the essays in the collection *Gaming as Culture*, edited by Williams, Hendricks, and Winkler, have a sociological bent, focusing on social reality and questions of identity. The closest thing to a literary study of the game can be found in Daniel Mackay's *The Fantasy Role-Playing Game*. Mackay calls role-playing games "a new kind of performance" (3) and draws on the language of drama and theater to understand the gaming experience. His analysis is, in his own words, "cultural, formal, and social" (121), but the last section of his book does explore the aesthetic possibilities of the role-playing experience, the "cathartic structure that encourages identification with its content and persists after the performance has disappeared" (122). According to Mackay, "The story has its own structure, narrative arc, tensions, conflicts, resolutions, mysteries, characterizations, themes, and denouements that are independent of the players, who have created it but, having done so, are only associated with it in the same biographical sense that artists are often associated with their work" (126). He arrives at this conclusion after retelling the narrative that emerged in a years-long role-playing game in which he participated with a group of close friends. He concludes that "performance [that is, the actual playing of the game], while quite possibly aesthetic in character, is not the aesthetic object. Rather, it is the interface to both the imaginary-entertainment environment and, ultimately, the distilled narrative" (129). In other words, the "aesthetic object is the residue left behind in the memories of the players" (129); it is the memory of the story that the game generated.

This is an important point, and I believe it is correct *if* we assume and apply standard definitions of what constitutes the literary and the literary aesthetic experience. But let us note, however, that the dynamic which Mackay describes reverses the one associated with the performative arts that he invokes. Dramatic literature traditionally moves from the page to the stage, and this transition generates a specific aesthetic experience: "The movement from script to performance liberates the play from its exclusively linguistic embodiment: language becomes speech, directions become *mise-en-scène*, implied presence becomes performance reality" (Garner xiv). That performance reality, as Stanton Garner has convincingly argued, is not passively received by the theater audience but is created through a complex "conceptual process designed to transform the stage and its activities into structured fiction" (xvii).

But this is not what happens in the role-playing game experience. If we continue with Mackay's performative arts analogy, we might say that the players collectively perform an improvised narrative for themselves–there is no audience–that can then be simply remembered or recorded as a textual narrative. From stage to, maybe, page. We must insist on that "maybe" because in the majority of cases the improvised narrative of the game is *not* written down except, perhaps, in the form of a few notes the gamemaster takes in order to facilitate the next episode of the game. And while Mackay undertakes to reconstruct, with the help of his fellow players, the narrative of the game he has been playing over the years, this exercise is not typical of the role-playing game experience. Role-playing games are by nature ephemeral. They last only as long as they are being played and are forgotten when they are not. They exist briefly, under special conditions, for a small coterie of participants, who are the performers and consumers of the narrative, and then they disappear.

Does this ephemerality, this oral performance, automatically preclude role-playing games from the literary? The groundbreaking work that Albert Lord did on Yugoslavian oral epic poetry, in his pursuit of understanding the composition of the Homeric epics, suggests otherwise. Lord demonstrated that the "oral epic" tradition uses a complex, and perhaps spontaneous, arrangement of preexisting formulaic expressions: "in a very real sense every performance is a separate song; for every performance is unique, and every performance bears the signature of its poet singer" (4). No two performances are the same. This means that the version of the *Iliad* that was written down and attributed to Homer, the work we think of *as* the *Iliad*, may have been one version of thousands that were not written down. There is no reason to believe that it was the best version. Nor should we assume that textual embodiment somehow solidifies the oral epic tradition into literature. This is to privilege text, to assume a hierarchy of literary forms that was meaningless in Homeric times, that remains meaningless in oral traditions, and that is becoming increasingly meaningless in a world of voicemail and emoticons. As Lord argues, "oral tradition is as intricate and meaningful an art form as its derivative 'literary tradition.' In the extended sense of the word, oral tradition is as 'literary' as literary tradition. It is not simply a less polished, more haphazard, or cruder second cousin twice removed, to literature" (141).

In the oral epic tradition and the role-playing game, performance and composition are inseparable because they occur in the same instance. This makes evaluative criticism difficult. The standards for assessing performance are different from those for critiquing a literary narrative. We have all seen productions of great plays, say by Shakespeare, that were ruined by bad performances. And, obviously, a good performance can raise a bad play to the level of tolerability. As literary critics, we may have a passing interest in assessing individual performances because, at least with a preexisting dramatic text, we have opinions on how we think they *ought* to be performed. But our training is in the analysis of the literary component. If that literary component is ephemeral, if it is never written down for close reading, we have two options. One, we assess on the fly, judging the narrative that is performed as it is being performed or immediately after it is complete and still fresh in the memory. This happens automatically in role-playing games. Once a game is over, participants tend to assess the session: "That was a great game; we killed fifteen orcs and saved the unicorn. And Niraka was moved to tears"; or "That game was awful. We just wandered around the dungeon for three hours. Nothing happened." Clearly this is not a profound hermeneutic, and the assessment could be more detailed, though the question of critical distance remains. It is, as we will see, almost impossible to assess the narrative generated by a role-playing game without participating in the game. But this participation puts the critic in an untenable conflict of interest, negating critical distance because the critic is part of the collective creating the text she would critique. A player whose character has died during a game may feel outraged at the turn of narrative events that led to that death, but those events may have contributed to a satisfying narrative for the game session as a whole. How can anyone fairly, or with the appearance of fairness, assess the death of Little Nell if she is playing Little Nell?

Two, we turn our attention to the formulas that allow for the performance. As Lord and Parry charted the formula that composed the *langue* of the oral epic's *parole* in performance, so we can turn to the rules and formulas that allow for the performance of the role-playing game. And these are written down. This latter approach makes more sense – a good set of rules will allow for rich, detailed, exciting performances or games; a simplistic, crude set of rules will lead to boring, predictable games – but a critical shift from the role-playing event to the rules that inform and define those events' individual utterances brings up the question: can rulebooks be literature? Let us begin by recognizing that all literature follows rules from the macroscopic (genre) to the microscopic (punctuation). Certainly many literary works became famous for breaking or abandoning those rules, but the majority of literature does not. And, to a large extent, "literary evaluation depends in part on our appraisal of the manner in which a text conforms to what we understand (at least historically) to be literary rules" (Reeves 15). There is also an argument that the "literary" is, to use Wittgenstein's term, a specific sort of "language game" and to understand it, indeed to recognize it, we must know the rules. English departments have taught texts of literary criticism for years, usually in an upper-level seminar with the ominous title of "Literary Theory"; would teaching rulebooks for role-playing games be significantly different? This question leads to several others and, I think, points to the future of criticism in the digital age: a shift toward metacriticism may be historically inevitable.

In 1967 Roland Barthes declared the death of the author. In 1970 Michel Foucault reduced authors to functions, "projections, in terms always more or less psychological, of our way of handling texts" (127). In the 1980s the New Historicism shifted critical emphasis away from the author to the dynamics of the culture which surrounded that author and in which literary texts circulated. These theoretical revelations had no immediate impact on the production of literary texts or, with the possible exception of Thomas Pynchon's attempt to render himself invisible, authorial status. It has been generally assumed that new technologies were required for these critical insights to become practice, and to a large extent this is true: the advent of hypertext allowed for texts that were defined by choices made by the reader, who clicked a path through the digital components of the works; blogs enabled anyone to become a "published" essayist; and Facebook made all young people into autobiographers. The advent of wiki technology has allowed for communal (and anonymous) authorship on a scale hitherto unimaginable. Digital technology has broken the author-text-press-reader formula asunder, but it has made its users dependent upon, and restricted by, the formal rules of software applications–that is, the actual computer programs–in ways that are not often recognized. Wikipedia and Facebook have been successful, while other such applications have not, because they have elegant interfaces that allow their users to easily enter their writings, pictures, etc. But that elegance comes at the cost of choice. Wikipedia and Facebook users must work within the preset, and largely immutable, parameters of those applications' codes. Because of this, all Wikipedia entries and Facebook pages look more or less the same and present their content in more or less the same ways. That content varies from user to user, but in the end the individual contributors, the "authors," are less important than the specific digital interface they employ, and they are regulated by its rules. Those interfaces are, de facto, manifestos; they have defined and spawned new genres.

There is little point in analyzing – even if one could – the millions of individual contributions posted to such applications. Any choice from among a million individual entries will be, to a greater or lesser degree, arbitrary. Increasingly, then, as digital technologies proliferate and evolve, we will no longer be able to assess individual iterations. We will, instead, have to turn our attention to the nature of the application. The critical questions will move from "Is this a good text?" and "Does it have literary value?" to "Is this technology or individual application – this set of rules and interfaces – sufficiently elegant, nuanced, and complex that it *could* produce texts of literary value?" To a large extent this is being done already by the user market: both Wikipedia and Facebook have succeeded where others have failed because their interfaces, their rules, work while others, no longer in use, did not.

While it has been assumed that it took digital technology to embody the theoretical speculations of the deconstructionists and New Historicists, I would argue that the role-playing game preceded and, to some degree, anticipated their theories. The timeline alone is suggestive: at the exact historical moment that Barthes and Foucault were deconstructing the author, Gygax and Arneson invented a system, a set of rules, which allows small communities to spontaneously generate narratives for and by themselves. Coincidence? Or fulfillment of a process of reevaluating the status of literature that began with the New Criticism's attack on the intentional fallacy, and a foreshadowing of the dissolution of authorial authority in the digital age? In the role-playing game, the author has been replaced by a game technology for producing narratives in a group setting. Not only is there no author, there is no text; there is only the creation of instant narratives that go off in spontaneous directions depending on the players and the occasional roll of the dice. *Dungeons and Dragons* may be proof that our literary interests should shift from the story to deep structures that allow the story to be what it is. Criticism necessarily becomes an act of metacriticism when the literary text is spontaneous or is one of a million entries in a computer program. Game rules and computer codes, therefore, have become the equivalent of aesthetic manifestos, critical adjudications that attract the creative adherents or charismatic works that inspire imitations, trends, or schools of writing.

It is easier to think of the role-playing game rulebooks than digital applications in this critical manner for two reasons. First, the rulebooks are, obviously, books. They are often expensive and lavishly illustrated and some are designed to look like ancient tomes or secret government documents. And these books are sometimes more than a collection of regulations, lists, and formulas for calculating actions and consequences within a game. Some aspire to a narrative themselves. That is, the rules are presented within a story that introduces the reader to the particular game world, be it one of medieval warriors or contemporary vampires. Second, people do read role-playing game books for pleasure. That pleasure derives, especially in the books that do not aspire to an internal narrative, from the engagement with the imaginary world that the books map for the gamemaster and players. The rules, character creation system, descriptions of the culture, lists of monsters and threats, all combine (if they are done well) to create a consistent and complex fictional universe. It is this environment, the postulating of all its contingencies, that readers of the rulebooks enjoy. So it is no surprise that, as mentioned, role-playing games have been created for a variety of preexisting fictional worlds from literature (*Call of Cthulhu*), film (*Star Wars*), and television (*Buffy the Vampire Slayer*). The rulebooks for these games attempt to extend the possibilities of these charismatic fictional realms, summarizing their internal logics and quantifying their contingencies so that readers can imaginatively move within them. The "success" of a given rulebook thus depends on how thoroughly and seamlessly it embodies the fictional world in its game mechanics.

But this swings us back to another author, the rulebook's author, or rather authors, because most of the role-playing game books are a collaborative effort of writers, designers, and artists. The *Dungeons and Dragons Player's Handbook* (Cooke, Tweet, and Williams), for example, has a three-person executive design team, thirty-four designers, twenty-eight "contributors," and an acknowledgment that the book is based on the original rules created by Gary Gygax and Dave Arneson. This is a team larger than on some film sets and there is no clear director who can be singled out as the auteur. Some role-playing game rulebooks are, of course, the product of one person, but the most popular, perhaps due to their complexity, are large team efforts just as most digital applications are now the product of design and coding teams. And if a particular rulebook is based on a preexisting fictional realm, then the writers (and in the case of film and TV, directors, designers, etc.) who created that charismatic world in the first place should also be considered part of the authorial team for the game that extrapolates from their vision. In the end, it would seem, there is no fixed, single author for the rulebook just as there is no fixed, single author for the story that is generated by game players using the book.

There may also be an argument for considering the gamemaster as the "author" of any given game-playing session. It is the gamemaster who sets up the basic parameters of the narrative and introduces minor characters, description, and plot points. And certainly a bad gamemaster, someone with no imagination, talent for description, or ability to interpret the rules, will result in a bad game and, hence, a bad narrative. A good gamemaster might be a type of auteur, rather like a film director, marshaling creative individuals into a collaborative effort which she, ultimately, controls through her superior knowledge (of both the rules and the narrative arc of a given playing session) and power (she adjudicates dice rolls). The response to this theory is twofold: first, while a gamemaster does steer and inform any given playing session, she cannot do so without the contribution of the players. The gamemaster marshals a team of players to construct the narratives; without those players she has no power or function. Second, while some gamemasters do create elaborate background narratives for the sessions they run, most do not, and indeed, no one has to. The manufacturers of role-playing game books also market (and sometimes give away) prepackaged adventures and rules for spontaneously generating a narrative through the rolling of dice.

So if we are going to evaluate a role-playing game, all we really have are the rulebooks. How do we evaluate them? As mentioned, readers engage with these books, when they are not using them as source material for actual games, in order to enjoy the construction, or reconstruction, of a complex fictional realm. Good game rules, then, are rules that accurately and consistently facilitate the imagining of that realm. More, they allow for a myriad of possible events and consequences to occur in that realm without straining its internal logic. In other words, they have systems that will accommodate a variety of imaginative events without collapsing the internal consistency of the world. And, I would argue, the best rulebooks strike a balance between relatively simple rules and the engagingly complex possibilities they allow. In other words, their game mechanics are elegant.

Now, for many role-playing game enthusiasts, "game mechanics" means the rules that govern the elements of chance in game play. That chance is usually governed by the rolling of dice. It is this element, as well as the improvised nature of the narrative, that marks role-playing games as "ergodic," a term coined by Espen J. Aarseth, "that derives from the Greek words *ergon* and *hodos* meaning 'work' and 'path'" (1) and is used to signify a type of literature in which the reader contributes to form or meaning by making consequential decisions: by choosing to click on a link or, here, to improvise a narrative consequence based on the roll of a die. So, for example, when a player says, "I swing my ax at the head of the goblin," the gamemaster will say something like, "Roll a D20" (a 20-sided die). The player does, scoring, say, 13. The gamemaster will then apply a numeric formula: "13 plus a strength modifier of 4 means you have hit the goblin. Now roll again to see how much you have injured it." This unique feature of the role-playing games is a mechanism for breaking down the contingencies of fictional realities into numeric formulas, to attempt, in essence, to quantify the chance elements of reality, albeit a fictional reality. This allows the narrative to move forward in unexpected ways and forces the players to improvise in response to the outcome of dice rolls, but the formulas that determine the effects of the dice rolls on the events and objects in the fictional world themselves have to embody the logistics of that world. If they are disproportionate in any way, they may collapse the fiction in which the game players are imagining themselves. So if, in the example above, a score of 13 on the die roll meant that the player not only hit the goblin, but caused it to explode, the internal logic of the universe would seem inconsistent. Why would a goblin explode? It makes no sense in that fictional realm. The game mechanics, then, would be faulty; the game rules inelegant; the games generated would never be satisfying, coherent narratives.

Can role-playing games ever be part of the academic study of literature? I have twice raised the question of the literary status of role-playing games in upper-division literary courses. In each case, the students who were familiar with role-playing games, who had played them or gamemastered them, were quick to argue for their potential literary status. They did, however, raise the question of appraisal. One student said, "You cannot critique a role-playing game by watching a group of people playing it, sitting back like an audience. That doesn't work because while playing the game is very exciting, there's nothing more boring than watching it being played. You have to be engaged in the process." This may be true, for those students who had never participated in a role-playing game were profoundly dubious about its literary potential. They found the rulebooks bewildering in their detail. I therefore arranged a role-playing game session for them; it encompassed one stand-alone adventure, and the students were assigned characters. One student was the gamemaster and I played with the students (my character was a warrior dwarf with a broken heart named Voltag Grimm). By the end of the session the students got it. They became interested in their characters and one actually applauded at the end of the adventure because her character received a reward. She was pulled into the fiction that she had helped create. Like my friend, she had entered a fictional world wholeheartedly. All of the students in the experiment accepted the possibility of the role-playing game as a literary experience, if not as a text, once they had played the game. After playing a game, they could appreciate the complexities and nuances of the game's rules.

Let us return to that game player sitting in her car thinking about paying her phone bill with the gold her character discovered during a role-playing game. She had engaged with and imaginatively moved within a complex fictional world for hours, a world made possible by the rulebooks for *Dungeons and Dragons*. That world was sufficiently compelling that her engagement carried into the real world. This is Coleridge's "suspension of disbelief" on steroids. It is total immersion in a narrative, a character, and a fictional world. I believe we would have to call that a literary experience. On the other hand, I, as a literary critic, will never have access to the story with which she was engaged. It is gone forever and cannot be critiqued. All I can do is study the rulebooks and imagine how they might help create a story so compelling that it, however fleetingly, becomes a surrogate reality. In a world without authors (or so many that the title has become meaningless), a world in which narrative and text are increasingly ephemeral (or so plentiful that the individuality of utterance is lost), the literary critic must turn to the deep structures that generate and inform the nature, complexity, consistency, and, yes, quality of those utterances. Literary criticism will become a metacritical assessment of potentiality, and individual articulations will be used as examples rather than as canonical texts. It was the role-playing game that freed narrative from the author-press-reader literary triptych; the new technologies are merely accelerating a process begun by people pretending to be elves. If literary critics want to stay relevant in the digital age, they must study the rules and learn how to play.

REFERENCES

Aarseth, Espen J. *Cybertext: Perspectives on Ergodic Literature.* Baltimore, MD: Johns Hopkins University Press, 1997.

Beowulf: A Verse Translation. Trans. Seamus Heaney. Ed. Daniel Donoghue. New York: Norton, 2002.

Cooke, Monte, Jonathan Tweet, and Skip Williams. *Dungeons and Dragons Player's Handbook: Core Rulebook I.* Renton, WA: Wizards of the Coast, 2000.

Featherstone, Donald F. *War Games through the Ages: 3000 B.C. to 1500 A.D.* London: Stanley Paul, 1972.

Fine, Gary Alan. *Shared Fantasy: Role-Playing Games as Social Worlds.* Chicago: University of Chicago Press, 1983.

Foucault, Michel. *Language, Counter-Memory, Practice: Selected Essays and Interviews.* Trans. Donald F. Bouchard. Ed. Donald F. Bouchard and Sherry Simon. Ithaca, NY: Cornell University Press, 1977.

Garner, Stanton B. *The Absent Voice: Narrative Comprehension in the Theater.* Urbana: University of Illinois Press, 1989.

Lord, Albert B. *The Singer of Tales.* 2nd ed. Ed. Stephen Mitchell and Gregory Nagy. Cambridge, MA: Harvard University Press, 2000.

Mackay, Daniel. *The Fantasy Role-Playing Game: A New Performing Art.* Jefferson, NC: McFarland, 2001.

Ong, Walter J. *Orality and Literacy: The Technologizing of the Word.* 1982. London: Routledge, 2002.

Rapp, Uri. "Simulation and Imagination: Mimesis as Play." In *Mimesis in Contemporary Theory: An Interdisciplinary Approach*, vol. 1. Ed Mihai Spariosu. Philadelphia: John Benjamins, 1984. 141–171.

Reeves, Charles Eric. "Wittengenstein, Rules, and Literary Language." *Neophilologus* 67 (1983): 15–20.

Williams, Patrick J., Sean Q. Hendricks, and W. Keith Winkler, eds. *Gaming as Culture: Essays on Reality, Identity and Experience in Fantasy Games.* Jefferson, NC: McFarland, 2006.

Wizards of the Coast. *30 Years of Adventure: A Celebration of Dungeons and Dragons.* Renton, WA: Wizards of the Coast, 2004.

2

Consider the Source: Critical Considerations of the Medium of Social Media

KIRSTEN C. USZKALO AND
DARREN JAMES HARKNESS

In 2009 Iran blocked its citizens' access to Twitter and Facebook in an attempt to quell social discord about its federal election. A Ryerson student was threatened in 2008 with suspension for cheating because of setting up a study group on Facebook. The U.S. Marine Corps has banned the use of Facebook, MySpace, and Twitter. New media studies, especially those concerned with social media environments, are investigating the constructions, roles, and effects of the media that are proliferating in the information age. The variety of social media available to those with high-speed internet connections means that those with an inclination can publish themselves online. These technologies do more than create a platform for speakers, however. The infrastructure and interface of social media influence how messages are created and sent. McLuhan couldn't have been more prescient with his assertion that the medium is the message; for social media, the software is the message. There are myriad social media platforms available, but this chapter will concentrate on the interfaces of three of the most widely used in North America: blogs, Twitter, and Facebook. Moreover, we will look at how the infrastructures behind the interfaces themselves construct, normalize, and proliferate the public images of the speaker. The technologies that run under the hood of popular social media help create and distribute online selves, cobble together communities, and share sound bites and narratives. A study of new texts on the boundaries of literature must consider the ways in which the medium creates the message. The interface defines new social media.

ONLINE IDENTITIES

The majority of scholars argue that blogs function as an online extension or even evolution of the autobiographical diary form; a number
have also conducted other such genre-targeted studies. Articles on
blogging emerged as early as 1998, when Yasuyuki Kawaura, Yoshiro
Kawakami, and Kiyomi Yamashita discussed the phenomenon in their
article "Keeping a Diary in Cyberspace." Kawaura et al. concluded
that online journals were "primarily a communicative behavior" and
that they were a form of self-expression and self-disclosure (244, 236).
In 2000, Philippe Lejeune wrote *"Cher écran—"* (Dear screen) and
Rebecca Blood published "Weblogs: A History and Perspective," which
gives an excellent, if brief, chronology of the development of the weblog. She starts with Jorn Barger's *Robot Wisdom*, which claims the first
usage of the term in 1997, and skims past some of the early names in
blogging on her way to discussing the rise of Pitas, one of the first blogging services; Blogger; and Dave Winer's Edit This Page. Since online
writing's rise in 1999, much critical and cultural work has attempted to
categorize and examine what it is. Critics have argued that blogs are
online diaries, online journals, new journalism, and "Hyde Park corner
blather" (Dvorak). Others, such as Julie Rak and Viviane Serfaty, have
looked at the content of the blog and its genre forms. These approaches
make it possible to teach online writing like epistolary writing, life writing, or (auto)biography. Particularly useful for this approach is a special
issue of *Biography*, published in the winter of 2003, which includes
several articles geared toward positioning the online journal within
the realm of biographical and autobiographical study.[1]

The ways in which we create online narratives are as important
as the stories they tell. It is necessary to understand that the media are
changing. They are changing in form. They are forming the broadcaster and the broadcasts. Their formats encourage users to communicate differently and to represent themselves in a specific format. Twitter is a 140-character, short-form message to a group of listeners who
can respond; it is the broadcast of a single thought. Individual topic
sentences, random musings, theses, and suggestions locate the author
within an introspective moment intended for mass communication.
Facebook is the corporatization of the self on pages filled with news

feeds, highlights, and personalized advertising. Facebook is a billboard of the self, a branded image of the "online me," which is sponsored by friends as an act of validation and crossover. The blog is the most like traditional periodical publications. The oldest and most stable form of social media, the blog is the blankest piece of paper, the least linked in of the online social media tools. However, blogs are not entirely form-less means of self-broadcast, and as such have the potential to construct meaning in equally invisible ways.[2] Beyond studying the communities that spring up from social media and the media's adoption as practical communicative tools inside and outside the classroom, it is impera-tive to consider how the infrastructure and interface, the mechanisms and the informational structures behind these influential media, work together to construct the experience and meaning of personal digital communication online.

danah boyd argues that when conceptualizing social media as "a medium instead of a genre, it is possible to see how blogs are more akin to paper than to diaries," because blogs "are flexible, allowing all different sorts of expressions and constantly evolving." Lined paper invites users to compose, sketch paper suggests a more unstructured use of the space, and a ledger implies the recording of business data; the medium influences the experience of and product of composition. If framed as medium instead of genre, the new infrastructures and interfaces become available for critical study. Richard Macksey argues that paratexts are "the liminal devices and conventions, both within the book (peritext) and outside it (epitext), that mediate the book to the reader" as well as the "framing elements" of the text which help create meaning for the reader (xviii). The software, the user, and her community should be understood as interrelated components, which also create and mediate the text. Genette uses the concept of paratext as something that "enables a text to become a book and to be offered as such to its readers" (1). Understanding the interface illuminates the mechanisms which construct online narratives.

AFFORDANCES OF INTERFACES

In making social media user-friendly, designers delineate paths for in-formation which also construct it. Interface studies extend the investigation of how publication platforms and their paratexts influence both content and audience. The interface is an "intermediary to communication" (Skjulstad and Morrison 413). It gives the user certain affordances, something Robert St. Amant defines as "an ecological property of the relationship between an agent and the environment" (135). St. Amant describes affordance as a function we can see that is intuitive: "we can often tell how to interact with an object or environmental feature simply by looking at it, with little or no thought involved" (135, 136) – for example, we instinctively know not only what a chair is for, but the best way to make use of it. He further breaks down affordance into four separate concepts – relationship, action, perception, and mental construct – and discusses how to incorporate the idea of affordance into a user interface by focusing on the connection between action and relationship (136–137). The last of the concepts, affordance as a mental construct, is most relevant to our discussion. St. Amant writes, "[T]hese mental affordances are the internal encodings of symbols denoting relationships, rather than the external situations that evoke the symbols" (137). In the authoring of a blog, meaning cannot be pinned on a single HTML control or text box; it is the process as a whole. The interfaces for LiveJournal and DiaryLand encourage users to create a personal journal, or online diary. Blogger does not. Twitter keeps your messages short. Facebook keeps your updates active.

ITS NORMAL(IZED) CONTENT

Despite its central position, the interface cannot be discussed without considering the software and data structures involved in its creation. We must move inside the machine to see the software behind social networking tools, to the interface and the infrastructure. The interface is what the user of social media software directly interacts with; it is the placement of form fields and buttons, the visual design, and the feedback received after performing an action. The infrastructure behind the interface is never directly seen by the blogger, but it drives the interface's development, defines its boundaries, enables a web page form to become a post and that post to be offered to readers. The infrastructure enables output. The output is, in part, the online self.

Programmers do not care about content. At Twitter, Facebook, Blogger, and Movable Type they develop software to make social networking a simple process; they listen to customer requests for features. However, developers are not concerned with whether a post will be an online journal, a political commentary, or a collection of cat pictures. They are concerned with memory allocation, disk usage, and transaction speed. Every shortcut taken in the source code, every data type or archiving scheme not supported, every function written, and every decision made by the programmer to achieve these goals influences the interface, and therefore influences the content produced. The developer is social media's *anima ex machina*, heavily influencing its development – and, by extension, the online identity of its users. To the programmer, language is a set of bits and data types sorted into different containers. How the programmer deals with data affects how she creates the interface; if she has no data structure in place to handle a certain kind of information, it cannot be accessed through the interface.

Data structure is created through a process called normalization – breaking data down and categorizing it into its smallest logical parts. Developers normalize data to make it easier to use and reuse in a database and to give it meaning within the infrastructure. To understand this process, we should look at how data is normalized: the title of an entry goes in one container, the body text goes in another, and so on. The structure of the data does not necessarily match the structure of its original context, however. Although a title and the body text are related to the same entry, there is no consideration given by the developer as to whether one comes before the other, whether it should be displayed in a specific style, or if one has hierarchical importance over the other on the page. The data structure is dictated by the individual pieces of data themselves. If we look at a typical blog entry, it is quickly apparent how the data might be structured. The developer takes the data within each of these containers and stores it in a database. This may be a simple database, such as a CSV or Berkeley DB file, or it may be a more complex relational database, such as MYSQL or Microsoft SQL server. Within the database is a series of tables; and a series of fields is contained in each table. A table describes a record of data – a

TABLE 2.1

· EntryID	· Category (integer)
· Title (string)	· ExtendedText (text)
· Date (datetime)	· PostStatus (integer)
· BodyText (text)	· Keywords (integer)

blog entry—and the table's fields hold properties of that data, such as the title or entry date. Figure 2.1 illustrates an example; a developer has created an Entries table with the fields EntryID, Title, Date, BodyText, ExtendedText, Category, Keywords, and PostStatus (also see Table 2.1).

When possible, such as with the Category and Post Status fields, the developer will replace a string (alphanumeric) value with a numeric pointer to the same data within another table in the database. For example, an author may create a set of categories for her blog (such as "Personal Life," "School," and so on), which are stored in a separate database table named Categories and associated with a unique ID (CategoryID). When an entry is marked with the Personal category, the software queries the database to see what the CategoryID of the Personal category is in the Categories table, and places that in the Category field in an entry's record in the Entries table (see Figure 2.2). This sets up a series of relations within a database, and helps keep the database smaller; an integer takes up far less space in the database than a string: one byte to store a single-digit integer, compared to eight bytes for the string "Personal." When you start working with hundreds of entries, this difference adds up quickly. It is also easier to maintain. If you want to rename the "Personal" category to "Stories from the Woeful Events of My Unexaggerated Life," for example, you would only have to update the entry once in the Categories table; because it is referenced by its CategoryID in each entry, it will automatically be updated in all records that reference it. Figure 2.2 illustrates the relationship between the Category field in the Entries table and the CategoryID field in the Categories table, and shows how data fall into the structure. By abstracting often-used data such as a category into separate database tables, data can be reused within the database, which keeps the database smaller. If we know we will be referring to a single category in multiple entries, it makes sense to create a table of

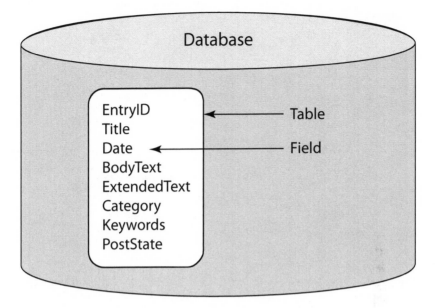

2.1. Database schematic displaying the relationship of fields and tables. A table holds records of data within the database, while fields describe the properties of each record.

possible categories and then point to their unique identifiers in each individual entry.

Each field in a database table is configured to accept a specific format of information known as a data type. For example, the Date field in the Entries table would be given a data type of DATETIME, while the Category field would be given a data type of INT (to specify an integer value). The body text of an entry would be placed in a binary data type known as a BLOB, since this is a type of data whose size is variable from record to record. Normalization conditions data to its purpose and ensures that the developer always knows what kind of data to expect when he retrieves it later. It also has the benefit of loosely validating the data by rejecting invalid data types. If there is an attempt to store a piece of INT data in the Date field, it will trigger an error, which prevents the data from being misused within an application.

The decisions made by the developer at this point, which involve configuring the tables and fields within the database, ultimately deter-

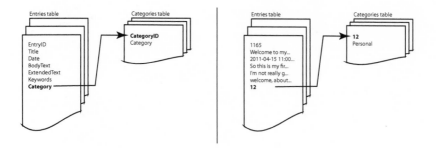

2.2. Relation between database tables based on an integer ID. The Category field in the Entries table creates a pointer to the CategoryID field in the Categories table. This allows for the easy reuse of data within the database without duplication. The value "12" in the Entries table provides a pointer to the category "Personal."

mine what will appear in the interface. If tables and fields do not exist in the database to support the categorization of an entry, for example, that entry is unlikely to appear in the interface since there is no facility to store the information (and, by extension, the interface will not prompt the blogger to categorize her thoughts).

ONE OF THESE THINGS IS NOT LIKE THE OTHERS

Different tools produce different social media, since many software packages are written for specific uses (for example, compare Live-Journal's emphasis on long-form journaling as opposed to Twitter's 140-character updates). The differences in their infrastructure—and therefore also in their interfaces—set one package apart from another. The code structures and the user interfaces developed by competing social media packages delineate information input differently, influencing the ways in which public identity is shaped and represented online. A software package created for diary writing, like DiaryLand, will reinforce the introspection of that style of writing. Twitter reinforces snippets of information, such as the user's location and activities. If a software package is for a more general audience, like Movable Type or Blogger, the blogger is given more latitude in her compositions, and identity may be formed around an external focus, such as politics.

A study of all available blogging packages and services is beyond the scope of this chapter: there are well over a million hits on Google alone for "blog software"; innumerable hosted services such as MySpace, Xanga, and DiaryLand; countless comparison charts of self-installed packages such as Movable Type; and dozens of applications for Twitter alone. This section will look at five broad applications—Blogger, Movable Type, LiveJournal, Facebook, and Twitter—focusing primarily on their differences to illustrate how the choice of software, and the development cycle behind it, can radically change a user's narrative output.

Blogger

Launched in August 1999 by Evan Williams and Meg Hourihan at Pyra Labs, Blogger is credited for the early growth of the blog medium. It was originally created as a simple tool to help the developers update their own websites, but they quickly recognized the potential appeal and retooled it for public use. Initially, Blogger's interface was very simple. It was a text box, a list of the most recent entries, and a calendar to look up entries from a specific date. Even today, Blogger does not tie the blogger to any specific kind of format, nor does it organize anything for the blogger. Like the page of a diary, the interface offers only a sequential means of finding and maneuvering through information.

Despite some cosmetic changes and its purchase by Google, the core functionality of Blogger has not significantly changed since its initial creation, although Blogger became far more style- and brand-conscious, placing more emphasis on branding the interface with the Blogger logo and creating a more visually appealing interface. Blogger has added labels that can be used to categorize a post, a rich-text editor that removes the need for any HTML knowledge, and comment functionality missing from early versions of the software, but it has not significantly changed beyond these. The page is still quite blank for the author, and she still can shape her blog however she sees fit. Unlike installed blog software, bloggers are not given direct access to Blogger's database structure or code. But much is said about both through its application programming interface (API), which is available for other programmers to write software to interface with Blogger.

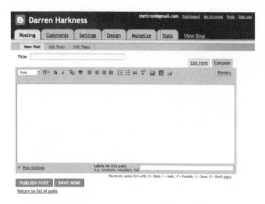

2.3. Blogger interface, April 2011. Note the addition of a title field, a rich-text editor, and post labels.

The lack of complexity in Blogger's data structure has to do with both its environment and its user base. Blogger supports millions of active blogs and must be conscious of its resources as a result, especially since the company does not charge for the service. Any functionality added to the system, therefore, must have as little impact as possible on the servers. This was first noticed by Evan Williams in 2001, when the popularity of Blogger caused its server to go down repeatedly; he eventually started a fundraising effort to purchase a new server to handle the additional load. Further enhancements were made to the core Blogger system to improve performance from 2001 to 2004. It was not until 2004, after its purchase by Google, that Blogger paid attention to the front-end interface.

Blogger is focused on the nontechnical internet user; although its users can customize their blogs' appearance and insert HTML into an entry, they are by no means required to do this in order to publish their blog. Madeleine Sorapure writes that an online diary "foregrounds the fact that the writer lives and writes in a context highly mediated by technology" (4), and this is apparent in Blogger. Blogger, like the other blogging packages, offers an affordance to its users: it becomes immediately clear that you are writing something that needs a title and a date. Blogger's interface – in contrast to LiveJournal – provides only a very basic affordance, and as a result has a minimal influence on what the blogger writes. She may be writing a diary entry, minutes of the latest council meeting, or a shopping list. Thus, the blogger mediates the content (but not always the presentation) of her own writing.

Movable Type

Blogger experienced a large amount of growth from 1999 to 2001, due to its low technical barrier to entry and its ease of use. It quickly started showing its limitations, however, in its lack of more advanced functionality, such as comments and the categorization of entries. In addition, some of its potential users were wary of entrusting their content to a company's servers. There were some attempts to create site-installed blog management software packages during this time, such as Noah Grey's Greymatter, but it was not until Movable Type's introduction in late 2001 that site-installed blog software gained traction. Ben and Mena Trott created Movable Type as a blog self-management tool for their own projects. It quickly gained interest among bloggers who wanted more from their blog software than Blogger was offering, or who felt uncomfortable trusting their content and privacy to a third-party host. The software offered the ability to host multiple blogs and authors, the categorization of entries, a built-in commenting system, the ability to draft entries, and a second output format (Blogger only offered HTML, while Movable Type offered HTML and RSS) ("About").

Movable Type is installed by the user (or her administrator) on the blogger's web server; as a result, it does not suffer from the same infrastructure and resource concerns that Blogger does. Movable Type has been developed for a small user base in each installation – generally a single blogger, but realistically no more than a handful of them. In 2001, this meant that Movable Type could have functionality Blogger could not, without worrying about how it would scale up to tens or hundreds of thousands of users.

The freedom that Ben and Mena Trott gained by writing a server-side application allowed them to better define how they wanted to blog. The decisions they made were to support the features they wanted to see in their own blogs, such as commenting and the ability to have more than one author (important for collaborative blogs, or for a website that contains more than one blog). As a result, they created a more complicated data structure. Because the database is hosted on the same server as the blog (or small collection of blogs), efficiency and database size are not as big a concern for Movable Type as they are for centrally hosted blogging tools such as Blogger. This allowed Ben and

2.4. Movable Type entry screen showing post options such as categories, keywords, post status, and comment options.

Mena Trott to create a more complex database structure that allowed for more data to be stored with an entry. Instead of Blogger's tabula rasa text box, more direction is given to the blogger (the entry screen for Movable Type can be seen in Figure 2.4). The blogger can specify a title, a primary category, and additional secondary categories; split her entries into Entry Body and Extended Entry fields, which will remove a portion of the full blog post from the front page; summarize the post in an excerpt; add keywords; decide whether or not the post should be published or kept as a draft; and finally, decide what day it should be authored on, whether that day is in the future or in the past.

This level of control over the process of blogging is of critical importance in the study of interfaces. Only a simple text box guides the

Blogger user. In Movable Type, the blogger is given specific tools. She is able to categorize her writing, which forces her to reflect on what it is she is going to write (or has written). Once that task is complete, and her entry is written, she can summarize her thoughts in the Summary field, reflecting on them again. So that she can more easily recall her writing later, she adds tags and keywords describing the content of the entry, and categorizes the entry within her own taxonomy. Finally she consciously publishes it by first previewing, seeing it as her readers will, then saving the entry. At every step in Movable Type, the author is made to reexamine her writing. Movable Type offers the same wide potential for development of identity as Blogger, but adds affordance for greater self-reflection. By focusing more attention on the publishing process, Movable Type helps the blogger be at once the observer and the observed. She can see herself seeing, as her audience does, and shape her identity accordingly.

LiveJournal

LiveJournal was launched at around the same time as Blogger, but it offered a much more delineated experience for its users. Brad Fitz-patrick, LiveJournal's creator, developed it as a community-based diary site; bloggers can create and update their own diaries, but they can also connect with others' diaries based on geographic area, based on group interests, or by including other LiveJournal users as friends ("What Is LiveJournal?"). LiveJournal has very similar infrastructure issues as Blogger: the system must support thousands of bloggers at any given moment (at the time of writing, for example, LiveJournal's statistics showed 160,251 updates over one twenty-four-hour period). As a result, its data structure must also be relatively simple. This is reflected in the journal entry page in LiveJournal (Figure 2.5), which is not significantly different from that of Blogger. Both supply the blogger with subject and body text fields, and both list entries by date. It is the differences between the two that change a blogger's experience, however. LiveJournal's interface offers a far different affordance than those of Blogger and Movable Type: the fields it brings forward from the data structure—mood, location, a customizable avatar with mood-based keywords, and the music currently playing—all put the blogger

2.5. LiveJournal entry screen, showing affect-specific elements, such as mood, location, and music, as well as comment screening and entry privacy levels.

in the mindset of creating an entry in a diary-like document. These additional fields encourage the blogger to give more thought to his emotional state when writing a new entry, and reinforce the autobiographical nature of LiveJournal. In addition, LiveJournal subscribers can upload multiple user pics, which can be assigned to entries as visual indicators of mood. One blogger, Kethryvis, has twenty-one avatars, each with different associated keywords, such as "I need a hug," "studying," and "do not fuck with me."

LiveJournal differentiates itself from Blogger and Movable Type by offering several ways for its bloggers to create entries: a blogger can use

LiveJournal's web-based forms, download a software application, send an email to her journal, or even call in an entry over the phone. Each of these ways of creating entries involves a different interface and, in the case of email and phone, carries different connotations and meanings that problematize the idea of the infrastructure and interface as shapers of identity. What does it mean for a blogger to send an email to her diary or talk to it on the phone? Although LiveJournal decentralizes its interface, all of the interfaces carry with them an undertone of confession. Where Blogger and Movable Type are centered on the individual, and reflect the individual back, LiveJournal is built around an anonymous gestalt, the community, to which the user is eternally confessing. In the email and phone interfaces, the LiveJournal blogger communicates directly to this confessor. In the case of the web-based forms, she communicates indirectly. Whether direct or indirect, communication is taking place between the blogger and her confessor. LiveJournal also offers the option to specify how private an entry is; it can be set as public, friends-only, or completely private (which mimics the traditional diary).

LiveJournal does not require highly technical knowledge to create and use its service. Its users do not need to secure hosting, register a domain name, or even learn HTML. Likewise, users only need basic web browsing skills to find and add other LiveJournal users who share their interests: from the user profile screen, you can click on either your physical location or any of your interests to receive a list of related communities or users. Once a blogger finds a user with shared interests, she can add them to her friends list by loading their profile and clicking on the Add button. The ease with which a LiveJournal user can create a community of fellow diarists helps further position her within the online diary genre.

Facebook and Twitter

Facebook and Twitter are a marked shift away from blogging, but still engage many of the same conceptual operators. Unlike a blog, however, which operates on a one-to-many model where you supply blog entries to a group of readers, Facebook and Twitter operate on a many-to-many publishing model. While you are offering updates, links, vid-

Share: Status Question Photo Link Video

What's on your mind?

2.6. Facebook status update.

eos, and photos to a group of friends, you are simultaneously seeing updates, links, videos, and photos from that same group of friends.

Originally, Facebook prompted its users with "Username is . . . ," suggesting that the user finish the sentence with a state of mind, activity, or adjective, such as "Darren James Harkness is writing a paper on Facebook." Since 2008, Facebook has twice changed its status update prompt, first by making the "is" optional in user updates, then by removing the prompt altogether, replacing it with "What's on your mind?" and combining it with the previously separate sections for sharing photos, videos, and links (see Figure 2.6). This marks a significant shift in Facebook away from simple status updates toward more of a microblogging service. What it also does is move Facebook away from identity creation and toward identity management, as suggested by DiMicco et al. Facebook becomes a composite space where all of the user's posts come together to advertise their social self (rather than create it). It operates with an eye to the business of social networking and places blatant cultural value on the often-invisible ways in which relationships have a stake in identity creation. Facebook users are often aware of their role in creating a financially viable and valuable social networking tool, and likewise strive to increase their cultural cachet on the site through compiling large groups of friends, the sharing of information (links, photos, and videos), joining groups, and managing events.

Twitter is a microblogging service founded in 2006 by Evan Williams and Biz Stone, both of whom were involved in the creation of Blogger. Twitter operates on the same many-to-many model that Facebook does, but is hyperspecialized. Twitter provides users the ability to post to its website short messages—referred to as tweets—generally focused around the user's current location and activities. In "The Psychology of Twitter," John M. Grohol characterizes Twitter as a "24/7

@stephenfry
Stephen Fry

Off on mammoth walk from Dublin town
centre to Joyce Martello tower - over 7
miles. Should be larky. Meeting someone
there for breakfast.

2 May 09 via Twitter for iPhone   ☆ Favorite   ↺ Retweet   ↩ Reply

@zeldman
Jeffrey Zeldman

Last minute gate change freakout. Had
run from one end of terminal to the oth
On board now, resuming normal
breathing.

2 May 09 via Twitter for iPhone   ☆ Favorite   ↺ Retweet   ↩ Reply

2.7. Tweets from Stephen Fry and Jeffrey Zeldman.

conversation that never ends," which takes on "more of an immersive, real-time feel of a talking conversation." The conversation metaphor is reinforced by Twitter's interface: you "follow" other Twitter users, and they "follow" you, very much like a regular conversation. Twitter is specific about what it expects from its users, prompting them with "What's Happening?" This encourages the user to think in terms of geography and activity, and induces tweets such as those in Figure 2.7 from Stephen Fry and Jeffrey Zeldman. The construction of a tweet–its brief nature and use of language when indicating a tweet's age–creates a sense of immediacy and intimacy among its users. Twitter imposes a limit of 140 characters per tweet, promoting what a few commentators have referred to as an "economy of words" (Conner). The limit was initially imposed because Twitter wanted to incorporate SMS messaging into its service (Rose), which has a 160-character limit. By limiting its users to 140 characters, Twitter can send a single SMS message for every tweet and include the user name of the person who wrote it. This limit is an excellent example of how the infrastructure of a tool has an overwhelming influence on the user's experience with it. It forces the user to write in short bursts and ruthlessly self-edit, and reinforces this by displaying the number of characters left in the tweet,

2.8. Characters left in tweet.

with the display getting darker as the number of characters rises until finally turning red as the tweet nears 140 characters (Figure 2.8).

Tweets that have appeared on the site within the last twenty-four hours are marked with the time elapsed since their entry, similar to Facebook (it is unclear which service first used this format). For example, Stephen Fry's tweet in Figure 2.7 shows that it was entered on May 2, 2009; new entries appear as "less than 5 seconds ago" or "10 minutes ago." This language gives users a sense of immediacy and intimacy, a sense made more prevalent when users post details about their own location and activities. Grohol, in "The Psychology of Twitter, Part 2," suggests that "while most people twitter while doing other things, the twittering makes a person feel even more connected to others who aren't with them at the moment than any previous technology ever has." Moses Ma writes that Twitter meets "a deep psychological need . . . for real community" that was "subverted by the Industrial Age." These reactions suggest that information normalization need not be read as detrimental, but can be seen as one way of establishing a shared method of creating community and communication. An awareness of the numerous ways in which information and identities are already normalized can likewise be brought into the classroom, as a way of conducting cultural criticism, creating a shared discourse, and looking at the ways in which digital platforms allow us to conduct new kinds of autoethnography.

PEDAGOGICAL POSITIONING OF THE INTERFACE

Hard-Copy Interfaces: Legally Normalized Identities

Information and identity normalization can be difficult ideas to address productively. Many students automatically bristle at the idea that their public identities online and offline are, in some sense, homogenized compilations. Calling attention to analogous examples can help address the ways in which we deal with normalizing interfaces on a daily basis. Students are provided with several interfaces which mediate their experiences as university students on a campus; the subjectivity shift is perhaps most prominent when they enter a classroom or lecture hall in preparation for a lesson. The concrete shape and organization of a classroom make it an unmarked interface (DePew and Lettner-Rust 175). Beyond the desks and chairs, which construct a type of self, students can be encouraged to find other interfaces that normalize them within the university, such as library cards, student ID cards, and transcripts, all of which support their subject position and validate their status to the greater community on campus and off. This normalization of physical identity continues outside of the university; other textual interfaces, like birth certificates, passports, insurance cards, drivers' licenses, and credit cards, all suggest pieces of public identity which are in the control of other agents. Identity, now more than ever, is normalized within corporate and governmental servers we will never see. These plasticized pieces of identity are analogous to the front and back ends of the social media platforms explored in this chapter; they are the visual output. Asking questions about what happens when we lose our wallets, when our credit records are somehow compromised, or when we apply for a job and have to signify that we do not have a criminal record allows us to see the very real ways in which biographies are being written about us and how little control we seem to have over their content.

In 1991 Donna Haraway pioneered analysis of the electronic body and how it muddies the borders of subjectivity in "A Manifesto for Cyborgs," where she discusses how the borders between the physical and the informational can blur. Haraway claims that each of us is a cyborg, an entity she describes as "a condensed image of both imagination and material reality" (150). Haraway spends much of "A Manifesto for Cyborgs" discussing how cyborgs live along the boundaries between human and animal, organism and machine, physical and nonphysical, and, finally, information and noise, and she applies this to the state of feminism in the early 1990s, arguing that it is creating fractured identities. Although Haraway's work predates the web, she provides a useful jumping-off point for looking at how social media – in fact, any electronic communication – works to blur the lines between author and reader, language and code, software and content.

N. Katherine Hayles extends Donna Haraway's cyborg theory in her discussion of post-humanism. She describes the post-human as that which "privileges the informational pattern over material instantiation, . . . thinks of the body as the original prosthesis we all learn to manipulate," and "configures [the] human being so that it can be seamlessly articulated with intelligent machines" (2–3). If the body is the "original prosthesis," then social media can be seen as an additional prosthesis we learn to manipulate as a way of extending our consciousness; it is an extension of the physical body into the electronic. danah boyd suggests that the blog itself is the blogger's identity, giving her "a locatable voice and identity in a community" ("Broken Metaphors" 11). In their study on weblog communities, Lilia Efimova, Stephanie Hendrick, and Anjo Anjewierden write, "weblogs are increasingly becoming the online identities of their authors" (2). The problem then is to place this within traditional models of literary theory; how does the online identity work with Lacan's model of identity, for example, when the subject has lost its subjective immediacy?

N. Katherine Hayles argues in "Virtual Bodies and Flickering Signifiers" that language becomes a code when made electronic due to the programming involved in transforming language from its original form into an "informational structure that emerges from the interplay between pattern and randomness" (30). Hayles invokes the traditional literary theory of Lacan, highlighting his statement "language is not a code" (30). However, Hayles claims, "in word processing, language is a code" (30). Lacan, she argues, wanted to keep a clear separation between signifier and signified. Unlike the paper-based text familiar to Lacan, however, electronic text is neither concrete nor static; it exists in a constant state of flux – encoding and decoding, continuously deconstructed and reconstructed through the blog software. Hayles continues:

> Information technologies operate within a realm in which the signifier is opened to a rich internal play of difference. In informatics, the signifier can no longer be understood as a single marker, for example an ink mark on a page. Rather, it exists as a flexible chain of markers bound together by the arbitrary relations specified by the relevant codes . . . a signifier on one level becomes a signified on the next-higher level. (31)

In short, signifiers flicker between signifier and signified, rather than float above the signified.

To illustrate how the signifier flickers, one only needs to follow a typical piece of social media from entry to display. Let's use the example of a blog entry. The first step is to enter it into the blog software's administrative interface. Unlike writing with a pen on paper, the form the entry takes in this interface does not necessarily match up to the form it will take when later read. It will go through several encodings and decodings between the time it is entered and when it is later viewed by a reader: it will shift from text in a content entry screen to query parameters, variables in source code, parameters in a SQL query, until finally being stored in a binary file, after three or four separate encodings. This is, of course, very different from the original text; though it does contain human-readable text, it is completely divorced from context.

The reverse process occurs when showing the entry a reader will see. Language has become code exactly as Hayles suggested it would, and goes through several stages of encoding and decoding between its author's creation and its viewing by the site user. At each stage of encoding, the text is divorced from its context, disassembled and reassembled anew. The presence of the author is divorced from the text itself in the time between the saving of the entry and its viewing by a reader. Sokari, a blogger at Black Looks, writes that "because of the medium, this presentation can never be complete. So many signifiers of ourselves are missing, the visual, our body language, our personal lives, anxieties, pleasures, family, friends, hobbies, work and the reality of our daily lives" ("Blogging from the Borders").

Lacan conceived of the floating signifier to describe how words within a sentence could move between sign and signifier, at least until the sentence is completed. Since language is in a constant state of flux in its electronic form, always shifting between text and binary, and the author can change the text at any time (with no literate record of its change), the division between sign and signifier is much more tenuous. Hayles uses the flickering signifier to discuss why there has been a shift from a focus on presence-absence to pattern-randomness, because the issue of presence-absence does not serve to "yield much leverage" when "the avatar both is and is not present" (27). In social media, the author is at once present and not present because the avatar of her identity is persistent through her blog entries, tweets, and Facebook statuses.

Fragmented Digital Journaling

In contrast to the hierarchically distributed physical signifiers of their public life, students have considerable personal power over the construction of a public, autobiographical, social self online. The web offers a number of platforms upon which students can assert their ideas and interact with one another, empowering them, within limits, to create a new self within interactive digital communities. Inside the academy some classes are maintaining class wikis or learning management systems as a way of communicating; however, there remain some problems with creating an intersubjective space when students are asynchronously collaborating (Larusson and Alterman 347). A great deal of communicative meaning happens in real-time conversations. Likewise, students do not naturally gravitate to wikis in their daily communications. Students in small classes or small tutorial groups should be encouraged to sign up with Twitter to facilitate communication over issues which might arise during the preparations for group work. Twitter can create an ambient awareness of community, and by having Twitter feeds on their phones (SMS) or desktops, students interact with interfaces which are familiar. Group communication is quick and easy, and can occur in real time; an added benefit is the potential for the tweet format to equalize effort and output. It is difficult to dominate a conversation conducted in tweets. Finding out if one can get one's inquiries and messages across in 140 characters should open up conversations about the kind of communications enabled in this just-in-time broadcasting.

Digital Autoethnography

Asking students to become active public intellectuals through a number of online media encourages them to consider how interface and infrastructure can shape the content and construction of their digital selves. One technique for examining this shaping is autoethnography, "a research method that utilizes the researchers' autobiographical data to analyze and interpret their cultural assumptions" (Chang 9) and that makes use of personal narrative and self-reflection as means of understanding a cultural process. Although this technique has been criticized by anthropologists such as Nicholas Holt,[3] it has been used with success by educators under different rubrics: journaling, reflective writing, inkshedding.

To use autoethnography, an educator would ask his students to create accounts on a number of social media platforms, including Facebook, Twitter, and a blogging tool, and to make use of those services over the course of the class. The educator would assign the students to keep a regular journal of their immediate experiences using social media tools, with the overall theme in mind of how these services influence the kind of content they are creating with them. For example, do students write primarily about what they are feeling on Facebook and what they are doing on Twitter? How does their writing change when it shifts from a short form, as on Twitter and Facebook, to a relatively long form, as in a blog?

The task should culminate in a summarizing assignment at the end of the class, where students collect their journal entries and analyze their use of social media over the life of the class. This assignment should examine shifts in the content of their writing over time, and how each service worked to enforce that shift. It would be useful, in terms of this assignment, to also give students some theoretical tools to analyze their writing; these might include autobiographical theory on the blog by Philippe Lejeune and Viviane Serfaty, post-humanist theorists like Donna Haraway and N. Katherine Hayles, and identity theorists such as Foucault and Lacan.[4] This capstone assignment should contain the student's reflections as well as selected posts from the various social media tools they used. In this way, the student has an individual picture of how her modes of communication and her public selves are constructed by the format being used to communicate.

CONCLUSION

Social media's growth is exponential, both among youth and young adults. According to a 2009 study by the Pew Research Center's Internet & American Life Project, 65 percent of American youth (12–17) make use of social networking sites, as do 67 percent of young adults (18–32). Overall, 35 percent of all online adults make use of social networking sites. Likewise, 32 percent of all online adults and 49 percent of youth read blogs, while 11 percent of all online adults and 28 percent of youth have created a blog (Jones and Fox 5). Of course, not all of those pages contain the kinds of narratives likely to appear in an academic classroom. However, the large-scale adoption of Twitter (11.5 million accounts, according to a June 2009 study by Cheng and Evans), Facebook (250 million accounts, according to its own statistics), and blogs (184 million, according to White and Winn) represents a substantial amount of writing. The amount of life writing, blogging, tweets, and Facebook updates exceeds the critics' ability to interact with it. However, its breadth suggests that the kinds of writing being done online deserves attention both inside and outside the classroom. Given that many students will have interacted with social media, educators should be giving them the tools to critically interact with those media and to understand how social media's construction works to shape the content they create with it.

This chapter has contended that one approach to looking at the kinds of literatures which appear online is to look at the platforms used to publish them and how those platforms influence their creation. The best way to understand the effect of a technology on the creation of meaning is to understand the technology itself. In the case of closed-source social media tools like Facebook and Twitter, where the infrastructure behind the interface is a trade secret and therefore unavailable for public viewing, scholars are limited to studying the interface and how it influences the creation of self. Open-source tools such as Movable Type give us a deeper look into how these interfaces are in turn influenced by their underlying infrastructure.

There is a steep learning curve in performing a more in-depth study of these tools and how their infrastructure influences the selves created within them. Scholars should have a basic understanding of the programming language the tool is created in, be it PHP, Perl, or Ruby. However, this deeper study is not necessarily required to explore how the construction of these tools shapes the creation of self within social media. Comparing the interfaces of various online publication platforms will give critics a better understanding of how the message and the self which produces it are normalized in order to be stored as data in the databases which run underneath the hoods of these tools. Studying the interface and infrastructure reveals how much of the online self is so freely offered up, how the messages about ourselves are prompted, and how our online literatures are influenced by the tools used to code and publish them. Information may be free, but it is being normalized, stored, published, and sold online. Social media may offer a potentially infinite number of ways in which to stand and be heard, but each platform influences the message ever so subtly. The key to reading this type of text is in understanding how the medium shapes the messenger, and therefore the message.

NOTES

1. A study by Hall, Hazel, and Davidson illustrated that blogging encourages positive exchange, mutual support, and peer aid in an educational environment. Publications are springing up encouraging the use of Twitter as a communication device, to teach succinctness, and as a collaborative writing tool. New techniques, tools, and methods to facilitate educational blogging are in the works. See Kim.

2. Various kinds of publication platforms run simultaneously online, sometimes even for the same person, in the same space. Those who Google themselves regularly will often be surprised at where and how they have been found by search engines; the use of multiple platforms multiplies this effect. Social media aggregators like Flock, FriendFeed, and Streamy speak to the new necessity of organizing electronic

social information; they speak to a desire to find a way to reweave some of the disparate narrative strands that compose part of distributed online identities and communities. However, finding and recompiling these disparate fragments is difficult, although sites like MIT's *Personas* will create an incomplete visualization of the electronic self. See the visualization at http://personas.media.mit.edu/personasWeb.html.

3. See "Representation, Legitimation, and Autoethnography: An Auto-ethnographic Writing Story," *International Journal of Qualitative Methods* 2.1 (2003).

4. See Lejeune's "*Cher écran –*" and *On Autobiography*; Serfaty's *The Mirror and the Veil*; Donna Haraway's *The Haraway Reader*, esp. "A Manifesto for Cyborgs"; N. Katherine Hayles's *How We Became Posthuman*, esp. "Virtual Bodies and Flickering Signifiers"; Lacan's "Mirror Stage"; Foucault's *History of Sexuality*, vol. 1:3.

REFERENCES

"About." *Movable Type* (5 Dec. 2001). Web. Accessed 1 Mar. 2011.

Blood, Rebecca. *The Weblog Handbook*. New York: Perseus, 2002.

Bochner, Arthur P., and Carolyn S. Ellis. "Communication as Autoethnography." In *Communication as: Perspectives on Theory*. Ed. Gregory J. Shepherd, Jeffrey St. John, and Theodore J. Striphas. Thousand Oaks, CA: Sage, 2006. 110–122.

boyd, danah. "A Blogger's Blog: Exploring the Definition of a Medium." *Reconstruction* 6.4 (2006): n.p. Web. Accessed 28 Feb. 2011.

Canwest News Service. "Facebook Student Spared Expulsion." *Canada.com* (18 Mar. 2008). Web. Accessed 1 Mar. 2011.

Chang, Heewon. *Autoethnography as Method*. Walnut Creek, CA: Left Coast Press, 2008.

Cheng, Alex, and Mark Evans. "Inside Twitter: An In-Depth Look inside the Twitter World." *Sysomos Resource Library* (June 2009). Web. Accessed 1 Mar. 2011.

Conner, Marcia. "Can Twittering Create an Economy of Words?" *Fast Company* (16 Nov. 2008). Web. Accessed 1 Mar. 2011.

DePew, Kevin Eric, and Heather Lettner-Rust. "Mediating Power: Distance Learning Interfaces, Classroom Epistemology, and the Gaze." *Computers & Composition* 26.3 (2009): 174–189.

DiMicco, Joan, et al. "Motivations for Social Networking at Work." In *Proceedings of the ACM 2008 Conference on Computer Supported Cooperative Work – CSCW '08* (San Diego, CA: 2008), 711. Web. Accessed 29 Nov. 2011.

Dvorak, John C. "The Blog Phenomenon." *PC Magazine* (5 Feb. 2002). Web. Accessed 1 Mar. 2011.

Efimova, Lilia, Stephanie Hendrick, and Anjo Anjewierden. "Finding the Life between Buildings: An Approach for Defining a Weblog Community." *Internet Research* 6.1997 (2005): 1–15.

Foucault, Michel. *The History of Sexuality*, vol. 1: *An Introduction*. New York: Vintage, 1990.

Fry, Stephen. "Twitter / @Stephen Fry: Off on mammoth walk from D . . ." *Twitter* (2 May 2009). Web. Accessed 1 Mar. 2011.

Genette, Gérard. *Paratexts: Thresholds of Interpretation*. New York: Cambridge University Press, 1997.

Grohol, John M. "The Psychology of Twitter." *PsychCentral* (23 Feb. 2009). Web. Accessed 1 Mar. 2011.

———. "The Psychology of Twitter, Part 2: World of Psychology." *PsychCentral* (11 Apr. 2009). Web. Accessed 1 Mar. 2011.

Haraway, Donna. "A Manifesto for Cyborgs: Science, Technology, and Socialist Feminism in the 1980s." In her *The Haraway Reader.* London: Routledge, 2004. 7–46.

Harkness, Darren James. "The Effect of Adding a Zero: The Blog and Identity." Unpublished M.A. thesis, University of Alberta, Jan. 2008.

Hayles, N. Katherine. *Electronic Literature: New Horizons for the Literary.* Notre Dame, IN: University Press of Notre Dame, 2008.

———. "Virtual Bodies and Flickering Signifiers." In her *How We Became Posthuman.* Chicago: University of Chicago Press, 1999. 25–49.

hippybear. "MetaTwitter? (or, Kill It While It's Young)." *MetaTalk* (21 Apr. 2009). Web. Accessed 1 Mar. 2011.

Holt, Nicholas L. "Representation, Legitimiation, and Autoethnography: An Autoethnographic Writing Story." *International Journal of Qualitative Methods* 2.1 (2003): n.p. Web. Accessed 28 Feb. 2011.

Hsu, C., and J. Lin. "Acceptance of Blog Usage: The Roles of Technology Acceptance, Social Influence and Knowledge Sharing Motivation." *Information & Management* 45.1 (2008): 65–74. Web.

Jones, Sydney, and Susannah Fox. "Generations Online in 2009." *Pew Research Center's Internet & American Life Project* (2009). Web. Accessed 1 Mar. 2011.

Kawaura, Yasuyuki, Yoshiro Kawakami, and Kiyomi Yamashita. "Keeping a Diary in Cyberspace." *Japanese Psychological Research* 40.4 (1998): 234–245.

Kim, H. "The Phenomenon of Blogs and Theoretical Model of Blog Use in Educational Contexts." *Computers & Education* 51.3 (2008): 1342–1352. Web.

Kottke, Jason. "On Twitter as a Rude Metaphor." *kottke.org* (3 Dec. 2007). Web. Accessed 1 Mar. 2011.

Lacan, Jacques. "The Mirror Stage as Formative of the Function of the I as Revealed in Psychoanalytic Experience." Paper presented at the Sixteenth International Congress of Psychoanalysis, Zurich, 17 July 1949. http://www-class.unl.edu/ahis498b/parts/week5/mirror.html. Accessed 14 May 2007.

Larusson, Johann Ari, and Richard Alterman. "Wikis to Support the 'Collaborative' Part of Collaborative Learning." *International Journal of Computer-Supported Collaborative Learning* 4.4 (2009): 371–402. Web.

Lejeune, Philippe. *"Cher écran–": Journal personnel, ordinateur, internet.* Paris: Seuil, 2000.

———. *On Autobiography.* Minneapolis: University of Minnesota Press, 1989.

Ma, Moses. "Understanding the Psychology of Twitter." *Psychology Today* (27 Mar. 2009). Web. Accessed 1 Mar. 2011.

Macksey, Richard. "Foreword." In Gerard Genette, *Paratexts: Thresholds of Interpretation.* Cambridge: Cambridge University Press, 1987. 1–15.

Olson, Eric T. "Personal Identity." In *Stanford Encyclopedia of Philosophy.* Ed. Edward N. Zalta (2010). Web. Accessed 1 Mar. 2011.

"Quick Tour." *Livejournal* (6 Apr. 2007). Web. Accessed 1 Mar. 2011.

Rose, Charlie. *Charlie Rose: A Conversation with Evan Williams, Co-Founder of Twitter.com* (27 Feb. 2009).

Web. http://www.charlierose.com/view/interview/10118.

Santana, Rebecca. "Iran Election, Uprising Tracked on Twitter as Government Censors Media." *Huffington Post* (15 June 2009). Web. Accessed 1 Mar. 2011.

Serfaty, Viviane. *The Mirror and the Veil: An Overview of American Online Diaries and Blogs.* New York: Rodopi, 2004.

SIGART/SIGCHI. 1999 *International Conference on Intelligent User Interfaces: Redondo Beach, Los Angeles, California, January 5–8, 1999.* New York: Association for Computing Machinery, 1999.

"Six Apart–History" (4 Mar. 2007). Web. Accessed 1 Mar. 2011.

Skjulstad, S., and A. Morrison. "Movement in the Interface." *Computers and Composition* 22.4 (2005): 413–433. Web.

"SMS." *Wikipedia* (2009). Web. Accessed 1 Mar. 2011.

Sokari. "Blogging from the Borders–My Blog and I." *Black Looks* (6 Oct. 2006). Web. http://www.blacklooks.org/2006/10/blogging_from_the_borders_-_my_blog_and_i. Accessed 8 Oct. 2007.

Sorapure, Madeleine. "Screening Moments, Scrolling Lives: Diary Writing on the Web." *Biography* 26.1 (2003): 1–23. Web.

St. Amant, Robert. "Planning and User Interface Affordances." *Proceedings of the 4th International Conference on Intelligent User Interfaces–IUI '99.* Los Angeles, CA, 1999. 135–142. Web.

Stone, Biz. "Twitter Blog: Changes for Some SMS Users–Good and Bad News." *Twitter Blog* (13 Aug. 2008). Web. Accessed 1 Mar. 2011.

"Twitter." *Wikipedia* (2009). Web. Accessed 1 Mar. 2011.

U.S. Marine Corps. "Immediate Ban of Internet Social Networking Sites (SNS) on Marine Corps Enterprise Network (MCEN) NIPRNet." *U.S. Marine Corps* (3 Aug. 2009). Web. Accessed 1 Mar. 2011.

White, Dave, and Phillip Winn. "Feature: State of the Blogosphere 2008." *Technorati* (2008). Web. Accessed 1 Mar. 2011.

Zeldman, Jeffrey. "Twitter / @Jeffrey Zeldman: Last minute gate change fr . . ." *Twitter* (2 May 2009). Web. Accessed 1 Mar. 2011.

Voice of the Gutter:
Comics in the Academy

TANIS MACDONALD

In none of the books on comics I have looked into . . . have I come on any
real attempt to understand comic books: to define the form, midway between
icon and story; to distinguish the subtypes. . . . It would not take someone
with the talents of an Aristotle, but merely with his method, to ask the
rewarding questions about this kind of literature that he once asked about an
equally popular and bloody genre: what are its causes and its natural form?

LESLIE FIEDLER, "THE MIDDLE AGAINST BOTH ENDS"

[C]omics are a wandering variable, and can be approached from many
perspectives. The restless, polysemiotic character of the form allows
for the continual rewriting of its grammar; each succeeding page need
not function in the exact same way as its predecessor. The relationship
between the various elements of comics (images, words, symbols) resists
easy formulation. The critical reading of comics . . . involves a tug-of-war
between conflicting impulses: on the one hand, the nigh-on irresistible
urge to codify the workings of the form; on the other, a continual
delight in the form's ability to frustrate any airtight analytical scheme.

CHARLES HATFIELD, *ALTERNATIVE COMICS: AN EMERGING LITERATURE*

PART I: SHUTTLE MEETS GUTTER: COMICS AS LITERATURE

Are comics "literature"? Should they be taught in our classrooms, and
if so, how? What literary functions might they fulfill? What can we

get from reading (and teaching) comics that cannot be obtained from other forms? What might we say to our students and ourselves about the reasons for expanding the boundaries of literature to include this form, once historically reviled as juvenile and trashy but now flying off the shelves of bookstores and libraries? What is the value of teaching a form whose very terms of signification (including "comics," "sequential art," "imagetext," and the well-intentioned but not always accurate "graphic novel") have not yet settled down to a final term upon which practitioners of the form, as well as scholars and historians, can agree? The cultural turn of the 1970s and 1980s, which saw mass culture blossom to proportions that alarmed some scholars and invigorated others, occurred well before the current undergraduates were born, yet these students too are sometimes mystified by the use of comics in university coursework.

Given the ubiquity of anecdotes about the new status of comics, anecdotes which often act as a starting point for serious discussions of comics, I will offer my own. In 1982, Raymond Briggs's *When the Wind Blows* arrived in the children's section of the library where I worked. The cover art resembled Briggs's much-loved and frequently circulated picture book *The Snowman*, but when I arrived at work, the librarian was recataloging the new Briggs book. Handing it over, she asked me to take it upstairs to the adult section. "It's not for children," she said. "I know it doesn't look like it, but it's a serious book about the bomb." Of course, I didn't take the book upstairs right away but read it first—such were the pleasures and privileges of that job. When I finished, I was less sure than the librarian was about whether *When the Wind Blows* was a book for children, though it was clear to me that it was not a book for children *only*. Despite this moment, it took me a long time to rediscover the graphic novel. I read Art Spiegelman's *Maus: A Survivor's Tale* only after it had won a Pulitzer Prize in 1992. When I returned to graduate study, I saw that *Maus* was included in the syllabus for "Fundamentals of Literary Study," the university's second-year survey course in English literature. Academia appeared to have changed very quickly; yet had the boundaries of literature actually moved?

The epigraphs for this chapter were originally published fifty years apart, in 1955 and 2005, respectively, and they outline some practical and still outstanding concerns about reading comics as literature. For a scholar as august as Fiedler, whose 1960 critical text, *Love and Death in the American Novel*, would establish him as an intellectual with a social conscience, to call for a sober consideration of the comic book as worthy of attention comparable to that Aristotle gave to defining tragedy, was remarkable, even coming as it did on the heels of Marshall McLuhan's discussion of Superman and Orphan Annie as cultural icons in 1951's *The Mechanical Bride*. A full five decades after Fiedler's essay was first published, Charles Hatfield's identification of the "conflicting impulses" of tradition and innovation in comics pinpoints the tensions and pleasures of reading comics, while addressing Fiedler's call for a methodology. Besides an interest in thinking about how comics function as literature, Fiedler and Hatfield share questions about how the prospect of regarding comics as intellectual material means that issues of class cannot be ignored. Fiedler's observation that "the fear of the vulgar is the obverse of the fear of excellence, and both are aspects of the fear of difference" (133) is followed up by Hatfield's warning that the comics subculture, especially the "underground" or "alternative comix" scene beginning in the 1970s, is "lowbrow and shabby in origin," though "it tends to be highbrow both in its material obsessions and in its self-conscious rejections of bourgeois norms" (xii). Hatfield notes, with some asperity, the "status anxiety" of scholars who may bring "traditional literary standards to comics without respect for the comics' unique origins and nature" (xii). Fiedler is equally respectful of comics' origin when he defends his point of view as being quality-based rather than an attempt to appear hip: "I should hate my argument to be understood as a defense of what is banal and mechanical and dull (there is, of course, a great deal!) in mass culture; it is merely a counterattack against those who are aiming through that banality and dullness at what moves all literature of worth" (128).

A still-steaming debate about what defines "literature of worth" is hidden behind the relative ease with which Fiedler invokes the phrase, and it would be foolish to ignore the five tumultuous decades that lay between Fiedler's comments and those of Hatfield. Those years saw, among many other political and social changes, charges of elitism in the university system and a rise in student activism, as well as feminist, Marxist, and postcolonialist challenges to the literary canon. Yet, given these seemingly sweeping changes, it is amazing how prescient

Fiedler was, or rather, how little has changed in the midst of so much social upheaval, so that Hatfield's comments are remarkably similar to Fiedler's. In the question of comics as literature, is this a case of *plus ça change?* What kind of defense can comics-friendly professors, students, readers, and practitioners of the form offer against Fiedler's accusation that comics as a form of literary "difference" inspire resistance manifested as "a drive for conformity on the level of the timid, sentimental, mindless-bodiless genteel" (133)?

The title of this chapter is intended to be a pun on comics' cultural history as popular text and on their future in scholarly study: a voice speaking from the "gutter" of disposable mass culture and also from the "gutter" that is the space between panels, the interpretive space of sequential art. That voice from the gutter, according to Scott McCloud in his 1993 nonfiction comics text, *Understanding Comics: The Invisible Art,* speaks through the "grammar of closure" (67); other critics concur, although on slightly different terms. Hatfield notes that panel-by-panel reading emphasizes the "art of tension" in comics (34), while Joseph Witek's sublime 1989 study, *Comic Books as History,* notes that the space between panels dictates the "unique rhythm of the medium of sequential art" to "create a movement [at] once pictorial and literary" (22). In the wake of this reading theory, I offer the "voice of the gutter" as an adjunct to the "voice of the shuttle," the phrase used by Geoffrey Hartman as a metaphor for the creation of written text, popularized (and ironized) by the online humanities research database of the same name: *Voice of the Shuttle* (http://vos.ucsb.edu). Citing Aristotle's *Poetics,* Hartman retells the Greek myth of Philomena, who, raped by her brother-in-law Tereus, who also cuts out her tongue to silence her, finds a way to inform her sister Procne of her abuse and imprisonment by weaving her story into a tapestry. Aristotle notes that Philomena's weaving is a form of writing, a way of communicating her plight silently, secretly, and over a long distance, and further notes that it is the "voice of the shuttle" that speaks to Procne: the weaving acts as a metaphor for written communication (Hartman 337). I note that this myth concerns one woman's need to communicate with another woman, and that the medium she chooses is associated with the women's culture and visual imagery, for Philomena's tapestry is illustrated with images of her assault. Many books on comics history seek to legitimize comics as art through early examples like the Bayeux tapestry, the cave paintings at Lascaux, or even the Stations of the Cross, but Philomena's use of the voice of the shuttle, so long construed as a metaphor for written language, is actually a more apposite metaphor for the use of pictures as language: imagetext using the conventions of sequential art. Aristotle's voice of the shuttle, then, also speaks with the voice of the gutter. The violence of Tereus's attack is revealed by the tension between the woven images.

As to whether comics are literature, it depends largely upon the comic, and upon the definition of literature to which one subscribes. The specter of Dr. Fredric Wertham, trailing his infamous 1954 book, *Seduction of the Innocent,* which condemned comics as unwholesome and dangerous for young minds, still lingers at the edges of our postmodern consciousness. Despite the fact that Wertham's reductive thesis that innocent minds were being corrupted by degenerate artists· seems quaint now, Matthew P. McAllister, Edward H. Sewell Jr., and Ian Gordon point out in their introduction to *Comics and Ideology* that Wertham's reading of the influential force of comics as subversive and radical was in many ways critically accurate, though his anti-progressive, conservative stance led him to moralize rather than theorize (6). (The best example from Wertham's text: in the twenty-first century, homoerotic readings of the Batman-Robin relationship may still be radical, but they are not particularly shocking, and readers would be hard-pressed to find any public intellectual willing to condemn the comic because of it. Wertham's condemnation of the Batman-Robin relationship as "a wish dream of two homosexuals living together" [190] was intended as a moral critique, but sounds today like a good beginning for a queer analysis.) However, we should not be smug or presentist about such matters. Much as it may be satisfying to think of ourselves as living in an advanced age where such bourgeois moralizations no longer apply, perhaps the furor over the "occult" imagery in J. K. Rowling's Harry Potter series should remind us to be alert to arguments concerning "appropriate" reading matter for children, who will grow into the young adults who then attend our university courses. For most scholarly examinations of comics as a genre, and for most writers and artists working in the form, the spurious morality offered by Wertham's 1954 book remains too close for comfort, and the Comics Code Authority that dominated the industry from the 1950s to the 1980s wrote a restrictive history that is – in the life of the form – much too recent to be casually dismissed.

Comics (and the much-debated term "graphic novels") gained their first real ground toward scholarly inclusion in the mid-1980s, buoyed by the publication of what have come to be acknowledged by nearly every comics aficionado as the "Big Three": Frank Miller's *Batman: The Dark Knight Returns* (1986), Alan Moore and Dave Gibbons's *The Watchmen* (1987), and Art Spiegelman's two-part *Maus: A Survivor's Tale* (1986 and 1991). Comics have begun to be used in school curricula; and materials for teaching *Maus* to students as young as five are readily available online (see the web sources in *Teaching Resources for Art Spiegelman's Maus*). With the inclusion of graphic novels in university courses, their multiple adaptations into art films, and their considerable impact on the publishing world, it would seem on the surface as though there were no issues at all about the boundaries that may have been breached in allowing the graphic novel to "invade" scholarly study. However, the place of comics in the classroom should neither be taken for granted nor assumed to be unproblematic; comics demand their own pedagogical ways and means.

PART II: IS THERE A CLASS IN THIS TEXT? COMICS AND INTERPRETIVE COMMUNITIES

For much of the relatively brief history of comics criticism, scholarly discourse has remained focused on the question of legitimation to the point of making it a mantra. There is an insistent chorus of justification in most critical texts composed by comics historians or critics, not to mention practitioners of the form: the authors, artists, and authors/ artists who write and draw sequential art, to use Will Eisner's term. For these practitioners, questions of legitimation are equally – or even more – concerned with questions of commercial and legal rights as they are with scholarly attention. Artists/authors are sometimes ambivalent about the mixed blessing of having their sequential art put under the scholarly microscope (Hatfield xiii). One irony of this hesitation is that the "secret club" of comics knowledge bears a great deal of resemblance to the "ivory tower" of academia, though the architectural metaphor for comics would be more in line with an underground hideout (basement? cave? comic book store?). You do not need a doctorate to enter this lair, but you will be tested rigorously about your knowledge of comics. Luckily the kind of cramming required to enter the cave is much like the total-immersion experience of reading to pass comprehensive exams, and more than one comics-friendly professor has become so because a comics fan (a student, a younger relative, or a long-time mature fan who is a peer) has impressed with the rigor of his reading discipline.

It must also be said that the resemblance between comics readership and academic study extends to their shared status as a largely white, male space. In *Reinventing Comics*, Scott McCloud points out the homogeneity of comics creators, fans, and, to a certain extent, their imagined protagonists, and he argues eloquently for the comics industry to make more practical and psychological opportunities for artists with female, nonwhite, and queer subjectivities (11). McCloud's point makes explicit the irony that has not yet been explored by many comics critics and historians: that claims of oppression issuing from middle-class, white, male authors (in any genre) who complain that their work is not taken seriously are astonishing to many readers and writers of other(ed) subjectivities.

The publishing boom of the 1980s brought literary notice to so much quality work in the comics genre that an embarrassment of comics riches is obvious to anyone teaching a contemporary literature or culture course. Like other genres and political modes that have fought for and won space in the academy—and I am thinking here of other specialties and genres with which I have worked: feminist literature and theory, avant-garde poetry and film, disability studies, postcolonial studies, Canadian literature—comics have won space and time in the classroom because they represent a mode of expression, and a style of art, whose time has come. Perhaps 100 percent acceptance in the academy is not currently available, but 100 percent acceptance is also not required. While it would be impudent to say that academically comics are a shoo-in, the inclusion of works of sequential art in the university classroom is no longer the cause for hot debate that it was in the 1980s, as discussed in McCloud's 1993 text, *Understanding Comics*, or the 1990s, as discussed in Joseph Witek's *Comic Books as History*.

The trend that appears to be emerging in the twenty-first century is less a battle over why professors may teach comics in the classroom and more about how to situate these texts with commensurate critical acuity. In the classroom, we must be able to assume the complexity of a text as a given, and proceed with analysis by examining the aesthetics, the politics, the intertwined complexities of form and content, the conventions it employs and those it resists, the tradition in which the text is situated, its social history, its artistic milieu, its innovations, its problems, its demands. I have reversed the terms in the title of this section to echo Stanley Fish's famous question, in order to remind readers that the work of situating comics as polysemiotic texts in the classroom requires professors not only to align their pedagogy to suit the work's complexities, but also to remain cognizant that assumptions of class cannot be ignored in the comics text. From their lowbrow beginnings in mass culture, to their occupation of a middlebrow, middle-class culture of acquisition and ownership, to the bourgeois social strata of their mostly male, mostly white creators and their long association with youth culture, comics are wreathed in issues of class that become magnified when the text is included in a syllabus. With this in mind, I offer six reasons to use a graphic novel in the classroom:

1. To discuss form
2. To emphasize genre
3. To introduce students to polysemiotic reading
4. To remind students that all literature uses both tradition and innovation
5. To illustrate that literary canons are both durable and mutable
6. To assert that reading is a series of skills, not a singular practice

There are more reasons, of course, but I will leave those to be identified by others. Suffice it to say that some comics are more worthy of study than others, and this discernment of worthiness may (and, some would argue, *should*) reflect the professor's bias, approach, politics, or sense of the classroom as an "interpretive community." Not for nothing does David H. Richter include in *Falling into Theory*, his 1994 text about working with critical theory in the undergraduate classroom, a section titled "Reading for Fun and Reading for Class" as an introduction to the section "How We Read" (Richter 205–208). Richter debates methodologies and practices here – not texts – and the various but not unrelated pleasures of reading "for fun" and "for class" undeniably have some overlap when reading comics as coursework. However, not every student will welcome the opportunity to read comics for or in class. Students' reactions to comics as university texts vary from the delighted to the cynical to the fearful. Some students will prove themselves to be good readers of comics; top students will transfer their skills to a visual-verbal text with little trouble, and many students who lag behind when reading a complex novel will shine when given a chance to display their complex reading of the visual code many comics deploy. Steven Johnson, in *Everything Bad Is Good for You: How Today's Pop Culture Is Actually Making Us Smarter,* notes that young people with the ability to adapt to dozens of new technologies often do well with texts that require them to "lean forward" and "fill in" the gaps in plot, much as is now required by complex television dramas and video games (Johnson 150–164). Graphic novels, with their gutters functioning as interpretive gaps and their storylines that feature the repetition of tropes, are yet more examples of technologically structured texts that require students to fill in the code as they read.

Other students, however, will struggle with the demands of sequential art, and will sometimes be frustrated by the fact that such an apparently "simple" text has exposed the gaps in their reading abilities. My colleagues who teach film tell me similar stories about beginning film students, and this has also been my experience when teaching poetry, making it clear that this struggle likely has more to do with the students' lack of familiarity with reading strategies than with the constitutive elements of the forms themselves. Some students resist reading forms with which they have not yet achieved a level of comfort, especially works that deviate from unified narrative and that place demands on readers to consider the structure, intricacies, or various levels upon which interpretation works. Despite comics' "coolness" factor, anyone teaching a graphic narrative should be prepared to discuss the form's complexities and entice students away from frustrations that may reflect what Fiedler identifies as the "politics [and] pathology involved in the bourgeois hostility to popular culture" (130). Pedagogically, comics are challenging texts. The professor must be aware of the seductive and mystifying qualities of the images and be willing to teach a sophisticated reading strategy to her students. Jeffrey A. Brown tells of an incident in teaching a comic book where he needed to pair up comics readers in the class with bewildered non–comics readers, who were having extreme difficulty understanding the codes of the comics (140–141). I have also noticed that teaching comics in a course with a variety of genres always changes the course for a handful of students whose relationship with written text is ambivalent at best, but who have illuminating and original approaches to reading polysemiotic code.

This takes some encouragement, of course, as students can be wary of the professor's intention in teaching comics. Is the professor trying (gulp) to be cool? Or is this a veiled test of reading skills? Will the students who display a level of comfort with reading the codes of comics be mocked or otherwise punished for displaying their long-cultivated and previously secret "geeky" skills? (Students will often apologize to me for their "geekiness," to which I have only one reply: in my class, geeky is good.) If students are stymied by the demands of reading the interactions between the images and the written portions of the text, we work together to establish and refine the vocabulary for discussing the text, which always deepens the classroom discussion of how texts work, how they present levels of debate, how they manipulate the reader, how they propose a political or social view, and what it means to write, and to read.

I appreciate Charles Hatfield's point that despite the popular emphasis placed on story in prose and in film, and to some extent in imagetexts, "narrative drive is not the only, nor always the best, criterion for evaluating a comic" (xiv–xv). The awkwardness of the term "graphic novel" is what we have invited by honoring the novel, that eighteenth-century upstart with its pretentious long narrative arcs, as the literary gold standard. Hatfield suggests, only a little facetiously, that the term "graphic novel" should forever appear in quotation marks (153). The use of the term is widespread, however, though not everyone can agree on its accuracy or its apparent prescription that comics should refashion themselves in the novel form. And then there is the matter of what kind of novel, as the world of comics has been for decades rampantly and gloriously trafficking in various genres and genre-blending, including horror, romance, detective fiction, mystery, science fiction, history, adaptation of classics, and verdant mixtures of all of these types. Clearly, the term "graphic novel" is useful only when it applies to the structure of the work in question; comics texts should be aligned with the literary genre they most resemble. Harvey Pekar's *American Splendor* has been much discussed as graphic autobiography, and Joe Sacco's *Palestine* as graphic journalism, so why not consider *From Hell* a graphic melodrama? Jason Lutes's *Berlin* a graphic ode? Alison Bechdel's *Fun Home* a graphic elegy? For scholars, this is surely an excellent way to direct students to think about the differences in form, format, length, style, context, and content in the works in question; as readers, this is surely what we owe the text.

Whenever I teach texts of sequential art, my background in poetics serves me better than any experience I have in novelistic analysis. Comics demand the kind of close reading that is best learned through poetry, and all analogies that equate the gutter between panels to the space between words in a poem, long a modernist and then postmodernist concern, are welcome. At "The New Narrative? Comics in Literature, Film and Art" conference held at the University of Toronto in May 2008, Canadian comics author Seth's keynote speech ("Seth Speaks!") refuted the often-asserted but poorly supported contention that comics are like film. (Robert Harvey also devotes an entire chapter to the differences between comics and film in his 1996 text, *The Art of the Comic Book*.) Seth asserted that comics, with their frame-to-frame movement, bear a much closer resemblance to poetry. Citing examples of how each panel focuses clearly on a single image, which may or may not be referenced in or given context by the previous or the subsequent panel (what Scott McCloud, in *Understanding Comics*, calls "aspect-to-aspect" movement), Seth noted that comics accrue visual imagery as poetry accrues verbal imagery. Seth's 2004 *Clyde Fans* offers a case in point; the first seventy-seven pages of this "picture novella," as its author calls it, offer a pictographic narrative in which action is sparse almost to the point of nonexistence. An elderly man walks through the living space, storefront, and warehouse of his long-closed fan store: eating, bathing, stepping into the street to light a cigar, and returning inside to sit at his desk and look at old receipts. The written narrative, the man's spoken monologue, relates the character's philosophy of salesmanship as an allegory for life, which is filtered through his memories of his career as a traveling salesman touring small towns in southern Ontario. Auden famously wrote that "poetry makes nothing happen," and in *Clyde Fans*, Seth dares to make "nothing happen" but the muted workings of memory. Though Seth positions the narrative neither as a Proustian meditation nor as a guilty revelation, *Clyde Fans* suggests a wealth of poetic, mimetic, and elegiac perspectives.

There is, undeniably, a wry irony in comparing sequential art to poetry: casting the popular against the esoteric, the "new" and "lowbrow" visual form against ancient elevated speech, the cutting-edge comic against the considerably less popular poetry. (But test this if you'd like: ask any passing person to name one living novelist, one living comics artist, and one living poet. Where do you think the silence will be?)

Perhaps the easiest way to situate comics as appropriate texts in the classroom would be to discuss the cultural centrality of superheroes, or the ubiquity of adaptations, or the challenge that alternative comics have made to the status quo of the action hero. But too little has been written about the experience of reading comics, and critics shy away from stating that a panel is more like a line of poetry in a long poem than it is like a sentence in a novel. Thankfully, plenty of comics artists understand this and demonstrate it very well, including Martin Rowson in *The Waste Land*; Canadian poet bpNichol in his "Allegories" cartoons of the 1970s; Peter Kuper in his two books of "picture puzzles," *Eye of the Beholder* and *Mind's Eye*; and Dave Morice in his anthology, *Poetry Comics*. Every critical text that offers a method of reading comics as complex texts (McCloud; Harvey; Inge; Witek; Hatfield; J. Brown) proceeds by zeroing in on the delicate features of the panels, their overlapping and multiple streams of meaning making, and the psychological tension and seemingly infinite potential of the slender gutter, what McCloud calls an "alchemy" of elements that appear to work in opposition but actually feed into a series of questions or possibilities about the subject matter. For the rebels among us, there is an added bonus in picturing the proponents of New Criticism roiling with disgust at their techniques being applied to a comic book. I find the mental image of Harold Bloom saying, "Well, *The Watchmen* tells us nearly everything we need to know" almost unbearably apropos.

But canon making, for a new form, is as much an exercise in tearing down structures as erecting them. Such a dynamic is vital to an emerging literature and to discussions about such literature in the classroom. As a Canadian literature specialist, I track the peaks and valleys of canon building as a national narrative and often question it as a national delusion; as a feminist poetry specialist, I spend long hours arguing that the innovative and the avant-garde deserve a place in our classrooms, even when (especially when) they disturb accepted meanings or rattle semantic certainty. The claim, repeated often in comics criticism, that comics are one of the last egalitarian arts, is inaccurate, of course: poets and short story writers, who also create alone with a pen and paper, or a word processor, do much the same thing. I note the blind spot that many comics creators have in not reading other genres or not acknowledging that they do; comics practitioners who complain of being the victims of genre prejudice could stand to remove the beam from their own eye. Exceptions to this complaint are plentiful and obvious, particularly considering the eclectic literary tastes reflected in the works of Spiegelman, Moore, and Miller. While an entire case for including comics as literature could not be built on the intensity of self-definition, it is valuable to understand that artists and authors think of their work as a literary genre with its own traditions and textual practices, canonical works, and authors, including dissent about those works and authors, and concerns about the politics of publishing that we have seen in feminist writing, in avant-garde poetry, and in the developing national or postcolonial canons. Detractors produce the same arguments in each of these emerging disciplines: this literature is not at all what we expect; it bears some resemblance to old forms but asserts itself too immodestly; it is attention seeking; it is politically suspect; it makes us uncomfortable. But as with other literatures that have received provisional acceptance in the academy, comics assert their legitimacy through their liveliness, their dissatisfaction with stasis, their restless energy, their sober acknowledgment of tradition, and their exuberant reimagining of the literary mode. The best texts, and the best authors, offer a profound engagement with the reworking of literary devices – some allusive, some historical, some postmodern.

PART III: CLASS TEXTS AS TEST CASES

If the proof of the pudding is in the eating, then the proof of a form's literary power is at least partially in the teaching. Can the work (poem, novel, drama, painting, music, etc.) stand up to analysis, to the varied reading skills of its audience, to the scrutiny of hours of instruction, to the parsing and hypothesizing of classroom preparation, discussion, and analysis? Can it stand to be roughly handled as it must be in the sometimes indelicate acts of analysis and interpretation? How will it endure the rigors of evaluation? Does it, in the end, extend its intellectual tentacles to probe the questions that literature asks in perpetuity: What is the work of human beings in the world? What can we make of love, death, birth, anguish, sex, faith, despair as this text has probed them? And why, after centuries of the printed text, are we still asking the same unanswerable questions?

I will look at two comics texts that I have used in the classroom, both published in 2003: a theoretical approach to Canadian alternative comics artist Chester Brown's *Louis Riel: A Comic-Strip Biography*, and a practical pedagogy for working with American Peter Kuper's graphic adaptation of Franz Kafka's long short story *The Metamorphosis*.

Comics as Historiographic Metafiction: Louis Riel

The decision to include Chester Brown's *Louis Riel* in a course on Canadian historiographic metafiction sprang from two overlapping ideas, one historical and one generic. Historian Albert Braz asserts, in *The False Traitor: Louis Riel in Canadian Culture*, that Riel is an elusive but enduring personality in Canadian history, largely due to the inability of twentieth-century writers to agree upon a single historical representation of Riel. Brown's subtitle of "a comic-strip biography" invites an unpacking of terms, suggesting parallel reading strategies: that a comic strip, as a popular genre, can support the cultural appetite for the contestable veracity of the "biographical" narrative, and, equally, that *Louis Riel*'s visual and verbal configurations invite a semiotics of contradiction that recalls the "twin impulses of realism and self-reflexivity" that Linda Hutcheon asserts are vital to any work of historiographic metafiction (20). Braz concludes that Riel has become "the ideal human bridge" by which white Canadians seek to "indigenize

themselves" through history and literature, so that non-aboriginal Anglo Canadians may at last construe themselves as native to the land
that they invaded (203). But Brown's *Louis Riel* does not engage Riel
as a bridge, but rather depicts a Riel self-consciously positioned as
a cipher in a metanarrative of nation. Throughout *Louis Riel*, the
concrete visuality of the images taunts the incompleteness of historical narrative, making Riel an unreadable factor, an aporetic figure of
impasse, both impossible and necessary to defining (or renegotiating)
Canadian national metanarratives. Brown positions Riel in the text as
a literary character constituted from the vicissitudes of historiographic
metafiction. His extensive endnotes to *Louis Riel* map out many of his
narrative and visual choices, citing a variety of works about Riel and
drawing attention to the multiple streams of Rielian discourse that
influenced this "comic-strip biography."

Brown's take on Riel proposes a number of challenges to the
graphic novel as biography and as journalism, to the Canadian historiographic metafictive novel, and to the wealth of historical discourse
about Louis Riel. Instead of presupposing the reader's presence as a
necessary active ingredient of the text, as a historiographic metafictive
novel does, Brown's *Louis Riel* presupposes a mode of resistance to a
national metanarrative. As Hayden White suggests in *The Content of
the Form*, "the plot of a historical narrative is always an embarrassment
and has to be presented as 'found' in the events rather than put there
by narrative techniques" (21). Brown sets himself up as both comic-strip
author and historical researcher in order to prove the unreliability of
both of these identities, inviting readers to dismantle the historical plot
and revealing its "embarrassing" narrative constructions. This comic-
strip biography uses its declared genres against each other and, in doing so, comments upon the effects of history on literature, the effects
of literature on history, and the ways that the graphic novel can fool
readers who presume a text's efficacy and readers who presume a text's
accessibility. Here, the polysemiotic features of a comics text introduce
additional complications to the reading of history, historiography, and
ideological nationalism.

Brown's *Louis Riel* is consciously, even voluminously, historiographic; the text's twenty-two-page endnote section documents Brown's
source material and discusses his reasons for favoring one source over

another, often on a panel-by-panel basis. Brown's precedent for this technique is Alan Moore and Eddie Campbell's historiographic opus *From Hell*, a text with a forty-two-page appendix of annotations outlining the historical, religious, architectural, and mythical allusions with which Moore has suffused the text. In addition, Moore provides a second appendix to *From Hell*, "Dance of the Gull Catchers," in which he offers a visual metaphor for his multiply fragmented postmodern text, complete with a fractal model of narrative proliferation using "Koch's snowflake" (Moore and Campbell "Appendix II," 23). In *Louis Riel*, Brown takes up this kind of narrative negotiation by foregrounding the techniques of historiographic metafiction – the unreliable narrator, the revisioning of history told from a politically oppressed or otherwise ignored source, the invasive voice of the self-conscious author – in the attempt to dismantle or disrupt historical certitude. But because Brown's text begins by assuming a third-person omniscient narrator, the endnotes – along with his frequent discussions of "the way [he's] drawn the scene" (263) – come as a surprise to those who read history as narrated rather than heavily, inevitably narrativized.

As is usual in historiographic metafiction, the author himself is multiply represented throughout the text: in this case, through the series of authorial selves offered by the endnotes. Brown is scholarly rigorous when he documents the "almost certain" lies told by Charles Nolin at Riel's trial (265), as well as when he relates William Sanderson's personal report of his treatment as a prisoner of the rebels in which Sanderson dismisses early reports of prisoner abuse as "a lot of damn lies" (249). In putting Riel's trial on the page, Brown painstakingly attributes every piece of dialogue to the appropriate pages of the published transcript of *Queen v. Louis Riel* (265). Brown also makes decisions that are less historically influenced and more indicative of artistic or personal political choices, such as his choice to draw William MacDougall as less robust than the historical documents suggest (writing, "I could live with that level of inaccuracy"; 246) and making other changes to the story for the sake of character and a cohesive narrative. Brown also makes an amusingly flippant, anachronistic inclusion of Charles Nolin into the group of men who make the trip south to collect Riel in 1884, and then asserts that Nolin clearly lied on the stand at Riel's trial (257). Brown is playful about the limits of his genre, cheerfully pointing out his own refusal to depict large and protracted battle scenes (261), a choice that looms large after reading Joseph Witek's account of Jack Kirby's painstaking drawings of American Civil War battles in *Comic Books as History* (13–47). Brown even abandons historical accuracy altogether at one point, adopting the pose of the overworked academic: "I'm pretty sure that I didn't make this up . . . but I can't find the reference right now" (266). In taking up a mock scholarly stance, Brown contributes to the instability of Rielian discourse by reminding us, as few other works about Riel have done, of its historiographic vulnerabilities. Rielian discourse is almost inevitably profoundly earnest–something Braz notes even as he falls prey to it himself–and while Brown takes Riel's story seriously, his bibliography listing twenty-seven primary sources about Riel (along with 150 people in the historical index) indicates that the limitations of form support a postmodern reading of Riel that highlights the perils of unacknowledged historiography.

By emphasizing the aesthetic of the graphic novel as it grinds against the contradictions of reading multiple histories of Riel, Brown foregrounds his visual and narrative choices, and suggests in doing so that this comic-strip biography demands an awareness of historiographic features hidden in the semiotics of reading literature, visual art, and history all at once. Engaging with a series of contradictory sources about Riel appears to position Brown himself as the unreliable narrator, not unlike Timothy Findley's Hugh Selwyn Mauberley in *Famous Last Words*, though Mauberley is a creation of both Ezra Pound and Findley, and Brown as artist, author, and amateur historian may juggle those roles but is not, in the end, a fictive identity. This too is a tradition in historiographic metafiction: the insistence to readers that even the dismantling of narrative is a narrativization in itself, that history can never be anything other than a construction of the historian, and that all the archival chaos encountered by the historian remains, despite its unreadability, the most accurate representation we have. No story tells itself without the disturbing observance of the author.

Brown draws from the self-aware, multiplicitous, historiographic archive of postmodern consciousness that has developed in Canadian historiographic metafiction, so much so that we could take the words that appear in Mauberley's handwriting in *Famous Last Words* and usefully apply them to Brown's text: "All I have written here is true; except the lies" (59). If we take the text's endnotes and introduction as evidence, Brown would be the first to agree that lies and truth are nearly indistinguishable in the panels of his drawn text, so that he must make room for their interstices and silences in his endnotes. If the pressures of historiography have effaced the differences between truth and lies, with potentially huge political ramifications for Canada and for the Métis nation, Brown's sometimes scrupulous and sometimes casual recording of reasons for his artistic and political choices in extratextual features foregrounds the shifting efficacy of the text, even as he asserts the significance of Riel as a hinge figure in Canadian history. In many ways, this is ground already covered by Linda Hutcheon and Robert Kroetsch, but the graphic novel brings its own bag of tricks to historiographic metafiction, as it lays claim to new perspectives in literary theory and, in the case of Louis Riel, historical criticism.

Kroetsch has pointed out that Riel is perhaps the ultimate subject through which the enduring national Canadian paradox may be construed as the national inability to agree upon a metanarrative, so that "the very falling-apart of our story is what holds our story together" (21–22). One of the problems with Kroetsch's undeniably attractive idea is that the need to dismantle the Canadian historical mythos is postmodern, and it may also be considered postcolonial, but it ignores the larger question of how dismantling the Riel myth would serve the Métis nation. Any transnational criticism that makes conscious the historical and social tensions that accompany a narrative of nation must also pause to consider what Riel has meant, and continues to mean, to Métis people. What Brown's text eloquently proposes is neither a narrative of nation nor a renegotiation of such a metanarrative from the Métis perspective. Instead, Brown shows us a Riel whose symbology remains undecipherable, an impossible but necessary figure with the blank eyes that Brown adapted from Harold Gray's *Little Orphan Annie*. The blank eyes do not quite represent a blank slate, but they cannot quite offer readers a historical bridge over which we can cross to meaning, indigenized or otherwise. Brown's *Louis Riel* is a metametanarrative, a text about how a metanarrative may be established, and a text that is perfectly positioned to teach students of emerging national literatures just how easily ideological narrative is offered as nation and how the pictographic code reveals the simultaneous opacity and transparency of Canadian history.

Comics as Adaptation: Peter Kuper's The Metamorphosis

If Chester Brown's Louis Riel functions in the classroom to introduce the instability of narrative, historical and otherwise, then a classic work of sequential art like Peter Kuper's adaptation of Franz Kafka's The Metamorphosis can function as a good tool to open a discussion of how interpretation works. When we offer one author's interpretation of another author's work, students can access the experience of interpretation as a function of adaptation, compare a visual/verbal text to a written canonical antecedent, and debate the capaciousness and limitations of both the short story and graphic narrative formats. The opportunities that students can be given to interrogate their own reading practices and interpretive strategies are nearly limitless in such a comparison. I will only offer one or two pedagogical strategies, working from the context in which I have used Kuper's adaptation of Kafka's short story, in a course that examined structure and form through an examination of transformation stories.

When introducing both versions of The Metamorphosis in the classroom, I emphasize choice. I announce that we will be reading the work in two versions, and that students are free to read either the graphic narrative or the short story first, with the proviso that I want them to make a conscious choice and be willing to discuss the impact of that choice in class afterward. In addition, I ask them to note the differences between the two forms and to speculate on how reading one text before the other might have influenced their reading of the second text. When I include an essay like Wilhelm Emrich's classic "The Animal as Liberating Self" from his 1954 Franz Kafka, the students have access to a ninety-year arc of literary history: the 1915 short story; the 1954 critical analysis which considers, among other things, Kafka's injunction that the "insect itself cannot be drawn" (Emrich quoted in Kafka 125); and Kuper's 2003 graphic narrative. The idea that Kuper has gone directly against Kafka's injunction and placed Samsa-as-dung-beetle in nearly every panel *and* on the cover of his adaptation invariably elicits debate in the classroom, with students taking up every position from anger with Kuper's defiance of Kafka's wishes to eloquent justifications about the availability of the short story as a cultural object with its own life beyond the author's wishes. At some point, a student always asks me "Can he do that?" meaning (among other things), "Is Kuper's drawing of the dung beetle a scholarly permissible way to treat a piece of canonical literature?" Given that literary adaptation has been with us for only slightly less time than original literary works, the answer can only be yes. This introduces a discussion about how a visual text makes meaning differently than a written text does; about how a visual text changes a written text for the reader, an argument familiar to many students who have read and viewed Harry Potter in print and on-screen; and, not least, about how different forms invite different but often similar reading strategies.

In offering the visual, the graphic adaptation must necessarily work with the limits of the visible, to use Judith Halberstam's term. The graphic adaptation cannot escape the potential for reductive readings of the visual, even as it must also contend with some of the rules of narrative. For both verbal and visual elements, sequence is crucial, with the visual aspects of the graphic novel form adding an extra degree of complication. Will the pictures "match" the words? Ought they to do so? Will what we see align (logically, ironically, dramatically) with what the words say? Not for nothing does Charles Hatfield describe the work of reading comics as predicated on the experience of "otherness," noting that the destabilization of the codified distinction between "the function of words and the function of images . . . is fundamental to the art form" (37).

To give students an experience of reading these tensions, I ask them to work in pairs on an exercise in close reading of parallel pages of Kafka's and Kuper's texts. The task is to focus on the features of each assigned passage, and then make comparisons and note the differences between the texts. The class as a whole will then discuss the interpretive significance of such differences. A point-form literary analysis of plot, foreshadowing, character development, use of narrative voice, image, and setting, along with tropes of monstrosity, change, the body, fear, and family dynamics may be set against a visual reading of light and shadow, bodies and faces, framing devices, dialogue boxes, manipulation of space or time, action or emotion portrayals. For example, a pair of students reading Kafka's account, at the end of chapter 2 of *The Metamorphosis*, of Mr. Samsa throwing apples at Gregor until one apple strikes Gregor so hard that it embeds itself in his back, where it remains for the rest of the narrative, noted the following points: (1) Kafka relates the entire incident in a single long paragraph that takes up more than two pages of written text; (2) Gregor notices that wearing the doorman's uniform seems to have re-enlivened his father's virility, and Gregor compares this with the older man's decrepit appearance when Gregor was the family's wage earner; (3) the older man's only spoken dialogue is a declarative "Ah!" upon entering the room; (4) the father's slow chase of Gregor around the room appears to last for several minutes; (5) Gregor is considerably weakened by the exercise; and (6) the apples are "lightly flung . . . without taking good aim" (Kafka 37).

Turning to Kuper's text to read the parallel passage, the student readers noted that Kuper takes nine panels covering three pages to show what Kafka wrote in approximately 1,500 words. The splash page that opens the sequence is dominated by the older man's large robust body as he flings his hat across the room (in Kafka's text) and across the span of two pages (in Kuper's). Kuper follows Kafka's dialogue-less narrative closely, rendering the chase scene around the family's small living quarters with an attitude of silent menace, set up by Gregor's thought balloon on the splash page, sputtering "C-could this be Father?? The same tired old man . . . ?" (Kuper 48). That finishes any semblance of dialogue as the stylized violence of the chase around the Samsa apartment is rendered by Kuper as a waking nightmare complete with the gaping jaws of all the other family members—Gregor, Grete, and Mrs. Samsa—held open in silent screams of agony and surprise, graphically depicting noise and chaos without actually voicing (or scripting) them. The chase ends after Mrs. Samsa, who is clad (as in Kafka's text) in only her chemise, throws herself bodily upon Mr. Samsa in an effort to stop him from hurting Gregor-as-beetle. The speech balloon containing her plea arcs out over the gutter away from the eighth panel, separate from her body blocking Mr. Samsa's access to Gregor. Her impassioned cry of "Spare Gregor, I beg you, spare him!" floats like a banner over the drawing of the wounded Gregor that ends this chapter, just as her "begging for Gregor's life" ends chapter 2 of Kafka's long short story. In Kuper's text, Gregor, wounded and with the embedded apple distorting the smooth carapace of his back, breathes out "Mother" in a wobbly speech balloon that indicates both his incapacitated state and his inability to speak a language that his family understands, as he spends all of Kafka's text speaking in a series of clicks and hisses, a dung-beetle language.

Students who compared these portions of the texts pointed out that seeing the apple embedded in Gregor's back was disturbing in a way that they had not experienced from the written text, and that the sexual vulnerability of Mrs. Samsa's intervention in her underclothes went unnoticed by them in Kafka's text but was impossible to ignore in Kuper's pictographic narrative. This fostered a discussion about the strengths and the ideological foreclosure of the graphic adaptation; this section of Kuper's text seems to favor Oedipal drama over political allegory, as well as emphasizing the waking dream aspect of Kuper's work over the original author's own contention that the story is about "the terror of art" (Kafka 108). Add to that the fact that Kuper's sequence with the apple is entirely silent, reminiscent of the silent tradition of Lynd Ward and Frans Masereel, both woodcut artists and early graphic novelists. Masereel is of particular interest as an intertextual influence on Kuper's art, especially considering that both Masereel and Kafka published with Karl Wolff in the years between 1915 and 1925. Kuper's adaptation of Masereel's style of stark faces and dense urban shadows to depict class oppression mixes with a sense of grotesque physicality that seems more reminiscent of Robert Crumb's work to produce a style that invokes the suffocation of being intensely embodied in a mechanized world, favoring critics who claim *The Metamorphosis* as a story about urbanized, mechanized class anxiety. It is important to point out to students that every adaptation necessarily tampers with the story, and that this neither condemns nor recommends the later version, though it suggests something of what is demanded of a discerning reader. An imagetext is fundamentally different from a written text, and our task is to investigate both the faithfulness to the earlier text and the deviations from it, the way the work serves both tradition and innovation in terms of the genre, the style, and the plot.

Sometime toward the end of our work with both texts, I will ask students to write a short paragraph about which version of *The Metamorphosis* is "better"; this open-ended and intentionally loaded question also asks them to defend their own terms for establishing a definition of "better." What is "better"? More creative? More original? More moving? More political? More fully realized as a narrative? More successful in reader reception? More complete as an allegory? Some students have argued that Kafka's short story is "better" because it is an older form, canonical and literary; some have argued that Kuper's adaptation is more nuanced, more contemporary, more accessible, more interested in keeping tradition alive; and still others have argued, eloquently, that quality judgments between genres are ultimately irrelevant, that ideas can and do survive transmutation—a good argument in a course that examines the literary traditions of transformation narratives.

* * *

While comics still strive toward literary acceptance and definition while insisting on being accepted on their own terms, it is indisputable that the history of the comics has been filled with literary lights who have been more than willing to trumpet the parallels between literature and comics. Comics may be challenging in the academy, but such obstreperousness has a long list of learned admirers. Among the modernists, William Faulkner patterned his own cartooning style on Aubrey Beardsley (Inge 79); e. e. cummings wrote passionately about George Herriman's *Krazy Kat* (Heer and Worcester 13–21); and Thomas Mann wrote the introduction to Frans Masereel's *Passionate Journey: A Novel in 165 Woodcuts* (Heer and Worcester 30–34). In more recent times, Palestinian postcolonial theorist Edward Said wrote the introduction to Joe Sacco's classic of graphic journalism, *Palestine*, calling it "a political and aesthetic work of extraordinary originality" (iii); American novelist Sherman Alexie provided a similar service, touting Jason Lutes's *Jar of Fools* in his preface to that work; narratology scholar Walter J. Ong wrote on Walt Kelly's Pogo and Walt Disney's Mickey Mouse; and postmodern novelist Umberto Eco touted the myth of Superman. In Canada, novelist and cultural critic Mordecai Richler wrestled with the "great comic book heroes" long before it was fashionable to do so. Finally, in the middle of Margaret Laurence's 1969 Canadian literature classic, *The Fire-Dwellers*, Laurence's protagonist, Stacey, trapped in a stultifying marriage and having never heard of

Betty Friedan, conjures up the subversive sexuality and genre-defying bravura of the Dragon Lady from Milton Caniff's *Terry and the Pirates*. The Dragon Lady appears "wearing Stacey's face and a slinky black velvet ensemble that clings to her gifted breasts and friendly thighs. What was it you wanted to know, McNab? She is addressing the customs officer. Did you say smuggling opium? But McNab (about thirty, muscles like wire rope) can only stand and drool, overcome by his impossible desire" (Laurence 87). Stacey's self-deprecating rejoinder to her own fantasy is that she is "either suffering from delayed adolescence or premature menopausal symptoms, most likely both," but the scene is familiar to comics readers, not just as a moment of fantasy, but also as a moment in which pictographic literature invades the world consciousness of a realistic character, or a real person. When we consider comics as literature, we should recall Charles Hatfield's metaphor of comics as an "ideal laboratory for the study of image/text relations," in which readers roll up their sleeves to delve into the fine workings of the "constitutive act of interpretation," participating in a "ceaseless interchange between popular genre works and more critically favoured ones" (xiii). The interchange is now too ubiquitous to ignore.

REFERENCES

Braz, Albert. *The False Traitor: Louis Riel in Canadian Culture*. Toronto: University of Toronto Press, 2003.

Briggs, Raymond. *When the Wind Blows*. London: Penguin, 1982.

Brown, Chester. *Louis Riel: A Comic-Strip Biography*. Montreal: Drawn and Quarterly, 2003.

Brown, Jeffrey A. *Black Superheroes, Milestone Comics, and Their Fans*. Jackson: University Press of Mississippi, 2001.

Eisner, Will. *Comics and Sequential Art*. Tamarac, FL: Poorhouse Press, 1985.

Emrich, Wilhelm. "The Animal as Liberating Self." In his *Franz Kafka*. 1954. Rpt. in Kafka, *The Metamorpho-* sis. Ed. Stanley Corngold. New York: Bantam, 2004. 113–129.

Fiedler, Leslie. "The Middle against Both Ends." 1955. In *Arguing Comics: Literary Masters on a Popular Medium*. Ed. Jeet Heer and Kent Worcester. Jackson: University Press of Mississippi, 2004. 122–133.

Findley, Timothy. *Famous Last Words*. Toronto: McClelland and Stewart, 1981.

Hartman, Geoffrey. "The Voice of Shuttle: Language from the Point of View of Literature." In *Beyond Formalism: Literary Essays, 1958–1970*. New Haven, CT: Yale University Press, 1970. 337–355.

Harvey, Robert C. *The Art of the Comic*

Book: An Aesthetic History. Jackson: University Press of Mississippi, 1996.

Hatfield, Charles. *Alternative Comics: An Emerging Literature.* Jackson: University Press of Mississippi, 2005.

Heer, Jeet, and Kent Worcester, eds. *Arguing Comics: Literary Masters on a Popular Medium.* Jackson: University Press of Mississippi, 2004.

Hutcheon, Linda. *The Canadian Postmodern: A Study of Contemporary English-Canadian Fiction.* Toronto: Oxford University Press, 1988.

Inge, M. Thomas. *Comics as Culture.* Jackson: University Press of Mississippi, 1990.

Johnson, Steven. *Everything Bad Is Good For You: How Today's Popular Culture Is Actually Making Us Smarter.* New York: Riverhead, 2005.

Kafka, Franz. *The Metamorphosis.* Trans. and ed. Stanley Corngold. New York: Bantam, 2004.

Kroetsch, Robert. "Disunity as Unity: A Canadian Strategy." In his *The Lovely Treachery of Words: Essays Selected and New.* Toronto: Oxford University Press, 1989. 21–33.

Kuper, Peter. *The Metamorphosis.* New York: Three Rivers Press, 2003.

———. *Mind's Eye.* New York: NBM Comics, 2000.

Laurence, Margaret. *The Fire-Dwellers.* Toronto: McClelland and Stewart, 1969.

Lutes, Jason. *Berlin: City of Stones,* bk. 1. Montreal: Drawn and Quarterly, 2004.

———. *Jar of Fools.* Montreal: Drawn and Quarterly, 2001.

MacDonald, Tanis. "'The way I've drawn the scene': History and Historiography in Chester Brown's *Louis Riel: A Comic-Strip Biography.*" Unpublished paper presented at "The New Narrative? Comics in Literature,

Film and Art" conference, University of Toronto, 10 May 2008.

Masereel, Frans. *Passionate Journey: A Novel in 165 Woodcuts.* 1919. San Francisco: City Lights, 1994.

McAllister, Matthew P., Edward H. Sewell Jr., and Ian Gordon. *Comics and Ideology.* New York: Peter Lang, 2001.

McCloud, Scott. *Reinventing Comics: How Imagination and Technology Are Revolutionizing an Art Form.* New York: HarperCollins Perennial, 2000.

———. *Understanding Comics: The Invisible Art.* Northampton, MA: Kitchen Sink Press, 1993.

McLuhan, Marshall. *The Mechanical Bride: Folklore of Industrial Man.* New York: Vanguard, 1951.

Miller, Frank. *Batman: The Dark Knight Returns.* New York: DC Comics, 1986.

Mitchell, W. J. T. *Iconology: Picture, Text, Theory.* Chicago: University of Chicago Press, 1986.

Moore, Alan, and Eddie Campbell. *From Hell: Being a Melodrama in Sixteen Parts.* Marietta, GA: Top Shelf, 2004.

Moore, Alan, and David Gibbons. *The Watchmen.* New York: DC Comics, 1987.

Morice, Dave. *Poetry Comics: An Animated Anthology.* New York: Teachers & Writers Collaborative, 2002.

Nichol, bp. *An H in the Heart: A Reader.* Toronto: McClelland and Stewart, 1994.

Richler, Mordecai. *The Great Comic Book Heroes and Other Essays.* Toronto: McClelland and Stewart, 1978.

Richter, David H. *Falling into Theory: Conflicting Views on Reading Literature.* Boston: Bedford, 1994.

Rowson, Martin. *The Waste Land.* London: Picador, 1999.

Sabin, Roger. *Adult Comics: An Intro-duction*. London: Routledge, 1993.

Sacco, Joe. *Palestine*. Seattle: Fanta-graphics, 2001.

Seth [Gregory Gallant]. *Clyde Fans*, bk. 1. Montreal: Drawn and Quarterly, 2004.

———. "Seth Speaks!" Unpublished lecture presented at "The New Nar-rative? Comics in Literature, Film and Art" conference, University of Toronto, 10 May 2008.

Spiegelman, Art. *Maus: A Survivor's Tale*. New York: Pantheon, 1986.

Teaching Resources for Art Spiegelman's Maus: A Survivor's Tale. Bucks Coun-ty Library, Doylestown, PA (2005). www.buckslib.org/onebook/maus. Ac-cessed 10 Nov. 2011.

Versaci, Rocco. *This Book Contains Graphic Language: Comics as Litera-ture*. New York: Continuum, 2007.

Voice of the Shuttle. University of California, Santa Barbara, English Department (1 Oct. 2001). Web. Ac-cessed 15 Nov. 2009.

Wertham, Fredric. *Seduction of the Innocent*. Port Washington, NY: Ken-nikat, 1954.

White, Hayden. *The Content of the Form: Narrative Discourse and Histor-ical Representation*. Baltimore, MD: Johns Hopkins University Press, 1987.

Witek, Joseph. *Comic Books as History: The Narrative Art of Jack Jackson, Art Spiegelman and Harvey Pekar*. Jack-son: University Press of Mississippi, 1989.

4 Television: The Extraliterary Device

DANIEL KEYES

Literary studies' extension from the study of printed texts into the study of screen culture is consistent with literary studies' analysis of how dramatic texts become theatrical events. The stakes for literary studies to consider screen culture as part of the extraliterary devices are consistent with the need to use criticism to excavate how screen culture reshapes our collective life world. As Raymond Williams in "The Analysis of Culture" so elegantly asserts:

> One generation may train its successor, with reasonable success, in the social character or the general cultural pattern, but the new generation will have its own *structure of feeling*,[1] which will not appear to have come "from" anywhere. . . . the new generation responds in its own ways to the unique world it is inheriting, taking up many continuities, that can be traced, and reproducing many aspects of the organization, which can be separately described, yet feeling its whole life in certain ways differently, and shaping its creative response into a new *structure of feeling*. (37)

Increasingly, the screens of televisions, computers, and handheld devices contribute to an emergent and immediate structure of feeling in a way that might not supersede print culture, but certainly complicates it. While Williams claims that each generation has its own innate competency for structuring feelings that it transmutes to the next generation, I sense in the current mediascape, which is dominated by a wide range of immediate and often interactive audiovisual media,

that the sense of discrete generational structures of feeling is less secure and more fragmented. For example, a Skype videophone call on
my laptop offers a different structure of feelings than the nightly news
program observed on commercial television (hereafter referred to as
TV).[2] The flow of vivid audio-image media shapes both developed and
developing countries' collective mediascape by generating ideological
and discursive formations that offer to structure the feelings[3] of viewers.
Implied in the complex communication web between advertisers, content providers, broadcasters, and viewers is that decoding and analysis
are necessary to navigate and challenge the structure of feelings and
interpellationoffered via these screen technologies. For example, older
"literary" narrative forms like nineteenth-century stage melodrama
inform the structure of feelings of narratives in the new, pithy, cell-
phone video webisodes,[4] where each one-minute episode ends with a
cliff-hanger. For television studies and perhaps for the next generation
of screen studies scholars, literary studies contributes a valuable set of
tools for interrogating and historicizing the emergent structure of feelings in this heterogeneous mediascape.

This chapter is an overview of the development of the relatively
recent academic discipline of television studies and will demonstrate
how literary studies and television studies both adhere to a commitment to interdisciplinary study that comfortably fits within a cultural
studies framework. This genealogy of television studies recognizes that
the visual and audio elements along with a focus on production, technology, form, and reception in some ways exceeds or at least challenges
the limitations of a strict formalist literary analysis of print.[5]

Although a relative latecomer to the academy, television studies in
the 1970s aggregated approaches from the social sciences and humanities around a medium in much the same way as literary or film studies.
This interdisciplinary move is consistent with how literary studies since
then has borrowed from other disciplines to hone its approaches while
tending to privilege the analysis of print text over the analysis of other
textual phenomena like performances or the visual arts.[6] Throughout
the 1980s and 1990s in North America, television studies emerged as
a field within communications, cultural studies, media studies, and
visual anthropology programs that tend to focus on commercial broadcast programming.[7] Michele Hilmes's account of television studies in

America from the late 1970s indicates how it has operated as a marginal program in communications departments at non–Ivy League universities while film studies has tended to be integrated into English departments at prestigious private American universities. English literature and more recent analytical newcomers, like film and television studies, operate in universities and colleges as ways of teaching argument and critical analysis, and displaying cultural capital. A more radical agenda also exists within media studies: television studies as not just about appreciation, but as media literacy and intervention (Kellner, *Television and Media Culture*; Kavoori).

Television studies' comparatively lowly and new status demonstrates how the academy reinforces what counts as cultural capital in a way that reflects Williams's impression that each "generation may train its successor" ("Analysis" 37) but that a new structure of feeling will emerge. In this case, this structure of feeling is supported by another medium with a distinct system of distribution and mode of production.

John T. Caldwell, in "Welcome to the Viral Future of Cinema (Television)" (2005), asserts that TV and film studies have merged in terms of both production and analysis: "Cinema, in some odd ways, has become television. Film scholars would benefit from considering how this shift has placed research on television's history at the heart of cinematic analysis" (96). Inevitably film studies, with a focus on aesthetics,[8] cedes to television studies' analysis of cultural form, which includes aesthetics. Caldwell champions television studies' combination of historical and formal analysis as the path that film studies should follow. Within Caldwell's narrative of the merger of film and television studies is the notion that this merger is driven not by a sense of an innate aesthetic affinity between film and TV, but by technological change and rampant corporate conglomeration that reduces the difference between the small and large screens. TV programs become feature-length films (e.g., the *Star Trek* franchise), and major serialized blockbuster films are, post–initial release, broadcast in edited form on TV (e.g., a new *Mission Impossible* release in theaters is preceded by the broadcast of the older films in the series on a major network that is owned by the same company that owns the *Mission Impossible* series). Moreover, both television and film texts post–initial release/broadcast will go to DVD or Blu-ray format for purchase. Thus the distance between the large communal screen of the movie theater and the suburban living room's flat screen is elided. Independent film and "quality" TV director David Lynch may rant that the iPhone has cheated film in his iPhone commercial, but conglomerates are increasingly moving toward viewing content as something that translates across platforms. Rather than academics merging these fields because of the affinity between them, it is as if the film-and-television industry under the influence of globalization's thirst for vertical and horizontal dominance have conspired to collapse this distinction in taste.

Television studies is undergoing its own textual crisis as the nature of TV and screen technology change. In teaching television studies that rely on material first broadcast in the 1990s, like *Twin Peaks*, I see how such landmark highbrow TV rarely resonates with my nineteen-year-old students, who were not born when the program initially aired. An English professor does not have to worry about whether Milton's *Paradise Lost* will vanish, or whether it can be taught by using a video file-sharing website like YouTube, which offers a radically cut-up version of a text. Increasingly I turn away from TV to look at webisodes as strange supplements to broadcast television or to examine activist television sites like *The Real News* or satirical parodies like *The Onion* that mimic the form of network broadcast news delivery to offer views not endorsed by mainstream journalists. The slipperiness of the text in television studies is both a challenge and an opportunity for the instructor seeking to locate a text that resonates with students. The tele-visual flow does not stand still, and thus television studies risks becoming the equivalent of "Sony Walkman studies" as the size and delivery of screen technology mutate along with viewers' structure of feelings. Television studies' future lies in morphing into a study of screen technology that engages with audiovisual screen culture and does not lose sight that all screen technologies are part art, part commerce, and part technology. Literary studies with its multidisciplinary approach to textual studies provides a gateway into grasping TV's supple and swift interweaving of art, commerce, and technology. Ott's *The Small Screen* and Davin and Jackson's *Television and Criticism* provide ample evidence of literary approaches to TV text and its persistence within television studies. I suspect that the market for television studies books responds both to fan culture and to academic interest as is the case with the critical anthologies about Comedy Central's *South Park* (1997–): two texts are dedicated to *South Park* and philosophy (Arp; Hanley), and two other texts fit a more literary model of criticism (Weinstock; Stratyner and Keller). This program, which focuses on four precocious, potty-mouthed boys, is open to a wide variety of critical approaches, and the literary approach of looking at one author and a series of texts resonated with the wave of *South Park* scholarship. Other approaches in television studies eschew this literary bent for approaches inflected by the social sciences.

Television studies asks questions not only about textual analysis but also about the technology and commerce that shape its delivery. I am wary of a hypothetical literature professor teaching a genre-based study of TV sitcoms that does not at least acknowledge the variety of approaches to sitcoms offered by television studies, but instead offers only an appreciation of character, plot, and a limited repertoire of grand themes. I would be equally skeptical of a literature professor who offers a course on Roman comedy and only discusses plot, character, etc., while ignoring histories of Rome, theories of comedy, Roman stage-craft, the relevance of Roman comedy's structures to TV sitcoms, etc. My practice of literary criticism is inflected by cultural studies' call to investigate representation as part of a wider reflection of ideology. Ideo-logical analysis can be derived by textual analysis, but I sense it gains more force when it confronts how audiences negotiate the embedded nature of aesthetic form in dominant white, straight, patriarchal, capi-talist economies and technologies.

In teaching both a first-year "Introduction to Literature" course focused on fiction and a second-year "Introduction to Film" (screen culture really), I am acutely aware that there is a logic whereby all the formal analysis offered in the first-year fiction course, like character, plot, theme, etc., is troubled in the second-year film course where stu-dents confront the audio-image text on the screen. For example, the traditional literary study of point of view in a novel shifts in discussing a sitcom that uses voice-over or shot-countershot sequences to establish and maintain a "first-person" perspective. The audio-image text of film or TV requires a different but complementary critical competency that most students who are attuned to screen technologies' structure of feel-ings readily grasp but may not easily articulate.

Television and literary studies share a rampantly multidisciplinary tradition. Literary studies in a post–I. A. Richards realm of formalist study absorbs other approaches and disciplines, including critical race theory, feminism, history, human geography, Marxism, philosophy, poststructuralism, psychology, sociology, and structuralism. The use of different approaches mirrors television studies' own multidisciplinary approach. Allen and Hill's comprehensive anthology, *The Television Studies Reader,* is divided into seven discrete approaches, "Institutions of Television, Spaces of Television, Modes of Television, Making Television, Social Representation on Television, Watching Television, and finally Transforming Television" (i). While pure textual studies may only be circumscribed by the section of *The Television Studies Reader* entitled "Watching Television," I sense that each of these divisions would not be out of place as a form of literary analysis. For example, if I were to slightly modify Allen and Hill's section titles and create a literary anthology with section titles like "Institutions of the Novel, Poetic Spaces, Making Poetry, etc.," I suspect most literature professors would accept these categories as being appropriate for the study of literature.

Literary studies and television studies should be subsumed under the title of "textual practice" or the "study of signifying practices" (Eagleton 40). In this paradigm, the status of a text may predetermine a number of approaches to it, but the status of the text does not delimit the approaches. For example, television studies must call forth a textual analysis that is aware of the audiovisual language of the screen, shot size, point of view, mise-en-scène, lighting, sound, timing of commercial breaks, structure of broadcast regimes, etc., that would be largely inappropriate as a textual approach to a novel, but this reliance on TV's formalist rules, the structures of its production, and the competencies required for its reception does not delimit the possible textual horizons or approaches to the text. I cannot imagine teaching a television studies course without some focus on how broadcast regimes regulate and control the flow of TV. Neither can I ignore how technology is radically altering broadcasts into narrowcasts and how viewers can become their own narrowcasters. These shifts in technology and commerce radically alter the definition of TV. While the book for the last four hundred years might be a fairly stable medium,[9] literary studies might do well to consider how its mode of production and dissemination influences literature.[10] Davin and Jackson's 2008 anthology, *Television and Criticism*, clearly aligns itself with exploring the relations between canonical literature and TV texts with one chapter by Len Platt titled "Our Common Cultural Heritage: Classic Novels and English Television" and another by Curtis Breight titled "Shakespeare on American Television and the Special Relationship between the UK & the USA." Yet I sense that literary criticism has more to offer television studies than connecting the dots between literary genres, their formation, and contemporary TV texts. Ultimately, television studies and literary studies operate in the arena of signifying practices, which is where the humanities and social sciences converge. Television studies and literary studies ultimately explore the production and reception of text within an ideological framework.

❉ ❉ ❉

When Homer Simpson, TV's straight, white, working-class, male, animated stooge, declares, "Television! teacher, mother, secret lover," he provides a definition of TV that suggests that the medium plays a number of conflicted incestuous roles for viewers as a source of education ("teacher"), *hiemlich* (mother), and *unheimlich* (lover). This troubles the attempt to define TV and place it in a literary framework of analysis where categories like the canon and genre operate stably. TV as an expression of late capitalism challenges the stability of these literary categories since it has come to define and delimit a phantasmagoric public sphere as a realistic dreamscape that regulates ideologies. Douglas Kellner offers a succinct assessment of the dominant American broadcast TV system that demonstrates how, unlike literature and literary study in the academy, TV is underpinned by a neoliberal commercial model where viewers' eyes are commodities to be bought and sold:

> Networks charge the corporations who purchase advertising time according to how many viewers watch a given ad and, in some cases, which viewers in specific demographic categories are supposedly viewing a given program (i.e., upscale women from 30–35). The corporations in turn pass these charges on to the viewers in the form of higher prices; because business can still, incredibly, take tax write-offs from advertis-

ing expenses, viewers pay for their free television with both higher taxes and growing public squalor. (*Television* 8–9)

This dominant model of broadcasting, though currently both waxing and waning, needs to be taken into consideration when evaluating TV's aesthetic content.

Since the 1950s, screen technology in the form of commercial broadcast television has become a mainstay in developed nations in most homes and elsewhere as screen technology becomes simultaneously small and portable (e.g., cell phones) and expansive and fixed (e.g., home theater, electronic billboards). The ubiquity and ephemeral nature of TV's content might suggest that it lacks a stable canon, but even though individual programs come and go, the format may remain reassuringly the same (e.g., professional sports), and the actual events operate as "new" spectacles (e.g., "the Vancouver Canucks versus the Montreal Canadiens"). Within this seemingly endless flow of new programming organized and advertised as new seasons, serialized genres operate to regulate viewing habits within a televisual day. While a critic of myth could regard literary genres such as tragedy and comedy as the stable expression of a collective unconscious, TV critics, like Kellner, assume that genres operate for television executives as a way of demographically organizing viewers' eyes for advertisers. Thus TV's professional sports programs operate as masculine melodrama, offering space to see men groan, cry, and cheer while daytime soaps serve an audience gendered as female with a slow pacing of narrative that elicits a similar range of emotions (Jenkins, "Never Trust a Snake!"). Genre thus serves as a useful and productive category for television scholars seeking to unpack how viewers are hailed by a set of expectations that aim to structure viewing pleasures.

Television studies has also generated its own sense of genre, as with Brian Ott's formulating the categories of hyperconscious and nostalgic, which operate as meta-genres. He theorizes that hyperconscious TV like *The Simpsons* (1990–) bends genres in self-reflexive gestures that embrace "an awareness and playfulness with our semiotic-saturated culture" (57), while nostalgic TV like *Dr. Quinn, Medicine Woman* (1993–1998) "says 'No' to the ever-changing social, political, and economic landscape and endeavours, instead, to recover and restore 'traditional' values, beliefs, and social relationships" (105). For Ott these categories of hyperconscious TV and nostalgic TV not only slot programs but are also symptomatic of two contradictory responses to the information age (106). Jason Mittell in "A Cultural Approach to Television Genre Theory" suggests that television studies complicates most genre theories, but he also notes the importance of genre in "shaping our media experience" (179). Genre is but one of the many tools television studies uses that dovetails with literary approaches.

* * *

Literary terms like the "canon" and the "author" can be applied to the shifts in broadcast regimes since the 1950s. TV in the developed world began with an oligopolistic model where a few networks broadcast signals via antenna (Boddy). In this first phase, starting in the post–World War II period, television operated in a fairly disorganized and ephemeral fashion. Scheduling and the notion of stable, segmented programming was haphazard (Ellis 26). Viewers tended to align themselves with programs and stars, not writers and directors. Networks encouraged brand loyalty by offering an appealing stable of programs. The vestiges of this scheduling logic can be seen with NBC's branding of Thursday night in 2007 as "Comedy Night Done Right." This appeal to genre serves as a unifying principle for viewers, who are assumed to be all white-collar workers, keeping banker's hours and working days, and thus seeking release from their work week by watching a slate of "office" sitcoms like *30 Rock* (2006–), *The Office* (2006–), *Parks and Recreation* (2009), and *Outsourced* (2010–) ("NBC Grooms").[11]

The advent of cable in the 1970s and, later, satellite TV; the proliferation of broadcasters; and the rise of relatively affordable video recording devices have allowed viewers to tape and control the flow of television. The VCRs and, later, DVDs provide a space for the notion of a canon of television with authors who are usually cast as writers/producers (Kompare). Some television genres like the sitcom appeal to a literary model of the "author function" with director's commentaries on DVD box sets giving rise to the notion of the auteur, who lovingly shapes her text for the viewer, rather than seeing the televisual text as the product of an industrial system of production bent on entrancing consumers.

In the 1980s, technology shifted to further stratify viewers through the emergence of specialty channels like music videos and pay-per-view television. For viewers willing and able to pay directly for extra channels, the multichannel universe offers a break from the dominant networks' televisual day, which is structured around a shifting base of viewers. Specialty channels speak to and for a specific group of viewers and anticipate the growth of Web 2.0.

The emergence of DVD box sets, as an improvement on VHS tape, has offered a more stable medium for collecting and readily accessing television programs. The box set generates a hierarchy of tastes and a stable canon of worthy texts for collectors or fans. Like Charles Edward Mudie's Victorian triple-decker private library subscription format,[12] which monopolized and controlled the distribution of fiction to middle-class England (Landow), box sets provide an afterlife for "free" serialized broadcast material that allows producers, directors, and stars to have yet another revenue stream after the initial broadcast. The box set, like the triple-decker subscription, is the perfect marriage of culture, copyright law, economics, and taste. My *Alfred Hitchcock Masterpiece Collection* DVD box set mirrors this Victorian literary conceit: its velvet-covered box with embossed writing offers the perfect sense that Hitchcock, the Victorian gentleman and "genius" filmmaker, produced a canon that is worthy of purchase and collection.

While the box set may be associated with specialty channels like HBO and quality programming like *The Sopranos*, which offer in true "cinematic" style the director's and actors' shot-by-shot commentary, box sets also exist for less prestigious "must-see" TV like the low-budget, grainy, reality program *Cops*.[13] Thus the canon of TV may no longer be the unstoppable ephemeral flow of pre-VCR television, but instead a digital Tower of Babel where each box set contains "scenes too hot for broadcast television," "never-seen-before highlights," director's comments, outtakes, bloopers, etc. So rather than controlling the rising tide of televisual texts, the box set gives rise to an endless mall of possibilities for the collector or fan. Concurrent with the emergence of the DVD box set has been the rise of other cross-marketed texts like video

games, movies, webisodes, theme parks, toys, books, etc., which complicate the scholarly task of isolating a text for study or the notion of a
reception study of a text by a group of viewers. The growing adoption
of Blu-ray technology, which offers five times the memory capacity of
DVDs, promises to further enhance the box set as a source of endless
fascination that might not need TV to pitch its magic.[14] The bundling
of Blu-ray with Sony's PlayStation 3 and Microsoft's Xbox 360 gaming
consoles as a portal for downloading high-definition film and television
content suggests a further melding of the forms of domestic screen
entertainment.

The DVD in its hyperlinked form with director's and possibly producers', writers', and actors' commentaries offers the promise of a radically expanded network of texts that work to illume the televisual text
proper. And when the DVD is tied to a TV program's website, which
links to other fan sites, the possible list of relevant texts further expands.
In terms of audience, TV programs can enjoy a curious afterlife as fans
generate websites that sustain a community of viewers. A vivid and
rich example of such devotion is the internet presence of the canceled
feminist western serial *Dr. Quinn, Medicine Woman* (CBS, 1993–1999),
which enjoys a curious post-production afterlife via numerous fan websites.[15] The canon of *Dr. Quinn* is not simply the DVD box set, which
contains hundreds of hours of programming and commentary, but all
of these websites and references, which provide a complex web of texts.
TV with box sets in the Web 2.0 era confounds notions of a text that is
limited and controlled by a director, producer, or TV network. For those
studying fan culture, a strictly literary approach that imagines television studies to be bound by the discrete study of programs or authors
would seem woefully inadequate. Discrete TV programs do not remain
bound by a particular medium (e.g., the DVD), but flow into a variety
of other media, where they are refracted by fan culture.

The promotion of television programming endorses notions of
authorship that, unlike literary forms, are corporate, diffuse, and dependent on a brand. The genre of reality television demonstrates how
the director seldom operates as an auteur; instead, a brand, like *Cops*, is
known not for its producer's artistic vision, clever camerawork, and deft
editing but by its faithful adherence to the genre's low-budget production values and its promise of exposing the raw underbelly of American

crime from the point of view of law enforcement.[16] The notion of an author of thirty-second commercials as creative genius may seem absurd, but much in the same way that Renaissance art was underwritten by the wealthy patrons who sponsored artists, a commercial is authored by its sponsor, which ultimately controls the creative content. Box sets like *Classic TV Commercials: The Ones We Never Forget* and *1001 Classic Commercials* might not support the notion of TV commercials as having an author or redeeming aesthetic value beyond nostalgia, but the marketing of the box set of Michel Gondry, Spike Jonze, and Chris Cunningham's music videos and films suggests that for these directors, their early music videos anticipated their "advance" into feature films. In this case, authorship operates as a way to construct a body of work by which to evaluate the artists' evolutions and as a commodity to appeal to fan interest.

"Authorship" persists with news programming that offers a sense of the corporation-as-author with tags that endorse the program as the product of a specific network or channel supported by an anchor and her news-gathering team. With TV, authorship extends to the star personality whether that is the news anchor or Oprah Winfrey. Television has a tendency to brand itself based on the cult of the star, who offers a way to gaze and builds a parasocial sense of trust with viewers (Horton and Wohl). Thus Winfrey appeared not only as the name of her show, but as a centralizing intelligence and portal that branded and shaped her content, guests, and studio audience. The lack of distinction between *Oprah* as a television program created by a team of researchers, camera operators, floor managers, editors, and director, and Oprah Winfrey as a surrogate for the home viewers' questions and reactions deliberately blurs the author function.

The rise of video-sharing services like YouTube and BitTorrent marks a shift from the dominant model of TV as viewers simply find programs without reference to the "network" as author, and increasingly moves viewers away from TV as it has been structured and regulated by major broadcasters.[17] Major TV networks recognize that internet spectatorship is not something to be feared and are struggling to put TV on the internet in a legitimate fashion that perpetuates the commercial business model where advertisers pay broadcasters for a measure of consumers' eyes. This form of branding and organizing of fans constitutes an attempt to regulate the author function of shows in order to target audiences (e.g., Fox's website for its speculative fiction thriller *Fringe*, 2008–). Commercial broadcast television had presented itself, up until the advent of mass-marketed VCRs in the late 1970s, as segmented ephemeral texts characterized by Raymond Williams's notion of flow: a seemingly ceaseless flow of texts (commercials, programs, etc.) designed to entice and ensnare viewers. As scheduled by individual broadcasters, TV's flow has tended to mirror and segment viewers' days (e.g., breakfast television, children's programming, daytime shows for stay-at-home parents, news programming, evening serials, etc.) while reinforcing the notion that the world is a series of readily accessible consumables. TV offers to shape a viewer's life world as a mall where each person is allowed to stroll, unencumbered by an empty wallet, provided they have access to a basic television set and a suitable domestic space. TV as the electronic mall would not seem to readily accommodate print's notions of a stable canon of texts underwritten by author-geniuses, yet these notions have crept into TV's arsenal of self-promotion such that networks proclaim individual programs as the products of stars and promote shows as belonging to a specific canon or subset of a "must-see" genre that will roll into a "must-buy" DVD collection for the ardent fan or a "must-burn" copy for the less copyright-respectful fan.

Generally, the dominant model for broadcast is based on a balance between national, regional, and often global interests where commercial broadcasters purchase a license from an arm of a federal government that allows them to broadcast to citizens provided they fulfill some concept of "community" service and standards. Thus TV, although a transglobal phenomenon, is often marked by an antiquated notion of nationalism where broadcasters offer viewers a sense of "deep horizontal comradeship"[18] (Anderson 7) while endorsing an agenda that reflects the values of its commercial sponsors. Viewers indirectly pay for TV via the products they buy, whose revenues fund the companies that pay for commercial space on television (Kellner, *Television* 8). Thus the content of "free" commercial television is underwritten by not only a nationalist agenda but a neoliberal, global, corporate agenda.

Via the internet and video-sharing platforms like YouTube and BitTorrent, TV's flow has been challenged by viewers who take control of the content, create their own dubs, and produce their own narrowcast version of television. In the various instances of copyright infringement, this form of television promises to change how content is not only produced, but also received in ways that fundamentally alter viewers' relations to the televisual text.[19] Alternatively, legal narrowcasting via electronic cookies, which collect data from the viewer/user's internet browser for the "broadcaster," is achieving an unprecedented level of surveillance over the viewer/consumer. Thus TV is changing and challenging the seemingly stable categories of author, genre, and canon, yet these categories are useful for the historical and critical mapping of shifts in the structure of feelings of the mediascape.

* * *

Students for television studies courses can be generally divided into two motivated groups: cultural theorists who savor critiques of mass media and fans who seek to justify and articulate their pleasures. While the cultural theory students will comfortably use articles derived from any number of disciplines, fans as students tend to provide detailed information based on hours of watching a particular program, participating in online forums, etc. In my third-year television studies course, which is cross-listed as both an English and cultural studies credit, I have cast myself as the equivalent of Jeff Probst, the host of reality TV's *Survivor*, in the way I mediate between these two "tribes," aiming to synthesize these two ways of knowing: the engaged fan and the critic, who grasp the ideologies of TV and the nuances of cultural form.

The first few weeks of this course are designed to value each tribe's knowledge and competencies. Initially, we read critical theory from television studies, and I introduce the notion that the course will focus on how different broadcast regimes, operating under different market conditions and regulators, shape content and form to produce TV that offers various worldviews. By discussing TV programming from Hong Kong and Africa, fans are taken from their comfort zone and made to challenge the constructions of their favorite programs. The next week, we explore the problematic practice of ethnography and how it can account for supple and resistant aspects of TV fan culture. Ethnography leads into autoethnography as students post online their synthetic reflections on readings and their practice of watching TV or watching others watch TV. The rest of the course is structured by genres of TV (e.g., week five is dedicated to daytime soaps) that are matched to scholarly articles. Genre also serves as a way of introducing, on the same topic, quantitative studies from the social sciences and qualitative research from the humanities, so we can explore the limitations and strengths of these approaches.

This mingling of audiovisual analysis and reading television studies articles has a number of advantages: (1) the two tribes enjoy a dialogue, (2) textual analysis of both the articles and TV is a given, and (3) there is more flexibility in terms of the TV texts discussed in lecture. For example, I may start with a TV text I am familiar with but add a text suggested by a student's discussion post. We also read articles[20] based on older programs or programs from non–North American broadcast regimes. For example, Iwabuchi's "Multinationalizing the Multicultural: The Commodification of 'Ordinary Foreign Residents' in a Japanese TV Talk Show" offers a glimpse of Japanese culture but also allows students to consider how much of North American reality TV and talk shows rely on a melodrama of racialized, gendered, and sexualized types. For each scholarly reading, I provide students with a single page that contains a list of short provocative questions about the readings and a list of terms used in the text with which students might be unfamiliar. The goal is for students to gain both a sense of specific critical jargon and its application to texts they have defamiliarized.

* * *

Aristotle's "The Poetics," perhaps an *ur*-text in terms of literary theory, suggests that literary analysis in the Western tradition has always focused on the words that escape the page to be spoken by actors and thus earn a cathartic reaction from audiences. He ranks "spectacle" as of least importance in the structure of Greek tragedy: "The spectacle has, indeed, an emotional attraction of its own, but of all the parts, it is the least artistic, and connected least with the art of poetry" (53). While Aristotle may see the "stage machinist" as more technician than the artist-poet, I sense this bias does not hold when examining TV (53). In my comparative study of how early 1990s daytime talk shows operate like the Greek tragic form in the way they formulaically structure the daytime talk-show host as choral leader, who conducts the studio audience as tragic chorus to react to the abject guest as tragic protagonist, I found that literary (drawing from the printed texts of extant Greek tragedy) and audiovisual cues from *Springer* et al. demonstrate that narrative form and spectacle necessarily combine in the agora of ancient Greek theater and in the home viewer's afternoon TV ritual.

I teach first-year literature as an introduction to theory with each week's focus being informed by a different approach to literature and a new text. By the end of week six in a thirteen-week course, students have been introduced to feminist, historical, psychological, and sociological readings, as well as to formalism and structuralism. These students have a sense that literary analysis involves structuring an argument where different contexts and reading competencies are employed to argue a position. The study of TV, or other forms of audiovisual culture, necessarily expands on this type of literary analysis by engaging with audio and visual codes. Literary analysis need not be bound by the notion that a text can only be a print text and thus accepts the notion that the world as a text is continually being produced, reproduced, and consumed.

Following Aristotle, I find the analysis of an audio-image text necessarily involves literary narrative elements. I doubt if literary analysis will ever be dubbed "print studies" in the industrial way that "television studies" has been, but I sense there is a virtue in this focus that involves students in dealing with the ideological elements of a text's production, dissemination, and reception as a logical extension of the aesthetic questions.

I favor literary analysis as a way of providing building blocks for performing an ideological analysis of a televisual text. In the case of TV, I encourage students to read or view against the grain of a program's structures by introducing the notion of TV programming as a structured system of hailing that follows prescribed narrative forms to shape viewers' feelings and worldviews. TV can hail viewers as willing docile subjects, but it often offers unanticipated subject positions for those seeking to view against the grain of TV's dominant message (e.g., a queer viewing of a straight criminal investigation program that reads the representation of straight homosocial police culture as rife with homosexual subtext). This approach to reading a TV text assumes that there is not one correct reading, but rather there is a multiplicity of readings in addition to the one intended by the producers of the program. Students can derive this notion from a "literary" source like Stanley Fish on Milton or Stuart Hall on the encoding and decoding of television. With Hall's article, the relevance of the argument tends to be more immediate.

I find TV commercials to be an excellent way to generate a case analysis for students because advertisements offer explicit, discrete, and compacted audiovisual texts. I like to use a comparative analysis that defamiliarizes students from a text and then brings their reading back to a more familiar everyday text. The advertisement I have selected as an example is decidedly not a complex or particularly "literary" text that resonates well with other texts and as far as I can see may contain only one rather oblique literary allusion. I have selected it because it is a quick teaching text where students are readily able to read the overdetermined dreamwork of the ad with the critical tools they have acquired in the course. Within the economical framework of a thirty-second advertisement, the narrative is semiotically complex and compact.

The Hong Kong police's recruitment advertisement "The Mark of Pride and Care," available via YouTube, offers a dream of law enforcement as a helping profession. Before screening the short commercial, I ask students about their associations with the terms "police," "law enforcement," and "Hong Kong police" to elicit a range of associations. While some students may think of law enforcement as society's way of controlling "bad people," I encourage other responses that might think of how police enforcement acts as a form of both soft and hard coercion. From the literary perspective of Fish's "reader response," this prescreening discussion helps locate viewers' assumptions and competencies, and thus might highlight how their preconceptions might structure their responses.

The "Mark of Pride" commercial blends strategic contradictions in terms of its form: it offers a dirty, noir-esque "Hong Kong" against which the bright, white police uniforms gleam as signs of moral purity; it offers slow-motion action supported by fast and sometimes deliberate nonsequential cutting. I ask students to locate these and other contradictions by making sense of the sumptuous audiovisual narrative's logic.

The advertisement's three narrative sequences champion police work as a highly ethical albeit gritty profession. I ask teams of students to work on each segment and to provide a description of the action that considers gaps in the narrative and the way the narrative achieves a certain emotional unity via first visual and then auditory cues. The first sequence of the ad opens in a decidedly non-urban muddy field: an eye-of-God perspective shows the police force disembark from a van en masse with the image cutting to focus on one male police officer who in slow motion tackles a civilian/criminal and gets muddy in the process. The editing bounces between images of the coordinated military teamwork and the individual action of the disciplined arresting officer; it alternates from eye-of-God shots to ground-level shots that demonstrate how this dirty police work is truly sublime and how this one officer's valor is part of a team's success. This message is reiterated when a superior officer wipes mud from the arresting officer's uniform; the camera angle has been restored to eye level from its former mud-level position. This congratulatory moment moves from an establishing shot of the two men to an extreme close-up of the uniform that clearly indicates that the "mark of pride" is the mud on this uniform. Metaphorically, the criminal "scum" has been cleaned up and purified by this heroic action that allows the officer to wear the "brown badge" of courage.[21] In this sequence, the point of view is both that of the noble officer and that of God looking down at the apparent chaos rendered orderly by this valiant officer.

The second sequence in the advertisement offers a case of domestic abuse initiated by a drunk and distraught father in an apartment complex that looks more like a grey-washed prison than a home for a young family. The police in this segment are female officers (women are absent from the first sequence, which offered "hard" policing) who reunite mother and child and provide a comforting shoulder for the sobbing child to cry on. In this case, the uniform is stained by grateful tears as the two are reunited, and one female officer looks on approvingly at the "mark of pride" of the helpful female officer. The arrest of the father and the resolution of this case of domestic abuse, poverty, and alcoholism are not revealed, but the music glosses over this glaring gap in the narrative to focus on a different type of emotional dirt that has been cleaned. In this segment, the Hong Kong police force is figured not as a rugged, masculine SWAT team but as a maternal force watching over its helpless citizens.

In the third and final sequence, we see the police force figured as a cyborg-panopticon with an opening shot of a police officer at a computer console dispatching officers to a car accident. There is a jump cut to the collision, where officers collectively work to free a helpless and anonymous man (unlike the very intimate portrayal of the mother and daughter as victims in the previous sequence) trapped in an overturned car. One officer in a motorcycle uniform has blood from the passenger or fluid from the car drip onto his motorcycle boots, which he later wipes clean as viewers are offered an extreme close-up of the black boots.

The motif of the extreme close-up on a human stain on the uniform, whether a shirt, blouse, or black leather boots, renders the uniform as fetish while curiously shifting the focus away from the idea of an individual working as a member of the police. In these instances, the uniform operates as a symbolic apparatus of the Hong Kong police force. From a Žižekian perspective, these human stains operate within the disciplinary code of totalitarian modernity to reveal "a 'stain of enjoyment' in the big Other of the Law, the perception of the domain of law as permeated with obscene enjoyment" (Žižek 12–13). The viewer is meant to identify with the uniform and gain pleasure from its contact with these human stains. Indeed the uniform as synecdoche for the Hong Kong police force rather than being besmirched by the human stain is completed by it. These three narratives manufacture an aura for the police officer's uniform that should leave civilians yearning to join the police force; viewers are hailed by these emotionally charged narrative vignettes, which situate the viewer not as the victim or criminal but as the future heroic officer wearing a stained uniform.

Rey Chow's *Sentimental Fabulations, Contemporary Chinese Films* asserts that contemporary Chinese[22] films tend to focus "on physical and material deprivation and psychological destitution" (21) that operate ideologically so that "*at the heart of Chinese sentimentalism lies the idealization of filiality*" (22). Filiality is not bound to "one's biological or cultural elders," but also operates as an "age-old moral apparatus for interpellating individuals into the hierarchy-conscious conduct of identifying with – and submitting to – whatever pre-exists them" (22). Clearly this ad operates within such a structure of fetishistic filiation in the modernist mise-en-scène of a noir Hong Kong.

In an undergraduate setting, I might hint at this Žižekian type of reading but would encourage students to generate their own readings by prompting them with questions. I also ask students to consider how civilians might read these three segments against the grain of the narrative's logic. I push them to think about how the characters who are not police officers are imagined in these sequences as either criminals or hapless victims.

I like to screen this clip once without sound and then with sound to see how students react to the addition of the triumphant militaristic orchestral music and to how sound cues action as each mini-climax is accompanied by an orchestral crescendo that seems to endlessly repeat the theme. I ask students how the commercial compensates for its lack of dialogue and character development with action-packed editing, camerawork, and music that focuses on the emotion of the mimed heroics. Aristotle may rate "spectacle" as unimportant in his appraisal of the key elements of tragedy, but this ad is quite obviously driven by television's melodramatic stage machinery rather than by plot, character, and dialogue. Given the direct appeal to recruitment in this ad, students need little prompting on the text's message. It is the subtext and reading against the grain of the ad's seductive logic that I try to encourage.

I ask students if they think this commercial is effective or not. I ask them to think about Canadian advertisements that use a similar narrative structure, perspective, visual palette, and music. I play a Canadian armed forces advertisement titled "Fight with the Canadian Forces" that in terms of narrative structure, lack of dialogue, authoritarian point of view, camerawork, mise-en-scène, editing, music, and mood seems to replicate the Hong Kong advertisement's structure of feelings. I ask them to consider how the Canadian armed forces commercial might play in Afghanistan and in Canada's north and how it reveals the contradictions between the myth of Canada as a nation of peace-keepers (Dorn) versus the reality of a military used to support paternalistic, neocolonialist operations abroad and within its own territories

(Razack). I also ask them to think through how race operates in each video clip (e.g., how does each video construct "terror" and its calming other, the authoritarian uniformed figure). Narrative certainly works in both ads, but it is strongly aided and abetted by Aristotle's lowly "stage machinists" who manufacture entrancing spectacles that provide the metaphor and metonymic punch of the ads' appeals.

For a research assignment that might stem from this comparison of the Hong Kong and Canadian recruitment advertisements, I might prompt students to research the advertising firms (e.g., Are they local or global agencies?) that produced the commercials, or to situate the Hong Kong advertisement within the legacy of the Hong Kong police force or Hong Kong cinema (Chow; Cheuk; Berry). I might suggest students examine other law enforcement and military recruitment ads produced in other broadcast regimes (e.g., Does the Iraqi army use the same style and narrative logic of North American recruitment ads? How are age, gender, race, ethnicity, and religion represented in the appeals to potential recruits?). These types of research prompts might lead to a more thorough examination of the institutional structures influencing the myth building in the advertisements.

* * *

I know of only a few professors of literature who encourage their students to create a poem, play, short story, or painting as part of the study of a literature. Typically, the creative and critical are divided. In television studies, because there needs to be a focus on production to grasp reception, such risks should be taken even though students might not produce captivating content. Increasingly, professors are using assignments that engage the creative impulse of students.

Anandam Kavoori's *Thinking Television* (2008) melds the creative and critical in what he dubs a "thinking television project," which blends critical race theory and media literacy to teach undergraduates (3). He describes the course structure in the following way: "the first half of the class is structured around focus groups in which the students watch stimulus material on television and multiculturalism. Different members of the class conduct the focus groups. The second half of the course is designated for the class to meet in focus groups to create a television show" (5). Students construct a hypothetical pitch for a TV show that must be "commercially successful" and "makes money" while expanding and diversifying the restrictive image gallery of mainstream broadcast TV (5). This project as "textual poaching" harnesses the critical to construct a notional program that would operate within the boundaries of commercial broadcast and does not require students to gain a grasp of production. From a more formalist perspective, Jason Mittell at Middlebury College runs an undergraduate course titled "Storytelling in Film and Media," which he describes as a "fairly traditional academic theory course, applying narrative theory to a range of examples in film, television and video games" ("Teaching"). In this course, his "video remix assignment" has students create a reinterpretation of a film or TV program by using editing software: "The goal is not to make a funny mashup or a fake trailer–instead you should manipulate the given footage to create a new fabula. It is an exercise to highlight how editing can tell stories, so you should feel free to be creative in how you recut the original" ("Storytelling"). Mittell and Kavoori both engage students in production to better realize the practice of critical theory. I sense there is virtue in encouraging students to become familiar with the practice of making TV in order to appreciate the interplay between theory and practice.

In my third-year undergraduate TV course, my "make TV" group assignment compels students to explore how broadcast regimes shape content.[23] The students in teams of three create standard broadcast-length thirty-second public service announcements for the university's closed-circuit television[24] around a preassigned relevant and controversial issue for the campus (e.g., the prioritizing of sustainability versus the ambitious building of roads, construction in a fragile semi-arid ecosystem, date rape on campus, troubling militarism). They produce these videos knowing that they will be vetted for broadcast by the vice president of learning and research, who will be concerned about community standards. They also know that UBCO-TV operates to boost the image of the campus for potential students, parents of students, and donors, and thus the internet broadcaster might shy away from a negative portrayal of life on campus.

Some of the submissions are rejected on aesthetic grounds while others violate "community standards"; some make it to air on the campus's closed-circuit television system and onto UBCO-TV's website under its "teaching and learning" tab, where a disclaimer precedes each video explaining that it does not express the views of the university and are part of a student project. This engagement with production and the tribulations of "broadcasting" demonstrates how institutions, whether a university or a large commercial network, shape the public sphere. The focus of this assignment is not on the quality of the content produced so much as on what is learned via the process of trying to air the short ads.

Such assignments occur in the humanities at the University of Sheffield, which has a media lab where students learn to work with video (Allam "Creative"). Sheffield provides an excellent "Toolkit" (Allam) where students can quickly learn the basic skills of planning, shooting, and editing. I sense that such endeavors might help give the humanities more relevance by allowing students to more widely disseminate their knowledge than with the fifteen-page term paper that remains on a memory stick or is posted only in a digital archive. We must not only equip students with the ability to critique and appreciate media, we must equip them and ourselves to work as activists in the emergent media sphere. The study of signifying practices involves a call to expand the type of media we use to signify analysis and critique. Offering students the ability to generate videos that offer a counterhegemonic structure of feelings is an exciting possibility for both student and professor.

NOTES

1. My emphasis here and later in the quotation.

2. By using "TV" as the term for broadcast television, I hope to limit the discussion to the dominant paradigm for television, which is currently being challenged by webisodes, YouTube, Bit-Torrent, and other forms of narrowcasting that television studies must necessarily embrace. See the online journal *Flowtv.org* to see a television journal committed to analysis of ephemeral screen culture.

3. Williams uses "structure of feelings" as a noun. In this instance, I use "structure" as a verb to indicate that advertisers, broadcasters, etc., participate in generating texts that attempt to structure audiences' reactions to the texts. The structuring of feelings represents a negotiation of affect by viewers that is part historically and part technologically determined.

4. For an excellent account of the emergence of webisodes, see Max Dawson's "Little Players, Big Shows: Format, Narration, and Style on Television's New Smaller Screens," which describes

how American television action serials like ABC's *Lost* and Fox's *24* create short, cheap television content for broadcast and purchase by cell-phone users that is seen as a supplement for fans of these programs.

5. I am conscious that with the introduction of handheld e-book readers that what has constituted print culture in the past may soon slip into screen culture as the book's look changes. I am fascinated that many e-readers attempt to reproduce the look of yellow vellum and older font styles to model the book on-screen, which suggests that the manufacturers of these technologies assume readers yearn for the tactile feel of Gutenberg's paper and ink.

6. There are of course exceptions to this general tendency with Marshall McLuhan demonstrating in the 1960s that print is but one form of technology. Since the 1990s we have witnessed a post-canonical turn with the definition of a text no longer bound by the printed page. Sidonie Smith introduced the presidential theme for the 2011 Modern Languages Association convention, "Narrating Lives," with this ecumenical sense of textuality:

> "Narrating Lives" captures this diversity of genres and media, encompassing medieval hagiography, letters, diaries, narratives of exploration and colonization, autobiographical and biographical texts, lyric cycles, and autobiographical fiction as well as the pictographs of native peoples, the oral traditions of indigenous peoples, testimonial witnessing, performance art, graphic memoirs, blogs, and autoethnography.

7. Since the 1960s, communications programs have produced television studies texts. See Horace Newcomb's reflection on his forty-odd years in television studies, "Studying Television: Same Questions, Different Contexts," which concludes with this circular logic about the value of studying television:

> I am unconcerned with whether one writes about episodes or series, genres or schedules, industry or policy, TiVos or cable, European public-service broadcasts, or economic shifts. I am concerned that we ask questions that help explain to others why television continues to be so important. That is what I look for when I read new work. That is just about all I care about, and if I do not find those critical questions, I stop reading. (111)

Newcomb's view of "importance" seems to insist that every work of television studies must proselytize for the discipline. I think we need to study TV because it is culturally relevant to many and instrumental in shaping ideological worldviews.

8. I am not entirely comfortable with the notion of film studies being characterized as being entirely about aesthetics because some film studies focus on production and history. However, American academic organizations like the journal *Film & History* tend toward the generation of close readings rather than a deeper cultural study of film that integrates questions of production, distribution, etc. See this journal's 2010 area chairs conference call at http://www.uwosh.edu/filmandhistory for a sense of the limitations of some types of film studies that adhere to a more formalist model of criticism ("Call for Area Chairs"). The Society for Cinema and Media Studies at http://www.cmstudies.org offers a more integrative approach

that mirrors Caldwell's synthetic approach to the analysis of screen culture.

9. The book and the marketing of literature have changed in the last four hundred years (e.g., serialized nineteenth-century novels), yet the basic format (bound paper), production via the printing press, and delivery via booksellers or libraries remains fairly consistent. As mentioned previously, e-readers may swiftly change these modes of distribution and production.

10. An exploration of the development of the graphic novel provides an example of how the bound "book" functions as an element of commerce, taste, and technology. Do fans demand that serialized comics be aggregated into graphic novels, or is this aggregation like post-syndicated versions of television shows remarketed in shiny new collector's edition box sets, a way to appeal to fans with yet another collector's item? Oprah Winfrey's "inspirational" book club offers another tantalizing interweave between media and notions of how old and new media in this late capitalist period profitably manipulate notions of taste.

11. These "office" programs, via laughter, trouble the anxieties of corporate America's declining fortunes. I think of *Outsourced* as the perfect expression of neoliberal globalization as it balances a standard storyline about a young white office manager out of his depth against the backdrop of a call center in India. The implied and explicit xenophobia in the program provide an excellent case study in how TV seeks to influence its anticipated viewers' anxieties about late capitalism.

12. The Victorian era's triple-decker lending of books (three volumes for each novel) via a private library resembles the now-vanishing video rental stores or the mail-order rental and online streaming companies like Netflix, which shape what is available by limiting their content to "mainstream" film and television. I thank the editors for suggesting this link that indicates, despite the difference in media, the long reach of modern consumer culture.

13. My box set of *Cops* does not contain a director's commentary. The usual format of a box set seems designed to facilitate the cross-marketing of upscale television programs like *The Sopranos* to fans who want to delve into a program. The *Cops* box set, on the other hand, is marketed with the promise of providing more uncensored, "raw" footage than what can be shown on regulated TV.

14. See http://www.blu-ray.com/faq.

15. A simple Google search of the string "Dr. Quinn Medicine Woman" yielded 255,000 hits in January 2009, 511,000 hits in December 2010, and 835,000 hits in November 2011. Many of these are fan sites.

16. Within the reality TV genre, the exception to this rule is Mark Burnett who, as the producer of CBS's long-running *Survivor* franchise, clearly marks each episode as his own despite the incredibly standardized formula that leaves little room for creativity and would not seem to require an auteur. Burnett's production of both *Survivor* and NBC's *The Apprentice* suggests that his positioning as auteur is a tactical case of branding.

17. For the devoted fans of a particular show, this sense of decentered texts is not their experience.

18. Some transnational types of satellite broadcast television operate regionally and thus avoid nation-states' regulatory regimes to offer a sense of horizontal comradeship based on linguistic or ethnic solidarity; for ex-

ample, Kurdish satellite television serves Kurds in Turkey, Iraq, Kurdistan, and elsewhere. See http://www.kurdsat.tv/english.aspx.

19. The closest analogue of fans' use of a TV text as raw material for recreation might be fan fiction. See fanfiction.net for examples. I have not been able to locate a university course dedicated to studying fan fiction, and I sense that many literature professors would resist the notion of studying such texts based on aesthetic grounds, yet Henry Jenkins's work on TV fans in *Textual Poachers* suggests that such ethnographic accounts of fan culture would be a rich and vital field for evaluating how fans negotiate the dominant ideology of serialized television.

20. The majority of the articles for this course are accessed from online journals like *Flowtv.org* and other jour-nals like *Television & New Media*, available via library databases like JSTOR and EBSCO.

21. My apologies to Stephen Crane's 1895 *The Red Badge of Courage*.

22. Chow uses "Chinese" film to include those produced in "the People's Republic of China, Taiwan, Hong Kong, and Shanghai" (x).

23. I have offered this assignment twice, in the fall of 2008 and the fall of 2010. The account offered here synthe-sizes these two iterations of the assign-ment in terms of topics and structure rather than detailing minute differences in the two versions.

24. See http://ubco.tv. This website and the closed-circuit television system on campus operate as part of the promo-tional arm of the university, although UBCO-TV does encourage students to make and broadcast content.

REFERENCES

1001 Classic Commercials. Mill Creek, 2009. DVD.

Allam, Claire. "Creative Activity and Its Impact on Student Learning—Issues of Implementation." *Innovations in Education and Teaching International* 45.3 (2008): 281–288.

———. "Filmmakers Toolkit." *University of Sheffield* (n.d.). Web. Accessed 15 Dec. 2010.

Allen, Robert C., and Annette Hill. *The Television Studies Reader*. London: Routledge, 2004.

Anderson, Benedict. *Imagined Com-munities: Reflections on the Origin and Spread of Nationalism*. Rev. ed. London: Verso, 1991.

Aristotle. "The Poetics." In *Critical The-ory since Plato*. Ed. Hazard Adams. New York: Harcourt Brace Jovanov-ich, 1971. 47–66.

Arp, Robert. *South Park and Philosophy: You Know, I Learned Something To-day*. London: Blackwell, 2006.

Benjamin, Walter. "Art in the Age of Mechanical Reproduction." *Marxist. org* (n.d.). Web. Accessed 14 Jan. 2008.

Berry, Chris, ed. *Chinese Films in Focus*. 2nd ed. Houndsmills, Hamp-shire, England: Palgrave Macmillan, 2008.

Boddy, William. *Television in the 1950s*. Champaign: University of Illinois Press, 1993.

Breight, Curtis. "Shakespeare on American Television and the Special Relationship between the UK & the USA." In *Television and Criticism*. Ed. Solange Davin and Rhona Jack-son. Bristol, England: Intellect, 2008. 37–48.

Burke, Kenneth. "Literature as Equipment for Living." *Direction* 1 (Apr. 1938): 10–13.

Caldwell, John T. "Welcome to the Viral Future of Cinema (Television)." *Cinema Journal* 45.1 (2005): 90–97.

"Call for Area Chairs Representing Love in Film and Television." 2010 *Film & History Conference* (1 Aug. 2009). Web. Accessed 14 Nov. 2010.

Cheuk, Pak Tong. *Hong Kong: New Wave Cinema 1978–2000*. Bristol, England: Intellect, 2008.

Chow, Rey. *Sentimental Fabulations, Contemporary Chinese Films*. New York: Columbia University Press, 2007.

Classic TV Commercials: The Ones We Never Forget. St. Clair, 2008. DVD.

Davin, Solange, and Rhona Jackson, eds. *Television and Criticism*. Bristol, England: Intellect, 2008.

Dawson, Max. "Little Players, Big Shows: Format, Narration, and Style on Television's New Smaller Screens." *Convergence: The International Journal of Research into New Media Technologies* 13.2 (2007): 231–250.

Derrida, Jacques. *Of Grammatology*. Trans. G. Spivak. Baltimore, MD: Johns Hopkins University Press, 1976.

Dorn, Walter. "Canada: The Once and Future Peacekeeper?" *Peace Magazine* (Oct.–Dec. 2006): 16. Web.

Eagleton, Terry. "The End of Criticism." *English in Education* 16.2 (1982): 48–54.

Ellis, John. "Scheduling: The Last Creative Act in Television." *Media, Culture, & Society* 22.1 (1991): 2–38.

Epp, Garrett P. J. "Chair's Message." *University of Alberta's English and Film Studies Department* (n.d.). Web. Accessed 27 Jan. 2009.

"Fight with the Canadian Forces." *YouTube* (n.d.). Web. Accessed 25 Jan. 2009.

Fish, Stanley. "Interpreting the *Variorum*." In *Debating Texts: Readings in Twentieth Century Literary Theory and Method*. Ed. Rick Rylance. Toronto: University of Toronto Press, 1987. 155–171.

Fringe. Prod. J. J. Abrams, Alex Kurtzman, and Roberto Orci. n.d. Web. Accessed 16 Dec. 2010.

Gondry, Michel, Spike Jonze, and Chris Cunningham. *The Work of Directors: Spike Jonze/Chris Cunningham/Michel Gondry*. Palm Pictures, 2008. DVD.

Hall, Stuart. "Encoding, Decoding." In *The Cultural Studies Reader*, 2nd ed. Ed. Simon During. London: Routledge, 2003. 507–517.

Hanley, Richard. *South Park and Philosophy: Bigger, Longer, and More Penetrating*. Chicago: Open Court, 2007.

Hilmes, Michele. "The Bad Object: Television in the American Academy." *Cinema Studies* 45.1 (2005): 111–116.

Horton, Donald, and R. Richard Wohl. "Mass Communication and Para-social Interaction." *Psychiatry* 19 (Aug. 1956): 215–229.

Iwabuchi, Koichi. "Multinationalizing the Multicultural: The Commodification of 'Ordinary Foreign Residents' in a Japanese TV Talk Show." *Japanese Studies* 25.2 (2005): 103–118.

Jenkins, Henry. "'Never Trust a Snake!': WWF Wrestling as Masculine Melodrama." In *Out of Bounds: Sports, Media, and the Politics of Identity*. Ed. Aaron Baker and Todd Boyd. Bloomington: Indiana University Press, 1997. 75–101.

———. *Textual Poachers: Television Fans and Participatory Culture*. New York: Routledge, 1991.

Kavoori, Anandam. *Thinking Television*. New York: Peter Lang, 2008.

Kellner, Douglas. *Media Culture: Cultural Studies, Identity and Politics between the Modern and Post-modern.* New York: Routledge, 1995.

——. *Television and the Crisis in Democracy.* Boulder, CO: Westview, 1990.

Keyes, Daniel. "The Performance of Testimonial Television on Daytime Talk Shows." Ph.D. diss., York University, Toronto, 1997.

Kompare, Derek. "Flow: DVD Box Sets and the Reconception of Television." *Television & New Media* 7.4 (2006): 335–360.

Landow, George P. "Mudie's Select Library and the Form of Victorian Fiction." *Victorian Web: Literature, History & Culture in the Age of Victoria.* Web. Accessed 8 July 2009.

Lynch, David. "David Lynch on iPhone." *YouTube* (n.d.). Web. Accessed 21 Dec. 2010.

"The Mark of Pride and Care: Hong Kong Police Force." *YouTube* (n.d.). Web. Accessed 25 Jan. 2009.

McLuhan, Marshall. *The Gutenberg Galaxy: The Making of Typographic Man.* Toronto: University of Toronto Press, 1962.

Mittell, Jason. "A Cultural Approach to Television Genre Theory." In *The Television Studies Reader.* Ed. Robert C. Allen and Annette Hill. London: Routledge, 2004. 171–181.

——. "Storytelling in Film and Media: Class Site for FMMC0357." *Blogdot Middlebury* (n.d.). Web. Accessed 15 Jan. 2011.

——. "Teaching Narrative through Remix" (17 Dec. 2010). Web. Accessed 15 Jan. 2010.

"NBC Grooms 'Must See TV' Heir: 'Comedy Night Done Right' Takes Place of Famous Motto." *Television Week* (Feb. 2007). Web. Accessed 29 Dec. 2008.

Newcomb, Horace. "Studying Television: Same Questions, Different Contexts." *Cinema Journal* 45.1 (2005): 107–111.

Ott, Brian. *The Small Screen: How Television Equips Us to Live in the Information Age.* London: Wiley-Blackwell, 2006.

Platt, Len. "Our Common Cultural Heritage: Classic Novels and English Television." In *Television and Criticism.* Ed. Solange Davin and Rhona Jackson. Bristol, England: Intellect, 2008. 15–24.

Razack, Sherene H. *Dark Threats & White Knights: The Somalia Affair, Peacekeeping and the New Imperialism.* Toronto: University of Toronto Press, 2004.

Smith, Sidonie. "The Presidential Theme for the 2011 MLA Convention: Narrating Lives." 126th MLA Annual Convention, Los Angeles, 6–9 Jan. 2011. Web. Accessed 4 Jan. 2011.

The Sopranos: The Complete Series. Amazon.ca (n.d.). Web. Accessed 28 Dec. 2008.

Stratyner, Leslie, and James R. Keller, eds. *The Deep End of South Park: Critical Essays on Television's Shocking Cartoon Series.* Jefferson, NC: McFarland, 2009.

Weinstock, Jeffrey Andrew. *Taking South Park Seriously.* New York: New York University Press, 2008.

"What Is Blu-Ray." *Blu-ray.com* (n.d.). Web. Accessed 25 Jan. 2009.

Williams, Raymond. "The Analysis of Culture." In *Cultural Theory and Popular Culture: A Reader,* 3rd ed. Ed. Tony Storey. Essex, England: Pearson, 2006.

——. *Television, Technology, and Cultural Form.* New York: Schocken, 1974.

Žižek, Slavoj. *The Plague of Fantasies,* 2nd ed. London: Verso, 2008.

Hypertext in the Attic:
The Past, Present, and Future
of Digital Writing

ANDREAS KITZMANN

In a recent expedition through my attic I stumbled (literally) upon my old Macintosh Classic computer. Curious and in dire need of some extended procrastination, I hauled the squat cube out of its box, set it on my desk, and plugged it in. After a lengthy period of whirring and clicking, the smiling Macintosh icon finally emerged on the tiny black-and-white screen. Given that this old computer had its primary use during my days as a graduate student, the contents were predictable enough—the usual assortment of overwrought fiction, the odd poem, goofy computer games, hastily written graduate papers, dubious freeware, and my Ph.D. dissertation, both in its final form and its numerous incarnations. What caught my eye in particular, however, was a folder labeled "hypertext fiction." Back in the day, which is to say the early 1990s, this folder represented in many ways the future promise of computer technology at its hyperbolic best. In that folder were the seeds of a veritable revolution, where the old traditions that guided written expression for centuries were to give way to a world of infinite possibility, variability, and unrestrained creativity. Written by daring pioneers of an emerging art form, the various authors were leading the charge to bring about the end of the printed book and replace it with a mode of expression that was joyously nonlinear and free to cross as many boundaries as the ever-increasing powers of the computer were making possible.

So what, exactly, was in that folder? By today's standard of computing power, not much—some black-and-white text with a few links, small grainy images, and the occasional audio clip that often caused the computer to crash. Indeed, as a revolution it seemed rather timid. Yet for those committed to using the computer for purely creative purposes, such as the creation of fiction or poetry, these early attempts did hold the promise of breaking the hold that more traditional forms of narrative had on the nature and form of written expression. Within academia, hypertext fiction, or hyperfiction, was often touted as concretely realizing many of the theoretical claims and concepts of contemporary critical theory, especially those associated with postmodernism and deconstruction. A case in point is the title of George Landow's influential book *Hypertext 2.0: The Convergence of Contemporary Critical Theory and Technology*. Hypertext–and more generally, the personal computer–somehow managed to make literary and critical theory real and offered "proof" that it actually mattered.

The aim of this chapter is twofold. First, I will address the question of whether or not hypertext still matters within the context of literary studies, and identify some of the major subgenres that fall under the general banner of hyperfiction or digital fiction as a means to chart where hypertext, broadly conceived, may be heading. Second, I will initiate a more general inquiry into the extent to which technological advances affect the very nature of human experience by offering new avenues for engaging with "the world" by employing technologically derived modes of expression that then depict or otherwise characterize this engagement. This is really just a fancy way of asking whether advances in media technology alter the way in which we see, experience, and represent (in this case, through literary expression) that which we understand as the so-called real world.

The question of whether hypertext still matters can be addressed in part by considering hypertext's connection to contemporary literary theory and analysis. Many of the literary approaches to hypertext take their cues from modern and postmodern experimental literature and theory. The majority of the books and articles that present hypertext as a major innovation in the evolution of "serious" writing point to the experimental hyperfictions championed by Robert Coover in his 1992 review and article for the *New York Times Book Review*, which first brought hyperfiction to the attention of the wider reading public. Coover's text enthusiastically embraces hypertext as a "truly new and unique environment," and details his various encounters with now-classic works of hyperfiction as well as his experience of teaching creative writing using specialized hypertext software such as Intermedia and Storyspace, the latter of which is the product of Eastgate Systems, one of the major (and arguably only) publishers of literary hypertext.

Eastgate has long declared itself as being dedicated to the creation of "serious hypertexts" and has become a champion for authors, both new and established, who wish to explore the potentials of electronic fiction, nonfiction, and poetry. Browsing through the Eastgate catalog does confirm the assertion that hypertext writing is a serious affair in the sense that the range of topics and approaches mirrors that usually encountered in the average English literature department–issues of identity, gender, cross-cultural intersections, high theory, intertextuality, and postmodernism, to name only a few.

Indeed, according to Jane Yellowlees Douglas, hyperfiction's common element is its tendency to follow the paths of late twentieth-century fiction, which is "characterized by multiple perspectives and voices, episodes linked with associative logic and memory, and rejection of conventional, often pat, final awarding of marriages, happiness, money, and recognition that wrap up narratives in mainstream and genre fiction alike" (8). Many authors are also united by a shared desire to explore what the technology can and cannot do in terms of presenting compelling and meaningful creative work in a manner that parallels the projects undertaken by the works that define the modernist and postmodernist canon.

Yet such an allegiance to the paradigms that arguably define what is recognized as serious literature does not universally characterize the nature of literary hypertext and its many incarnations on platforms that include the web and the cell phone. From the perspective of an academic wishing to explore such a terrain for teaching or research purposes, this presents quite a challenge. For one, there is the nasty question of what to include within the category of literary hypertext, plus the equally pernicious question of defining what, exactly, literary hypertext is (and is not). Then there is the matter of the ever-changing nature of digital expression itself. As media systems converge and mutate, and as new programs, phenomena, practices, and technologies fall in and out of the market, the sheer mass of what might need to be considered, if only for a moment, increases exponentially. Whether one is a digital immigrant or native, there is always something "out there" that potentially merits attention and that might just be the next trend to completely transform the expressive landscape. Thus, any attempt to create categories or somewhat stable interpretive systems is fraught with the ever-present threat of obsolescence and outright ignorance (on the part of those making the categories). That said, I will take the risk of creating a few categories of literary hypertext with which to, at the very least, offer a temporary zone of interpretive security:

1. Text-based hypertext: completely text-based, conventional hypertext
2. Modest hypermedia: sites that incorporate visuals and sound as supplements to textual content
3. Dynamic hypermedia: sites where text has given way to primarily visual or game aesthetics and structures
4. Web 2.0 environments: phenomena such as blog fiction, wovels, and wikinovels that are based on collaboration and peer-to-peer creation
5. Hybrid hybrids: variations that collapse the above categories, especially via nonconventional uses of technology, such as cell-phone novels

The above taxonomy may also be useful for providing a basis with which to formulate a pedagogical approach to teaching hypertext fiction and poetry within the context of a university-based literature course. While rather broad, the five categories parallel the functionality of genres as they are often used within literary scholarship and education by highlighting common conventions, formats, styles, approaches, material conditions, thematic elements, and structures. By creating such categories and deliberately isolating common characteristics and structural elements for the purposes of sustained critique and analysis, the seemingly wild and unfamiliar terrain of hypertext becomes framed within an interpretive system that draws on the particular strengths of literary scholarship, namely the ability to discern categories and trends, to apply historical knowledge of form to new and emerging genres, and to engage in close readings to determine value and cultural relevance. Accordingly the question of how to teach this stuff becomes a little clearer. Hypertext, like any other art form, has its major genres or groupings that manifest in identifiable patterns, formal structures, codes, conventions, and styles. Lines can therefore be drawn between the pre- and postdigital, between trends in other media and cyberspace, between historical conditions and thematic commonalities within the digital literary landscape, and between the materiality of the technology itself and the formalized expressive content that emerges within and around it. In short, the average literature professor should be quite comfortable teaching hypertext in his classroom, given that once you remove the gloss of technological marvel, the terrain becomes quite familiar.

TEXT-BASED HYPERTEXT

The first category could be considered the "classic mode" in that the initial forays of hypertext were almost exclusively text-based, which can perhaps be attributed mainly, but not exclusively, to the limits of early hypertext technology and display terminals. That said, the exclusivity of text is a matter not just of constraint but also of conscious choice on the part of writers. It is important to remember that hypertext technology such as HyperCard or Storyspace is considered by many to be a new medium for *writers* and *readers,* and as such it is primarily a medium with which to experiment with the written word itself. Images and sound effects are merely window dressing. What counts are the words.

Such a sentiment is certainly emphasized by Robert Coover who in his keynote address for the 1999 "Digital Arts and Culture" conference in Atlanta, Georgia, mourned the passing of what he termed the "Golden Age of Hypertext" – an age when pioneering hypertext writers "explored the tantalizing new possibility of laying a story out spatially instead of linearly, inviting the reader to explore it as one might explore one's memory or wander a many-pathed geographical terrain, and, being adventurous quests at the edge of a new literary frontier, they were often intensely self-reflective" (Coover, "Literary Hypertext"). With the advent of the World Wide Web and multimedia computing, such noble pursuits have given way to meaningless "image surfing" where the art of letters loses its substance and becomes reduced to "surface spectacle." Coover is no doubt overstating his disdain for media-rich hypertexts in an effort to point out what he believes to be truly revolutionary about hypertext, namely the manner in which it has served as a platform for radical experiments in narrative, fiction, or poetry. In his commentary on Shelley Jackson's *Patchwork Girl*, Coover reminisces about what he feels was truly remarkable about so-called classic hyperfiction:

> These early multidirectional webworks of text spaces had the alleged disadvantage – a disadvantage that has all but disappeared – of having to click a mouse and read from a screen, relatively new experiences then, but they challenged the constraints and conventions of centuries of printbound reading in very exciting ways, offering the writer vast new formal possibilities and redefining the relationship of the reader to the text. (Coover "Literary Hypertext")

Coover has been accused of being overly nostalgic about this apparent golden age, which is something that he readily acknowledges in the course of his address. Indeed, there is much to take issue with regarding Coover's negative assessment of hypertexts that integrate visual and audio material but for now, what is noteworthy in Coover's emphasis on classic hyperfiction is the fact that such works compel us to focus on what hypertext means in terms of reading and writing. Such a focus is crucial, given that it serves as a basis for much of the theoretical and creative work within the domain of digital media as a whole.

Some examples of hypertext novels that keep to Coover's classic ideal are the hyperfictions of Adrienne Eisen, Judd Morrissey, and Judy Malloy. Eisen's works contrast the tactics of many normative hypertexts in the sense that there are few links and the narrative is usually framed within the first-person account of a particular character and his or her life situation. While the reader has some choice with respect to what text portion to read, these choices are quite limited so that getting through all the links is not a burdensome project as it is with the more complex hypertexts that initially defined the genre, notably Michael Joyce's *afternoon, a story*. There are no images, only text, and the narratives are quite personal and seemingly autobiographical, dealing with broad themes such as adolescence, relationships, sexual tensions, pregnancy, childhood traumas, etc. The stories have closure in that the reader does eventually end at a final screen. The structure for "Considering a Baby?," for example, is extremely simple by hypertext standards, offering the reader three links for each month of a pregnancy. Clicking on any of the links moves the month forward by one. The texts are for the most part pithy comments and observations on the nature of pregnancy from a woman's perspective, favoring a wry, cynical viewpoint as opposed to one that is overly romanticized and naïve.

Judd Morrissey's hyperfiction *The Jew's Daughter* offers a more dynamic media experience, although the overall experience is still text-based. Described as an "interactive, non-linear, multi-valent narrative," *The Jew's Daughter* uses a simple but ingenious linking mechanism in which the act of selecting a linked word changes only a portion of the page that one is reading as opposed to taking one to another page altogether. The result is subtle and somewhat disarming because the effect is to render the text into an unstable form that changes in ways that are not predictable. In contrast to Eisen's work, Morrissey's prose is abstract and poetic, eschewing descriptive language for evocative phrases that do more to create a mood than to provide a concrete sense of narrative development. In this way, *The Jew's Daughter* is typical of many literary hyperfictions that favor a more experimental and abstract approach to the art and thus is in line with Coover's preference for "classic" hypertexts.

As an established figure in the hyperfiction community, Judy Malloy's work also keeps to the idea of classic hyperfiction, using the text as the primary medium. Many of Malloy's works are representative of the subgenre of database narratives, which "use a computer database as a way to build up levels of meaning and to show many aspects of the story and characters, rather than as a means of providing alternative plot turns and endings" (Malloy "From Narrabase"). The experience of reading such a work is akin to repeatedly plunging into a pool of information from which a reader emerges with "a cumulative and individual picture" (Malloy "From Narrabase"). By the standards of contemporary graphic design, Malloy's hypertext novels, such as "Revelations of Secret Surveillance" (2004), are not that much to look at. The first page of "Revelations" features a simple black box within which, written in white, is the first scene of the novel. Around this block of text are arranged (against a rather acidic green background) a series of chapter titles and phrases that serve as links. The reader can go through the work either by clicking on these links or by reading the work sequentially by way of the blue bar at the bottom of the page. The links on the right side of the page take the reader to various points within a particular "canto," whereas the links on the left allow the reader to traverse the ten major sections of the novel as a whole. As the reader clicks on a link on the right, the text in the center changes and an additional link is added to the list on the bottom. Eventually the links begin to repeat themselves and at that point the reader can move on to the next canto.

The narrative structure of "Revelations" is relatively conventional in that it follows the familiar pattern of alternating between the memories of the main characters, in this case Gwen and her memories of how she met her husband, Gunter, in Germany, and the stories and recollections of Gunter's parents, who were forced to flee Nazi Germany. In between such reflections is an additional narrative strand that concerns the life of the two main characters and their friends as they spend part of the winter in a New Hampshire cottage. Thematically, the novel draws parallels between the censorship and persecution of artists in Nazi Germany and the increasingly restrictive conditions for artists in post-9/11 America. Given the relatively simple structure of the interface (and the option of the blue bar), Malloy's novel is a rather straightforward reading experience in the sense of not overwhelming the reader with a multitude of links or fragmented narrative strands. Indeed, one might question whether the novel would work just as well as a conventional book, given the comparatively linear organization of the hypertext structure. Nevertheless, "Revelations" remains a satisfying experience due to the fact that the various narrative sequences, which are compelling in their own right, are not overshadowed by an overly complex interface and linking structure.

MODEST HYPERMEDIA

Taking advantage of the computer's ability to render a variety of media experiences, my second category for hypertext is characterized by works that privilege an approach that uses sounds or visuals mainly to supplement the textual content. The work of Robert Kendall is exemplary here in that many of his hypertexts, which are primarily poems, employ low-key Flash animations that while certainly part of the experience, are still secondary to the textual material. The hypertext poem "In the Garden of Recounting" reveals itself as the reader moves the cursor over the words "memories," "fall," "like," and "rain" and over the faint outline of plants situated in the middle of the screen. Hovering causes phrases to emerge in a fluid motion, and then they recede back to their point of origin once the reader moves on. The apparent simplicity of the interface is somewhat deceiving in that the images and emotions conveyed through the ever-circulating words are woven together in a complex fashion. What is particularly striking about the work is that the themes and implied narrative of the poem become gradually more concrete as the phrases drop in and out of focus.

A different approach is taken with Kendall's poem "Faith," which is not "proper" hypertext in that it is not structured around a network of nonlinear links that the reader must access through active participation. Instead, Kendall, again using Flash, has the words of his poem trickle down into formations that are reminiscent of the broad genre of concrete poetry in that the words take on a multitude of patterns that to varying degrees represent the poem's content or mood and, as well, point to the basic instability of language and representation in general. The poem is cumulative, meaning that as one moves through the sequence, phrases and words are added to what is already on the screen or, in some cases, certain words and phrases crowd out others by merging, mutating, or outright pushing them away. Accompanying the textual material are discrete musical effects that punctuate the movements of the individual words and phrases. At the very end of the poem, the reader is left with a pile of jumbled words with the final act being the headline word, "Faith," falling to the bottom of the screen leaving the words "just to sum up" as a wry conclusion to this statement about faith in contemporary society.

Caitlin Fisher's "These Waves of Girls" (2001) is another work that effectively integrates visual and audio material into a nonlinear hypertext where the reader actively determines the process of the reading experience. The narrative concerns a young girl struggling with her sexual identity and is structured as a confessional autobiography that parallels, to some extent, the experience of someone reminiscing about childhood experiences while flipping through old photographs. This use of autobiographical forms is fairly typical for hypertext authors, especially in cases where nonlinearity and a reader-driven narrative progression are the major structural elements. One likely reason for such a preference is that the confessional mode lends itself well to a multivalent hypertextual environment, given that the act of remembering and recounting one's past is often a nonlinear experience where memories are triggered by a variety of cues, such as old photographs, comments by listeners, and random daily events.

Fisher's "hypermedia novella," as she has labeled it, begins with a splash screen of a video of a cloudy sky set in fast forward and the sounds of somewhat forced laughter. After a few minutes the screen changes to offer the reader a menu of largely suggestive choices, such as "kissing girls," "school tales," "I want her," and "she was warned." Passing the mouse over any of these options causes a small text window to open on the right and an image on the left. Actually clicking on any of the menu options takes the reader to another screen, which presents another array of links and menu options. Throughout the work, audio and visual elements are used intermittently. A few of the images allow for a rudimentary form of manipulation in that passing the mouse over a particular image causes it to distort and stretch. This device is used most with an image of a female breast, the effect of which is to simulate the act of squeezing someone's breast, which in the context of the story lends a certain "tactility" to the experience. The audio elements are relatively sparse in comparison, with recorded laughter being one constant. In one instance the reader is presented with a screen that has twelve audio players that can be played either individually or simultaneously to create a cacophonous experience of competing stories. The effect is quite powerful in that it concretely renders the multiplicity of memories, identities, and perceptions that often compete with one another in terms of becoming part of an "official" life narrative.

"Inanimate Alice," written by Kate Pullinger and Chris Joseph, is a multimedia novel aimed at a younger readership. The ten-episode story has a pedagogical element to it with supplementary websites, blogs, and other material available for teachers and parents. The story itself, which once again is in the form of a first-person autobiography, is told from the perspective of a young girl who travels with her parents around the world as her father takes on positions with various oil companies. Each country constitutes a separate episode and represents Alice at a different age and stage of life. As one moves through the episodes the multimedia elements become more complex and interactive, and game elements are included in the mix. This increasing complexity mirrors Alice's development as an animator and game designer, which is ultimately what she becomes as an adult. The narrative is linear and while readers propel the narrative forward by clicking on an icon or completing simple tasks, the story itself must be read in sequence. The text is sparse and concise but in combination with the sound effects and other elements offers a compelling experience in terms of drawing the reader into Alice's unfolding story. The increasing complexity of the gaming elements also point to some form of story/game hybrid in that they eventually become interdependent, meaning that the reader must negotiate both successfully in order to continue with the story. This interdependence between story and game relates to the fact that the main narrator is herself immersed in gaming and graphic design, which will eventually be her chosen career. In this respect, the inter-section between game and story becomes a fitting paradigm for the manner in which Alice herself relates and works through her experiences and passage into adulthood.

DYNAMIC HYPERMEDIA

The third category of literary hypertext is made up of works that often stray very far from the written word and employ techniques and aesthetics taken from film, game design, conceptual art, and electronica, to name only a few influences. Yet despite such diverse influences, the works that I am including in the category of dynamic hypermedia continue to represent "literary" approaches to hypertext in that "text" and, to a lesser extent, narrative remain central and defining components. What is especially noteworthy of such works is that they actively attempt to redefine the literary experience by directly engaging with the paradigms and fundamentals of digital technology. In other words, the computer here is much more than a delivery vehicle but rather is a dynamic co-determinant in the overall nature, aesthetic, and experience of the work in question.

Exemplary here is Bebe Molina and Daniel Howe's "Roulette," which, as the title suggests, is informed by one of the fundamentals of gaming, chance, which by extension has also played a role in experimental fiction, such as the "cut-up" technique used by William Burroughs or some of the techniques employed by the Dadaists and the Oulipo group. Upon opening "Roulette," the reader is presented with three rotating cubes, within which are contained a dozen or more bouncing cubes, the behavior of which is reminiscent of the balls in common lottery machines. By clicking on one of the larger cubes, a small cube is drawn out and superimposed on the surface of the larger cube. Each small cube represents a single word, which when selected also appears highlighted in a passage below the cube interface. The passages, as one might expect, are typically abstract and do not initially appear to be part of any narrative sequence. Indeed, given that the reader has little control over which small cube is actually extracted, the sequences of the text are the product of mere chance. While certainly innovative in its delivery, "Roulette" is a relatively crude example of what computer scientists are pursuing in the fields of computer-generated writing, natural language generation, and to a lesser extent artificial intelligence, which can all be broadly characterized as fields that are attempting to empower the computer with increased agency and the ability to self-evolve.

Mary Flanagan's "The House" literally pits the reader against the computer in that the reader must actually struggle with the interface in order to maintain some control over the narrative, which emerges in piecemeal fashion. Structured around an architectural metaphor, the "story" of "The House" revolves around a troubled relationship between two people who are confined to a small space. The struggle with the interface is intended to mirror the struggles of the two characters contained within the space of the work itself, and thus is said to create an "intimate, interactive, screen-based piece" (Flanagan). Rendered in a 3D environment, "The House" is a "computer-based spatialized organism world" that apparently is regulated by the computational process of the sine wave—a fact that is probably lost on any reader not familiar with computer programming or mathematics. The text, which is mainly a collection of sentence fragments, is "written" on or beside rooms that are arranged in a random pattern. With the mouse, the reader can move the entire assemblage, which has the effect of bringing some of these rooms, and their accompanying texts, closer to or farther from view. After a time, the system as a whole seems to regenerate itself, although it is unclear if the actions of the reader had any influence on the newly emerging patterns. In the author's description accompanying the work, Flanagan asks, "how does everyday spatial practice bring into focus the relationship between code, language and relationships? What are the key characteristics of digital relationships as seen through this light? Does the recurring emphasis on process, chance, and interactivity also function as an indicator of larger questions about the chance writing of the text?" These are all good and profound questions, however the ability of "The House" to offer even partial answers is debatable, at least beyond the level of a very general spatial metaphor. In other words, yes the experience of moving the assemblage around and glancing at the fragments that come into view may indeed approximate the frustration that one may experience with a relationship going down the tubes, but that is about as far as things go, at least from my experience. As a purely conceptual work, "The House" is interesting and worthy of attention in that it provides a concrete platform from which to experience a dynamic where narrative gives way to a complex interplay between the computer and its user. Indeed, what is notable and frustrating about "The House" is exactly the fact that the level of influence a user may have on the overall system remains resolutely unclear. Yes, one can move the boxes around, but what does that mean exactly, and what are the consequences? Again, this may replicate the experiences of so-called real life, but is this enough?

Donna Leishman's intriguing and evocative "The Possession of Christian Shaw" is similarly obtuse in terms of providing readers with a straightforward narrative experience in which the cause and effect of reader choices can be immediately experienced. However, from the opening screen, which features a stylized modern cityscape rendered strangely haunting by a brooding musical soundtrack, the reader (or participant, as Leishman prefers) is effectively transported into a world that is as engaging as it is perplexing. As part of Leishman's doctoral dissertation ("Creating Screen-Based Multiple State Environments: In-vestigating Systems of Confutation"), "The Possession" is loosely based on a seventeenth-century Scottish account of an eleven-year-old girl who was believed to be possessed by a particularly persistent demon. Several members of the local community were implicated in the case, with the ultimate result being the execution of six adults. Leishman's version of this story is neither representational nor historically accu-rate. The piece is rendered in the style of a minimalist cartoon with Christian Shaw depicted as a wide-eyed innocent with a particularly large head. Upon entering the environment the participant, to use Leishman's term, is not presented with any navigation tools or clues. It is only by passing the mouse over various parts of the screen that the participant begins to uncover possible links and interaction zones. There is little or no text in "The Possession," and the narrative is gradually constructed via a series of small vignettes, almost puzzle-like in their quality. Some of these vignettes are fairly detailed and engag-ing, but offer little in terms of adding to the narrative or providing clues about Christian's situation. They are merely digressions, which Leishman defines as "spaces in which the extra emotion and sensual explorations exist."

The sparse yet highly intuitive nature of "The Possession" reflects the primary research question of Leishman's dissertation ("Creating"): "How does the artist develop an interactive style and visual vocabulary, which evokes rich responses from the participant whilst challenging them to counter conventional interaction tropes?" Judging from the work itself, one response to this question would be to create an envi-ronment where the participant/reader must gradually and intuitively learn or discover the various methods and modes of interactivity. For example, after closing a given digression or vignette, the participant is returned to the main screen that upon closer inspection has changed in a very minor way. Often these changes are in the form of added links, which are almost imperceptible to casual or quick observations. However, as one becomes familiar with this tactic, the process of uncovering the story and moving through the narrative becomes in-creasingly easier and, I would argue, compelling. There are moments, however, where the "wrong decision" will abruptly end the experience, returning the reader to the original position.

Unlike many other works of hyperfiction that offer complex audiovisual environments and nonlinear navigation methods, "The Possession" does not create an experience where the reader is left feeling helpless, ineffectual, or confused. Despite the lack of actual text and explicit narrative cues, "The Possession" manages to captivate because of its almost poetic ability to immerse the reader within a satisfying environment of gradual discovery and well-structured meandering. Eventually, should one get to the end, a written epilogue is offered that presents the account of the actual Scottish case and additional reflections on its meaning within a contemporary context. This epilogue, when encountered after the experience of moving through the interactive environment, has an additive effect in terms of providing some of the encountered interactions with added meaning and tangential significance. "The Possession" is very much a participatory narrative where the reader, through her interactions and moments of reflection, digression, and intuition, gradually pieces together a story that is as much the product of individual interpretation and active construction as of the designs of Leishman herself.

WEB 2.0 ENVIRONMENTS

Much has been made of hyperfiction's ability to engage with the reader on a level that actively invites input, interaction, and various degrees of co-authorship. Indeed, it is this type of engagement that prompted many scholars and writers to proclaim that hypertext would eventually end the tyranny of the text and usher in an age of mutual authorship and collaborative modes of expression and creativity. It is certainly arguable whether such claims have any bearing or not, especially within the context of so-called serious or literary hypertext, which remains very much a fringe activity enjoyed by a relatively small and elite group of enthusiasts. However, with the increasing popularity of Web 2.0 applications, such as social networking sites, blogs, and wikis, the range and complexity of collaborative forms of writing have certainly increased. While the bulk of what is out there is far from significant in terms of literary merit or even basic readability, there are some notable examples that point to potentially significant developments in the nature of online creative expression. Within the context of mainstream publishing, Penguin's "A Million Penguins" can be credited as bringing the genre, if one can call it that, to the wider public's attention and possibly providing some form of legitimacy to writers attempting to merge the usually solitary act of literary expression with the interactive multiplicity that characterizes the web itself. Created in partnership with De Montfort University in Leicester, England, "A Million Penguins" was launched in February 2007 and formally put to rest one month later, after about 1,700 people actively took part in the exercise. By most accounts, the actual novel was a dismal failure, with Jordan Jacks's comment in the *Yale Herald* ("the worst book I've ever read") being representative of the overall reaction from critics and the wider public. However, there was far greater enthusiasm for the project as a social experiment and as an important cultural exercise in and of itself. In the research report published by De Montfort in April 2008, the project was framed as less of a literary experiment and more of a social experiment. "The research focused on two questions: what was the role of the discussion around the writing, and what patterns of social behaviour occurred among the contributors? Framing the research questions in this way allowed us to approach *A Million Penguins* as a cultural text and, inevitably, led us to critique the question underlying the wikinovel experiment—can a community write a novel?" (Mason and Thomas 1).

Among the most interesting findings of the report was the observation that "A Million Penguins" "challenged the 'garden' metaphor so widely used to characterize behaviours in wikis." Instead of participants carefully tending to the creation of a site in a manner analogous with the tending of a real garden, the wikinovel took on the character of a carnival with moments of excess "featuring multiple competing voices and performances" (Mason and Thomas 2). The site was populated by individuals ranging from serious "gardeners" earnestly attempting to mutually create a meaningful work to attention-hungry pranksters, hackers, pornographers, vandals, and narcissists who kept Penguin's editorial team working literally around the clock to keep the site from crashing or deteriorating into an uncontrollable tangle of disparate voices. Despite such editorial efforts, "A Million Penguins" was deemed a literary failure because of the sheer volume of so many non-integrated elements and voices. In one of the many blogs created within the project, it was noted that "A Million Penguins" "felt like 21 short stories with all the same character names, not one cohesive piece of literature" (15). Similarly, the project was considered faulty in terms of it being a collaborative, community-driven event, mainly because the novel itself is an inherently noncollaborative form. "The problem with A *Million Penguins* in a nutshell is that the concept of a 'wikinovel' is an oxymoron. A novel is probably as un-collaborative a literary form as you can get, while a wiki is inherently collaborative. Wikipedia works because encyclopedias were always in a sense collective works – distillations of collective knowledge – so the wiki was the right tool for reinventing that form. Here that tool is misapplied" (19).

So was the project a failure? In terms of creating a collaborative novel that could actually be read, the answer would be yes. But as a social experiment and as an effort to explore the potentials for using the collaborative powers of the web to create new forms of expression, the results were arguably positive. "The contributors did not form a community, rather they spontaneously organized themselves into a diverse, riotous assembly. We have demonstrated that the wiki novel experiment was the wrong way to try to answer the question of whether a community could write a novel, but as an adventure in exploring new forms of publishing, authoring and collaboration it was, groundbreaking and exciting" (Mason and Thomas 21).

The website *Ficlets* offered a model of collaborative writing that was perhaps less fraught with the kinds of ego-driven disputes and actions that drove the editors at Penguin to drink. Aptly described as "literary legos," the aim behind *Ficlets* was to provide a forum for the creation of very short stories (no longer than 1,024 characters). Once created, the stories were posted to the site as modules, which could be augmented by others in the form of prequels and sequels. What distinguished *Ficlets* from the wiki approach is the fact that once posted, the original stories could not be edited or changed but only linked to additional stories that might (or might not) carry the narrative forward. In addition to prequels or sequels, comments from registered users were displayed below the ficlet, creating a kind of forum for discussion, support, and mutual admiration. While the results were unlikely to win a Booker Prize, the site did appear to be successful as a community of engaged writers who, for the most part, were supportive and genuinely engaged with one another's efforts. *Ficlets* could, in fact, be likened to the workshop model commonly used in creative writing courses, with the notable exception that there was no authority figure, such as a teacher or published writer, leading the course of events. It was this workshop paradigm that arguably lent a certain legitimacy to the website in that it had the potential to serve as an incubator or forum for budding writers who might eventually bring their work out of the website and into publication. What was significant there was not so much the writing, but the environment that was created by such a communal website.

A website which makes its role as a type of incubator for new writers more apparent is StoryMash, which also includes financial rewards in the form of revenue sharing and regular contests. StoryMash has no limits on word count or genre, proclaiming that "novels, screenplays and new creative writing forms yet to be name[d] are accepted." The basic unit of authorship is the "chapter," to which is attached a discussion forum that allows the author and his readers to engage in an extended discussion of the material. Once the author is happy with the work, it can be officially "published" on the site and made available for peer review via a ranking system.

Stylistically, the bulk of what is written on these sites is not overtly different; however it is worth considering the impact of such communal, networked environments on the status or definition of "authorship" in the conventional sense. With so many voices participating or at least providing varying degrees of input and reaction, who is writing what? All of this contrasts with the romantic notion of the individual writer struggling with her book in a lonely attic somewhere. Writing, like many things, has become a form of social networking, and I anticipate that this trend will continue as technologies evolve and as their integration into creative practice increases. Perhaps we can expect more works along the lines of Toby Litt's "Slice," published by Penguin's digital series, We Tell Stories. Using blogs and Twitter as the main delivery vehicles for the narrative, "Slice" tells the story of Lisa (Slice to her friends) from the perspective of parallel weblogs, one written by Slice and the other written by her parents. The reader was also briefly given the option of mailing the characters through text messages on Twitter. Although the ability to interact with the characters was limited to a four-day period, all the exchanges are archived on the site. The success of "Slice" as an engaging experience can be attributed to its ability to use a common networking tool as a medium for storytelling.

It should be noted that Penguin's We Tell Stories is part marketing exercise and part experiment. In the former aspect, the six stories that make up the series are based on six classics in the Penguin archive, with the aim being to encourage new readers to pick up these books once they are inspired by the digital adaptations on the web. In terms of experimentation, We Tell Stories "reflects the ways in which publishing is reinventing itself, rethinking business models, emerging forms, cultural needs and, perhaps most significantly, design issues as the book blossoms from its traditional format as text on pages into new, experience-based explorations" (Willis).

HYBRID HYBRIDS

This final category is a bit of a mashup and is driven more by speculation than concrete examples and verifiable observations; as such, it provides a platform for bringing this chapter to its conclusion. The major element here is the actual technologies employed to create and consume literary material, which offer a glimpse into possible futures as opposed to established trends in the present. What I hope to make clear here is the importance of thinking through the experiential nature of technology itself and its ability to foster behaviors and existential conditions that depart from previous conventions. Such a move is important because it provides a way of thinking about hypertext and digital fiction that is not confined solely within debates grounded in poststructuralist literary theory and postmodernism, which tend to obsess about the changed dynamic between reader and writer that hypertext brings about. Accordingly, hypertext can be explored through a greater range of theoretical models and, as well, shift the debate from comparisons between print and hypertext to a discussion that is more inclusive of issues important to the continued development of digital media. A cue can be taken from Espen Aarseth who, in his book *Cybertext: Perspectives on Ergodic Literature*, argues for the need to move hypertext beyond the parameters of literary theory and the altered relationship between readers and writers. Aarseth's term "cybertext" is defined as a "machine for the production of a variety of expression," with the computer interface being understood as a "mechanical device for the production and consumption of verbal signs" (Aarseth 3). The point here is to direct our attention to what readers are reading from, as opposed to only what is being read, which is to say that the form, in the case of hypertext and other digital media, is as important as the content–indeed it is perhaps now meaningless to make a distinction between the two. Equally useful to the present discussion is Aarseth's term "ergodic," which he defines as the "non-trivial effort required to allow the reader to traverse a text" (1), which basically means that readers must make concrete decisions about how they are going to read the work in question, as opposed to following a preset reading paradigm, as in the case of a printed book.

One immediate result is to downplay the overreliance on literary theory as the major tool with which to conceptualize hypertext, literary or otherwise. For Aarseth this is not intended as an attack on literary theory but rather is a move to defend it from becoming "useless" by extending it far beyond its conceptual borders:

> I wish to challenge the recurrent practice of applying the theories of literary criticism to a new empirical field, seemingly without any reassessment of the terms and concepts involved. This lack of self-reflection places the research in direct danger of turning the vocabulary of literary theory into a set of unfocused metaphors, rendered useless by a translation that is not perceived as such by its very translators. (14)

Such thoughts resonate with the media scholar Mark Hansen, who emphasizes the need to consider the material and phenomenological nature of technology and its participatory role in defining what we experience as "reality." For Hansen, media technology is an active and tangible agent in the shaping of experiential reality itself. Drawing from Walter Benjamin, Hansen argues that technology functions as a "material force of natural history" through its role as an "agent of material complexification" that necessitates a "corporeal and physiological adaptation" on the part of human beings (234). In other words, media technology cannot be explored by only emphasizing discursive constructions, which has been the overriding tendency in humanist scholarship for a number of decades. Rather, according to Hansen, theorists must also consider the ways in which specific media technologies "complexify" both human life and the world in which we live. It is for this reason that Hansen advocates an approach that emphasizes physiology as opposed to linguistic constructions, thereby redirecting the "linguistic turn" to what might be called the "material turn." There is more to media than discursive constructions, and technology does more than just influence modes of representation and communication. Rather, as Hansen asserts, "technology impacts our experience first and foremost through its infrastructural role" and thus "informs our basic ways of seeing the world" (3). Technology, then, is an interwoven part of human culture itself, a dynamic part of the whole experiential realm of the human condition and thus not separate, not explainable in terms of purely discursive statements (Kitzmann 3).

In terms of hypertext, what this means is that it takes on the function of a material presence that potentially alters the trajectories of both human society and technological development. Hypertext, like any technology, is part of the real world in terms of having a material presence and in terms of being part of the general matrix of human activity and culture. Thus, the act of thinking about and theorizing hypertext requires one not only to consider the specific material conditions of the medium and its relationship to prior modes, such as print, but also to realize that hypertext is situated within a very complex dynamic that is beyond the ability of any one academic area to fully capture. A sentence from Katherine Hayles's brief but highly informative and evocative book *Writing Machines* is worth repeating at this juncture: "Medium and work were entwined in a complex relation that functioned as a multilayered metaphor for the relation of the world's materiality to the space of simulation" (42). Hayles wrote this passage in response to her reading of M. D. Coverly's hypertext novel *Califia*, which prompted a type of theoretical epiphany through which she realized that her reading of *Califia* was initially limited by the fact that she was focusing on the words alone rather than on "an integrated perspective in which all components became signifying practices." These components included not only the text, of course, but also the "layered images, complex navigation functionalities, and simulated documents" (41). Such thoughts led to Hayles's concept of a media-specific analysis that argues for the need to consider the material conditions of the medium as well as the content when engaging in any form of analysis or critical reflection. Based on the preceding discussion of Hansen, I advocate that Hayles's approach be augmented by considering also the material conditions and dynamics between the medium and the "world" in which it is situated. Thus, considering the material specificity of hypertext involves also the consideration of topics such as the information economy, the technological infrastructures of a given society, the dynamics of human-computer interaction, the environmental consequences of information technology, and the ideological conditions around which particular technologies were brought into being and others were left to fade into obscurity. This list could extend into infinity, which might lead one to argue that what I am proposing here is a practical impossibility. However, my point is not to encourage forms of scholarship that attempt to be utterly comprehensive in terms of taking everything into consideration. Such a task is reminiscent of one of the unfortunate characters in a Borges story who toils away at projects that literally have no end. Rather, my aim is to draw attention to the rather simple concept that the material conditions of a particular medium extend far beyond the specific confines of the technology and also involve the materialities of the world itself.

This brings me to the cell-phone novel – a "literary" phenomenon that has taken Japan by storm and is beginning to show up on North American shores with the *Textnovel* site discussed briefly in this volume's introduction. The cell-phone novel is perhaps the most concrete example of hybrid hybrids, given that it is an actual genre that is enjoyed by a very large audience, at least in Japan. As the name suggests, cell-phone novels are works of fiction that are initially written on a cell phone but then later republished in print form. Given the constraints of the medium, such as the small keyboard and screen, as well as the discursive conventions associated with text messaging, the language of cell-phone novels is sparse and devoid of lengthy descriptions and complex character development. The emergence of the phenomenon can be traced to the website *Maho no i-rando*, a blogging portal popular among Japanese youth. The site's administrators noticed that many bloggers were writing novels on their blogs and in response created a new feature that allowed users to upload their work to cell phones and to permit readers to post comments. *Maho no i-rando* claims that over a million novels are now listed on its server, which is really quite astonishing.

According to Norimitsu Onishi, writing for the *New York Times*, the popularity of cell-phone novels can be directly attributed to the material conditions of the technology itself: "The boom [of cell-phone novels] appeared to have been fueled by a development having nothing to do with culture or novels but by cellphone companies' decision to offer unlimited transmission of packet data, like text-messaging, as part of flat monthly rates." A more complex argument is presented by Chiaki Ishihara, whom Onishi quotes: "It's not that they had a desire to write and that the cellphone happened to be there. Instead, in the course of exchanging email, this tool called the cellphone instilled in them a desire to write." Given this fact, it is not surprising that most cell-phone novels are written in the first person and are highly autobiographical, mimicking for the most part the diary form. Accordingly, the majority of cell-phone authors are young women writing about troubled relationships, adolescent anxieties, teen pregnancy, unrequited love, and generational conflict. What is surprising, at least to me, is the success of cell-phone novels in their printed form. Justin Norrie, writing for the *Sydney Morning Herald*, reports that half of Japan's top ten novels for 2008 were cell-phone novels, with the bulk being written by first-time authors. The average sale for individual novels is 400,000 copies with *Koizora* (Love Sky), written by Mika, selling more than 1.2 million copies in less than a year. Such success is made even more curious by the fact that many purchasers would have already read the cell-phone novel in its original, serialized form. Mayumi Sato, an editor at Goma Books, credits the communal aspect of cell-phone novel culture as the force behind such sales figures: "It might seem strange that young readers are going out and buying the book after they've already read the story on their mobile. Often it's because they email suggestions and criticisms to the author on the novel website as the story is unfolding, so they feel like they've contributed to the final product, and they want a hardcopy keepsake of it" (Norrie).

Japan's literary establishment bemoans the success of these novels, citing their limited vocabulary, thin plots, rampant clichés, and underdeveloped characters as not befitting a culture that has produced some of the world's oldest literature. News reports on cell-phone novels point out that the bulk of the readers do not read "real" novels and limit their cultural experiences to those available in popular culture, especially comic books, TV serials, manga, and video games. Leaving aside questions of taste and the legitimate concerns over tradition, craft, and creative complexity, what needs to be acknowledged is that cell-phone novels exemplify, in a very concrete manner, the influence that technologies have in reconfiguring the creative landscape. Furthermore, the phenomenon points to the importance of a technology's materiality and the existential infrastructure that is created around its use and adoption into mainstream culture.

To date, the cell-phone novel's success is limited to the Japanese market, but it is probably safe to assume that the phenomenon is a harbinger of things to come on a global scale. The popularity of text messaging is hardly confined to Japan, and the conditions seem ripe for the cell-phone novel to develop elsewhere. Yet what is particularly significant is not so much the specific subgenre of cell-phone novels but rather the fact that new communications technologies are functioning as a force for new creative literary endeavors and, moreover, as a fierce challenge to the very foundations of the publishing industry and the conventions surrounding authorship, editorial work, distribution, and financial remuneration, to name only a few key elements. In this respect, it is worth paying close attention to how established and emerging handheld and wireless technologies are being deployed and situated within or against the publishing industry and what this may mean in terms of how writers write and readers read. A particularly intriguing example, I think, is Amazon's Kindle device, which was released in November 2007. The Kindle is an electronic book reader, which in and of itself is nothing new, given that such devices have been on the market, with limited success, for a number of years. What makes the Kindle significant is its free, built-in wireless connection, which allows the reader to directly access Amazon's ever-expanding online bookstore, which makes the device far more commercially viable than its predecessors.

Amazon is also breaking new ground by recognizing, in a concrete manner, "the importance of the connectivity between our differing modes of reading, the fact that readers might like to follow up references within the text or to conduct a related search" (Lloyd 33). The

Kindle's ability, while relatively limited, to connect to web-based content, such as blogs, online newspapers, and search engines, is, as Sara Lloyd observes, significant because it acknowledges "the fragmented, always on nature of most people's reading habits today, allowing readers to move seamlessly from reading a few pages of a novel, say, to snacking on some news, before picking up a couple of blog feeds" (33). That said, Amazon's approach to the Kindle is still far from what the "think-and-do tank" the Institute for the Future of the Book has dubbed the "networked book," which is evocatively described as an "evolving entity within an ecology of readers, authors and text" that is never finished and always a work in progress. Amazon's model is still tied to the downloading of relatively static content (i.e., published works), as opposed to designing the Kindle as a portal to the web itself, where a given work could potentially exist in a fluid, networked environment of constant interaction, exchange, and augmentation. To this end, many publishers are paying close attention to the ongoing development of the smart phone and whether such devices will be deployed and adopted as viable reading and writing platforms. The advantage that such technologies have over the likes of the Kindle is their ability to fully access the web, which means that instead of distribution, which is Amazon's model, the emphasis is on access and search, which is arguably the main challenge to the stability of conventional print culture. "Google and Apple, between them already have the solution for eBooks (and it's not a download solution). Read and search on your iPhone and access via a web browser, anything in print can be handled that way. More to the point: everything in print can be handled that way. Everything will be searched via the web, everything will be accessed via the web. Downloads are pretty much of an irrelevance" (Hodgkin qtd. in Lloyd 38).

The emergence of tablet computers, with the Apple iPad leading the pack, has encouraged much speculation over the future of the book and the publishing industry in general. However, the bulk of these debates are centered around what could be termed logistical and financial considerations, which is to say questions of how e-publishing will affect the conventions of a publishing industry that is rooted in print culture. Will bookstores eventually be obsolete and will readers favor electronic books over printed books? Will the traditional role of the publisher as an arbiter of cultural value give way to an on-demand world where authors deal more directly with their reading audiences in terms of both creative output and financial compensation? To a large extent the answers to such questions are in the affirmative, given the demise of many bookstores both large and small and the increasing ubiquity of tablet computers in the market. In Canada two notable instances also point to the manner in which electronic publishing has effectively undermined both the authority of the publishing industry to determine cultural import and its ability to meet the demands of the reading public. In the first instance, a work by Terry Fallis, the winner of "Canada Reads," an initiative by CBC radio in which notable Canadians engaged in a kind of verbal sparring match to defend their choice of a book that all Canadians should read in a given year, was first made available as a podcast because it had been rejected by a host of publishers. Responding to positive reader feedback, Fallis self-published the novel, which then went on to win a major Canadian literary award at which point the book was picked up by a major publishing house. In the second instance, the 2010 Giller Prize–winning novel, *The Sentimentalists* by Johanna Skibsrud, caused a turmoil due to the fact that the small publishing house that first released the novel was unable to keep up with the demand for copies by readers. As a result, most readers accessed the novel as an e-book, which effectively promoted the e-reader as a legitimate and more efficient publishing and reading platform (Patch).

What is less clear at this point is the extent to which sophisticated multimedia tablet devices, such as the iPad or RIM's PlayBook, have ushered in new conventions of literary creation that parallel those realized and attempted by the hyperfiction community. In other words, when it comes to electronic books, the primary differences from their print counterparts are a few search functions and occasional links or embedded video. The structure and literary conventions remain unchanged, indicating that such devices have to date been employed primarily as delivery platforms as opposed to opportunities to experiment with the essential nature of reading and writing.

The million-dollar question, then, is not if people will read books in digital form but rather how they will read them and, as well, how authors and readers will relate to one another via the technology that provides the access. To a major extent, we already have some answers to this question. In the future (the very near future), readers and writers will have the potential to coexist in a fully networked environment that is ubiquitous and portable. As Peter Brantley notes, such an environment "stands to profoundly disrupt scholarship and reading," and he elaborates further:

> It is not the issue merely of having content digitized, but rather the near-constant availability of that information combined with the means to find it with search, that enables disruptions in how we use books, and ultimately how we write books. Network ubiquity makes Amazon's Kindle ebook reader distinctive enough to prove that content acquisition can be serendipitous; that Googling on a powerful mobile phone or computing device can be deeply utilitarian rather than merely demonstrative of cool technology; and that research and education are being profoundly reshaped by the ability of users to engage with information from anyplace, and at anytime, where they can provide sufficient attention to the task. (2)

Clearly, for the academy, the continued maturation of the e-book, in whatever form, will radically affect not only how content is delivered to students and faculty, but also pedagogy itself. The "textbooks" of the near future will likely gravitate en masse to electronic platforms and thus be understood more as databases of content than as stand-alone texts that maintain their authority and validity by virtue of conventional notions of authorship, expertise, and reputation. Moreover, such platforms will become "smart" in the sense of being able to respond to the reading habits and needs of their readers, to automatically update themselves as new editions become available, and to provide feedback to instructors, who will not only be able to monitor students but also engage with them directly via the e-reading platform. Such dynamic, interactive, and individualized platforms will no doubt influence how faculty structure their classroom or lecture experiences. Already existing devices, such as "clickers" and other interactive tools, will encourage classroom environments that mirror the responsive environments encountered in the online world (Cole).

The traditional role of the publisher as the only legitimate arbiter of verifiable content and "good" (or marketable) culture will rapidly fade away, giving way to the almost mob-like, peer-to-peer system that dominates much of what is known as Web 2.0. This is not to say that the traditional book and the conventions of solitary reading (and authorship) will cease to exist. There will always be a need, context, and market for such work. However, the landscape of what we today call the literary establishment, with its coterie of authors, critics, publishers, agents, reviewers, and readers, will change dramatically in the near future. This will not only engender new forms of writing that both accommodate and further develop the always-networked environments of the web but will also define what we know and appreciate as capital-L Literature and the values and traditions associated with it. Whether this is a cause for lament or celebration remains to be seen.

NOTES

This chapter expands on some of the ideas explored in my book *Hypertext Handbook: The Straight Story* (New York: Peter Lang, 2006). Specifically, this chapter elaborates on or incorporates extracts from 33–37, 40, 84–86, 99–101.

REFERENCES

Aarseth, Espen. *Cybertext: Perspectives on Ergodic Literature.* Baltimore, MD: Johns Hopkins University Press, 1997.

Brantley, Peter. "Introduction: Homes for Good (Orphan) Books." *Library Trends* 57.1 (Summer 2008): 1–7.

Cole, Stephanie. "Quit Surfing and Start 'Clicking': One Professor's Effort to Combat the Problems of Teaching the U.S. Survey in a Large Lecture Hall." *History Teacher* 43.3 (May 2010): 397–410.

Coover, Robert. "The End of Books." *New York Times Book Review* (21 June 1992), sec. 1, 23–25.

———. "Literary Hypertext: The Passing of the Golden Age." Keynote address, "Digital Arts and Culture," Atlanta, GA (29 Oct. 1999). Web. Accessed 13 Nov. 2008.

Coverly, M. D. *Califia.* Watertown, MA: Eastgate Fiction, 2000.

Douglas, J. Yellowlees. *The End of Books or Books without Ends: Reading Interactive Narratives.* Ann Arbor: University of Michigan Press, 2000.

Eisen, Adrienne. "Considering a Baby?" *Adrienneeisen.com* (n.d.). Web. Accessed 8 Sept. 2010.

Fisher, Caitlin. "These Waves of Girls." *York University* (22 Feb. 2001). Web. Accessed 8 July 2009.

Flanagan, Mary. "The House." *Electronic Literature Collection*, vol. 1 (2006). Web. Accessed 8 Sept. 2009.

Hansen, Mark. *Embodying Technesis: Technology beyond Writing.* Ann Arbor: University of Michigan Press, 2000.

Hayles, Katherine. *Writing Machines.* Cambridge, MA: MIT Press, 2002.

Hodgkin, A. "Amazon versus Google for eBooks?" *Exacteditions* (24 Nov. 2007). Web. Accessed 3 Sept. 2009.

Jackson, Shelley. *Patchwork Girl*. Watertown, MA: Eastgate Fiction, 1995.

Joyce, Michael. *afternoon, a story*. Watertown, MA: Eastgate Fiction, 1987.

Kendall, Robert. "Faith." *Wordcircuits.com* (2002). Web. Accessed 25 Sept. 2009.

———. "In the Garden of Recounting." *Drunkenboat.com* (2004). Web. Accessed 25 Sept. 2009.

Kitzmann, Andreas. *Hypertext Handbook: The Straight Story*. New York: Peter Lang, 2006.

Landow, George. *Hypertext 2.0: The Convergence of Contemporary Critical Theory and Technology*. Baltimore, MD: Johns Hopkins University Press, 1997.

Leishman, Donna. "Creating Screen-Based Multiple State Environments: Investigating Systems of Confutation." Ph.D. diss., Glasgow School of Art, Sept. 2004. Web. Accessed 23 Oct. 2009.

———. "The Possession of Christian Shaw." *6amhoover.com* (Sept. 2004). Web. Accessed 23 Oct. 2009.

Lloyd, Sara. "A Book Publisher's Manifesto for the Twenty-First Century: How Traditional Publishers Can Position Themselves in the Changing Media Flows of a Networked Era." *Library Trends* 57.1 (2008): 30–42.

Malloy, Judy. "From Narrabase to Hyperfiction: Uncle Roger." *Well.com.jmalloy* (1991). Web. Accessed 24 Oct. 2009.

———. "Revelations of Secret Surveillance." *Well.com.jmalloy* (2004). Web. Accessed 23 Oct. 2009.

Mason, Bruce, and Sue Thomas. "A Million Penguins Research Report." *Institute of Creative Technologies* (24 Apr. 2008). Web. Accessed 16 Nov. 2009.

"Mission Statement." *Institute for the Future of the Book* (n.d.). Web. Accessed 23 Mar. 2010.

Morrissey, Judd. *The Jew's Daughter* (n.d.). Web. Accessed 3 Dec. 2009.

Norrie, Justin. "In Japan, Cellular Storytelling Is All the Rage." *Sydney Morning Herald* (3 Dec. 2007). Web. Accessed 15 Dec. 2009.

Onishi, Norimitsu. "Thumbs Race as Japan's Best Sellers Go Cellular." *New York Times* (20 Jan. 2008). Web. Accessed 15 Dec. 2009.

Patch, Nick. "Scarcity of Giller-Winning 'Sentimentalist' a Boon to eBook Sales." *Toronto Star* (12 Feb. 2010). Web. Accessed 20 Mar. 2010.

Pullinger, Kate, and Chris Joseph. "Inanimate Alice." *Inanimatealice.com* (2006). Web. Accessed 30 Sept. 2009.

Willis, Holly. "We Design Stories: The Digital Fiction of Six to Start." *AIGA* [*American Institute for Graphic Arts*] (22 July 2008). Web. Accessed 23 Oct. 2009.

Zuiker, Anthony, and Duane Swierczynski. *Level 26: Dark Origins*. New York: Dutton, 2009. See also http://www.level26.com.

6   The ABCs of Viewing: Material Poetics and the Literary Screen

PHILIP A. KLOBUCAR

My software did this to me.

CHRISTOPHER T. FUNKHOUSER, 2009

To date, relatively few analyses of the screen as an aesthetic form in its own right have been produced. Critiques of web design and interface usability maintain strong historical attachments to print and typographic disciplines, conceiving electronic communication as page- and document-based. The very term "screen" continues to prioritize the cinematic arts, often implying, whether intended or not, that the methods and ideas of film criticism are equally applicable to current programmable writing practices on the computer. However, as an increasing number of visual culture historians and film theorists realize, the screen as art object invites an increasingly wide array of cultural analyses, corresponding to the medium's growing significance as both a mode of social interface and knowledge construction. Such developments, cinema theorist Haidee Wassan points out, tend to be addressed within film studies through critical explorations of malleability and multiplicity—metaphors, in other words, "wherein screens are reconceptualised as windows that shrink and expand on cue" (74). As a formative attribute influencing how the screen work is to be engaged, perhaps even interpreted, physical dimension, for Wassan, contributes to an effective materialist schema, according to which various traditional approaches to film-based media can be interrogated over a greater number of cultural contexts. As video emerges in newly consumable formats via devices and environments as divergent as Jumbotrons perched high above freeways and cell phones and iPads clutched in crowded subway cars, no single mode of usage seems dominant. How is it possible, Wassan asks, for traditional methods of film criticism to account accurately for this radical shift in the medium itself?

> Against claims to the contrary, cinema scholars must do even more to integrate into their critical frameworks the multimediated environment that is clearly forcing a new definition of cinema. We can no longer retain film's monopoly on our understanding of cinema in particular or moving image culture more generally. Neither celluloid, movie theatres, nor modernist ideas about art adequately account for the dynamic shifts ushered in by media culture in the last two decades. (75)

These new signifying forms continue to elude common genre-based approaches in arts criticism, upending the very concept of the film arts as exclusive practices to include creative work in broadcasting, software production, and cellular data networks, not to mention critical studies in information economics, globalization, and science and technology theory. The screen, we find, carries its own unique array of visual, aural, and verbal constraints, constituting a distinct objectivity—or at least one decidedly divergent from the page. Of course, the revisionary influence of these technologies works both ways, since it also invokes a clear mandate to introduce methods and devices from film criticism to both interpret and evaluate works composed for an increasingly wide variety of different screens. Cinema as both a discipline and a practice helps new media viewers accommodate language on-screen by providing a familiar critical context for its visual animation. Perspective, composition, and narrative subgenres emerge handily as chief attributes guiding our interpretation of even the most complex screen poetic constructions, while content itself becomes free to acquire the forms and gestures of a basic mise-en-scène. Beyond the cinematic field, social media technologies have refashioned the screen as both a new interface for mediated communication and a portal for interpersonal networking, establishing at least two more fundamental models for the interpretation and assessment of the screen work.

These three frameworks of cultural production for the screen help to establish the medium's uniquely multilayered approach to artifice and aesthetic meaning in general. To engage the screen as a mode of communication automatically invites an array of media-specific questions, not to mention the various uncertainties intrinsic to the technology at hand. The dispersed, decentered, explicitly fragmented nature of presentation format is certainly not as easily disregarded compared to works in print. Where the printed page renders an effective symbolic continuity (at times, even linearity) in its arrangement of content, the screen openly asks viewers to discount all notions of conclusion or end point. Note here that even mainstream cinema cannot escape the structural (and economic) demand for endless sequels or serialization. Concepts of time and process remain essential to interpretation, as all content appears automatically in view of some kind of update, either projected or preceding.

Not only is no "text" effectively finished on-screen, but the technical structure of the medium as a "network" continually invokes multiple sources of authorship, most of them indiscernible to the viewer. Whether one engages the screen from a laptop, desktop, or mobile device, it is difficult to ignore the sense of a manifold complex of semi-hidden authorial presences directly connected to the same documents. Current advertisements for the telecommunications corporation Verizon are especially significant in this respect in that they may constitute one of the first explicit efforts to promote the official redundancy of telephony as a private mode of communication between individual clients, marketing its services instead as a 24/7 mass surveillance system for customers who appreciate a network with both the will and the capacity to monitor and respond to all activities on-grid. Rather than fear this kind of system as a potential threat to individual privacy, customers are meant to take solace in the security and supervisory facilities it proposes. Such campaigns are meant to complement the increasingly common public conception of the screen as a mode of connection rather than representation. Of course, to realize in the screen its chief design and function as a kind of portal, inherently signifying access to an unquantifiable "web" of independent activity, removes any final traces of referentiality in its structure. Any pretense to the reflective aesthetic framework it inherited from the printed page – a medium that continues to represent the symbolic expression of individual consciousness/voice – seems effectively erased. Much like the old broken-mirror gag popular from the time of vaudeville to early Hollywood slapstick films (where an actor's double tries to convince him or her that a normal doorway or window is reflective glass), the viewer facing today's networked screens cannot but realize that the images peering back at her are not her reflection, in fact bear almost no relationship to her either expressively or existentially, but instead signify a rather thinly disguised, remote other – a passage, in other words, to separate spaces and separate visions, never fully visible, yet always present.

To write, to work, to communicate within this particular framework – this non-reflective, decentered, apparently borderless environment – invites us to reconsider some of the more fundamental precepts informing arts practices, whether literary or visual in form. Pedagogical questions concerning teaching and interpreting the particular artifice of the screen tend thus to benefit from earlier critical lineages and revisionary formalist experiments in modernist and postmodernist writing. Studies emphasizing important historical and theoretical relations between modernist and postmodernist writing practices and developments in information technology have appeared with increasing frequency and increasing complexity in argument since the emergence of new electronic media formats. As artists and writers purposefully pursue a more media-centered practice, critical work within the field begins to warrant a substantive, as opposed to instrumental, approach to the technology itself, understanding technological developments to have social and intellectual effects on society rather than merely mechanical ones. An important early explorative work in this vein, Jerome McGann's *Black Riders: The Visible Language of Modernism* (1993), for example, argues that many of the visually and spatially sophisticated uses of language in early modernist poetics evolved specifically in relation to late nineteenth-century advances in book design and print technology. As McGann writes, "To the extent that such bookmaking foregrounds the importance of writing's signifiers, the work exhibits uniformities and coherences. Different presses, however, generate distinct sets of coherences" (12).

McGann's critical work has been of particular importance to many contemporary poets who continue to explore more formal, semantic relationships in language as part of their aesthetics. Specific to the first decade of the twenty-first century, writers Steve McCaffery (*Prior to Meaning: The Protosemantic and Poetics*), Barrett Watten (*The Constructivist Moment*, 2003), and Darren Wershler-Henry (*The Iron Whim*, 2005) all contend to varying degrees that research into experimental literary formalisms of the modernist period must consider changes in media technology – especially as they pertain to new typographic environments – to appreciate fully the aesthetic challenges posed by poets like Ezra Pound, Gertrude Stein, and Laura Riding Jackson, among others, to more traditional verse forms.

Such studies tend to be categorized within the literary arts as material histories, acknowledging how different modes of representation in terms of media technology and design help determine a work's cultural meaning. These histories support a semiotic approach to language, where meaning occurs at the level of the signifier and not as a form of extralinguistic reference. This distinction is vital, offering what many field scholars prefer to call (after Jacques Derrida) alternative grammatologies. McCaffery, for example, follows Levinas's theories of textuality to consider writing itself as an actual moment of cognition that is durational and rooted as much in experience as in its signification – in Levinas's words, a sense (*le sens*) by which one confronts or engages with an emergent other (*autri*). McCaffery develops an original history of early literary experiments in what linguists now term semantic or semiotic structures. Such "protosemantic" interests in writing, as McCaffery terms them, are of special import to modern literature, as they provide critical insights into modernity's dual, at times conflicted, relationship to writing as both a mode of notation and a record of verbal utterance. The mode of signification is important. Where works of literary import follow science discourse's general dependence on semantic and syntactic form, language's capacity to function as a notational structure attuned to the variousness of human experience becomes quickly evident. McCaffery's useful grammatology presents a much more complex intertwining between what he calls the phonetic and pictographic "linguistic impulses" that define writing's literary lineages throughout Western culture (*Prior to Meaning* 119). Acknowledging Jacques Derrida's seminal analyses in this area, along with his critical identification of the phonetic "impulse" with the philosophical and political impasse of logocentrism, McCaffery nevertheless critiques *Of*

Grammatology as historically incomplete. "The history of logocentrism is portrayed as basically three leaps," McCaffery writes, "from Plato and Aristotle through Rousseau to Saussure and Lévi-Strauss . . . an axis that's partial, to say the least" (*Prior to Meaning* 107). Labeling Derrida's methodology of deconstruction as a "fashionable metatextual practice," while comparing its ubiquitous presence within North American academies to "Attila the Hun's entry into Rome," McCaffery makes it clear that his own project is driven partially by the challenge to "adumbrate [Derrida's partial] lineage and complicate any claims to a logocentric subservience of writing to speech in Western thinking" (107). Evidence of writing's visual capacity, its ability to signify a spatial orientation to language and thus a pictographic concept of meaning, appears regularly in writing from the Middle Ages onward, and there were significant manifestations even earlier in Hellenic culture (McCaffery, *Prior to Meaning* 59).

For McCaffery, a grammatological recognition of writing as distinct from (but in no way secondary to) language as speech offers an invaluable, even liberatory, conjugation of semantics with aesthetics. As such, the page and all it composes acquire a unique metatextual significance, divergent from the logocentric metaphysics of presence supposedly conveyed through verbal-based systems of communication. Freed from what McCaffery calls in an early essay on language and form in the poetry of bill bissett, *North of Intention* (1986), the "fetish of reference," where language is "[p]roposed as intentional, as always 'about' some extra-linguistic thing," the signifier becomes instead "an active, local agent functioning within a polymorphous, polysemous space of parts and sub-particles. . . . it commands hierarchy, subordination and postponement" (98). The attributes McCaffery invokes recall again Levinas's theoretical views on writing as a kind of inessential echo or, perhaps better, a tracing of something other than language, and yet not the literal thing, that is, the referent, that language as speech attempts to represent. Consistent with this emphasis on writing as programmatic construction, the very object of the book itself emerges newly imagined as an ideologico-historical practice. To write, for both McCaffery and Levinas, is to exercise or somehow use space and sound toward particular language-oriented objectives. Levinas may not be specifically considering poetry and the literary arts as exemplary usages, but McCaffery's emphasis on "hierarchy, subordination and postponement" successfully confers to language many fundamental visual and spatial components. Several of McCaffery's aesthetic arguments, in fact, allow us to imagine explicit attributes of the page as especially relevant to discussions about language and its representation via screen. In this context, the issues that the page invokes concerning the metaphysics of presence in meaning seem, in this sense, formally suspended, while certain aesthetic concepts respectfully advance to another level.

We can see this kind of development in one of the more popular efforts in contemporary screen writing, Young-Hae Chang Heavy Industries' intriguing animated piece "Dakota" (2002). Conceived and directed as a Flash composition, "Dakota" presents a robust (if abrasive) introduction to programmable text practices. Young-Hae Chang Heavy Industries comprises two writer/artists, Young-Hae Chang and Marc Voge, based in Seoul, Korea, where they have continued to produce, both stylistically and structurally, a remarkably consistent oeuvre since 1999. "Dakota" shares with Young-Hae Chang Heavy Industries' other pieces many basic attributes, including the medium – Flash-encoded animation with sound. The design is simple: black text nearly filling a white background, punching through the screen at a pace quick enough to obscure most of the narrative flow. The lettering appears in a simple sans serif font, usually Monaco, in contrasting black and white with intermittent use of various shades of grey. These colorless narratives move forward loudly and quickly, spilling out various motifs, some political, some satirical, with the subtlety of air raid sirens in the middle of the night. "Dakota's" narrative begins with the mandatory countdown that opens all Young-Hae Chang Heavy Industries' Flash works, a sequence of numerals alternating with spelled-out numbers. Each screen is filled out with portions of prose lines strung together against a pounding sequence of jazz drumming by Art Blakey. The final lines of narrative describe a series of rapid cut-away shots of what one presumes is a typical urban night street scene in Seoul. The narrative thus evokes autobiographical elements relevant to both writers, especially Voge, the American member of the Young-Hae Chang Heavy Industries team. Marc Voge's text describes at a surface level an emotionally difficult coming-of-age moment that he experienced growing up near Detroit, Michigan, when he and his friends embarked westward for their mandatory post-adolescence road trip. Like most tales of this genre, Voge's narrative derives from a particular instant in

READY TØ HIT THE RØAD,

6.1. Still from "Dakota" by Young-Hae Chang Heavy Industries.

his own life when memories of his youth combined with growing fears of an all-too-looming adulthood to impart a series of harsh personal assessments. What sets Voge's reminiscences apart from the usual journey of young male self-discovery is its overlaying structural and rhetorical references to the first two sections of Ezra Pound's epic *Cantos*.

Written out on the page, with em dashes (–) representing screen transitions and forward slashes signifying line breaks within single screen displays, an immediate parallel to Canto I instantly emerges with the opening sequence:

FUCKING – WALTZED – ØUT – TØ THE / CAR,
    LEANED / IN – AND / TURNED ØN – THE /
IGNITIØN, – READY TØ / HIT THE / RØAD, – WE RØLLED / BACK
THE / TØP, – DØWN THE / WINDØWS,
    – PUT BEER / CASES IN / HER TRUNK, – ØUR BUTTS / ØN
HER / UPHØLSTERY, –
WHØØPIN' – 'N – HØLLERIN', – THE SUN – HIGH – ABØVE –
    PØURING – DØWN – ØN ØUR – HEADS – AND – THE – HØT –
HØØD[1]

Pound's Canto I begins with the following lines:

> And then went down to the ship,
> Set keel to breakers, forth on the godly sea, and
> We set up mast and sail on that swart ship,
> Bore sheep aboard her, and our bodies also
> Heavy with weeping, and winds from sternward
> Bore us onward with bellying canvas. (3)

More than a simple update of Pound's *Cantos*, "Dakota" specifi-cally engages many of the same metatextual historical conflicts found in the modernist epic's relationship to previous translations of Homer's original song. As critics have long pointed out, the first canto interro-gates the *Odyssey* as much as it offers a translation of it. More specifi-cally, it incorporates interrogative forms of critical analysis and cross-examination into the procedure of translation. We have in Pound's version not so much an update of a classical Hellenic work, but rather an intriguing set of complex, trans-historical encounters between in-dividual texts. The famous bibliographic commentary that ends Canto I serves as more than a kind of playful authorial intrusion within the narrative. It helps reframe the very practice of translation as less of a "trans-scriptive" practice than an actual physical engagement with the Homeric tradition as a material artifact. Pound's first encounter in this way can be said to co-surface with Tiresias's own initial emergence in the poem:

> "A second time? why? man of ill star,
> "Facing the sunless dead and this joyless region?
> "Stand from the fosse, leave me my bloody bever
> "For soothsay."
>   And I stepped back,
> And he strong with the blood, said then: "Odysseus
> "Shalt return through spiteful Neptune, over dark seas,
> "Lose all companions."

As we see in the passage above, the moment Tiresias makes his fateful appearance, upon seeing Odysseus, the soothsayer instantly rebukes him for returning to the mouth of Hades. Of course, the original Homeric narrative never suggests that Odysseus has met Tiresias pre-viously. Clearly a case of mistaken identity. Or is it? Pound's deviation from the text neatly overlays the original poem with a record of his own encounter with Homer. Such an intrusion is made explicit in the next few lines when Pound literally cites the text he is reading:

Then Anticlea came.
Lie quiet Divus. I mean, that is Andreas Divus,
In officina Wecheli, 1538, out of Homer.
And he sailed, by Sirens and thence outwards and away
And unto Circe.
     Venerandam
In the Cretan's phrase, with the golden crown, Aphrodite,
Cypri munimenta sortita est, mirthful, oricalchi, with golden
Girdle and breat bands, thou with dark eyelids
Bearing the golden bough of Argicida. So that: (3)

It appears we have at least two Odyssean journeys at hand here, one literal, one literary. The literary allusion casts the *Odyssey* as an important metaphor for all journeys, whether physical or psychological, as pursuits of knowledge, while simultaneously literalizing it by invoking Pound's own experience. Like Odysseus, Pound, too, seeks knowledge. "Sitting on the Dogana's steps" in Italy in 1920, an expat exiled from most American literary traditions, facing the beginning of what would be a lifelong poetic project, Pound feels similarly stranded between two worlds. Such a division will not be easily reconciled by advice from the souls of men long dead, but rather in the writings he is in the very live process of consuming (much like Tiresias consumes the calf's blood to engage in soothsaying). It is only in this sense that it seems accurate to say that Odysseus has returned to the mouth of Hades, for Pound's act of reading has brought them together again.

The lexical encounter is then specifically highlighted in the bibliographic reference that follows: "In officina Wecheli, 1538, out of Homer." It is a Latin translation by Andreas Divus, printed in 1538 by Wechel. At such points, the ancillary material effectively weakens the primary retelling of the poem. We are no longer being sung to, but instead find ourselves in situ within a specific printing history, the details of which suggest that the canto's primary "odyssey" may be that of the text itself as it is materially, that is, physically, produced through time. Pound makes it clear that this canto is dealing with a distinct material object, not just the text's content. It is a particular construction of

Homer identified first by the translation work of Andreas Divus and the press of the French printer Christian Wechel.[2] Implied in Canto I, therefore, is a much more complex material history of this canonical "pillar" of Western poetry. In Pound's hands—again, literally and figuratively—we find not just a book, but a particular artifact, significant of Western Europe's earliest reintroduction to classical culture and history. In fact, the Wechel press remains within early modern press history especially emblematic of humanist Europe's centuries-long struggle to bring about the modern renaissance, signaling the prominent political role of printing technology in the general secularization of the continent's intellectual spheres (Ditchfield). Read in this context, Pound's particular interest in Homer as a bibliographic event clearly acquires a profound cultural politics. Pound's decision to reference these histories in his reworking of Homer's poem shows nothing less than a conscious reenvisioning of culture as specific material events in history composed by and through concrete acts of determination. Canto I is meant to appear similarly—that is, as a concrete event of production, signifying the continued pursuit of humanism and humanist cultural concerns.

Divus's presentation of the *Odyssey* provided Pound with both a narrative and a presentation format upon which he could superimpose and redevelop his own experiences as a modern traveler turned storyteller. With respect to the format, the very structure of the epic as a reproducible printed document helps transform the traditional oral myths of Hellenic culture into a material artifact of trans-historical significance. Conveyed as such, Odysseus's epic wanderings end up serving Pound's own poetic travels as well. His masterful, metrically sophisticated interpretation of book XI, the Nekyia, further refines Divus's original record into an aesthetic ode to modern individual political and cultural alienation. To read the *Odyssey* through Canto I is to engage necessarily with the central themes of modernity itself with its plight of the subject as individual, cast off in a sea of self-doubt and constant questioning.

Pound's work obviously presents Voge and Chang with a cultural event of similar significance. "Dakota's" screen-based interpretation effectively reopens Pound's original interrogation of the epic form, advancing both the metrical structure and subsequent motifs into a new set of contexts. Young-Hae Chang Heavy Industries' fast-paced visual and aural assault converts Odysseus's travels across the Mediterranean into a reckless road trip through the Dakota states in the American Midwest, providing an updated, if somewhat crude, rendition of Pound's reversioning of book XI of Homer's *Odyssey*. In fact, the coarseness of Young-Hae Chang Heavy Industries' narrative in many ways matches perfectly much of Canto I and II's own aesthetic voice, for it is arguable that the spirited "whoopin' and hollerin'" of "Dakota's" drunken, belligerent characters recalls faithfully the mood and actions of Odysseus's crew as they hurriedly cast their sails away from Circe's island to the western edge of the world—"To the Kimmerian lands, and peopled cities / Covered with close-webbed mist, unpierced ever / With glitter of sun-rays." Pound's voice is powerful and strong. Where in Canto I, Pound's Homeric voice recounts how

> Here did they rites, Perimedes and Eurylochus,
> And drawing sword from my hip
> I dug the ell-square pitkin

"Dakota" reports,

> — HERE — THEY — BRØKE — ØUT — A — CASE, — PEPPY — AND — ED,
> — AND — UNZIPPING — MY — FLY —
> I — PISSED — ØNTØ — THE — NEXT — SPACE.

If I continue to confine my translation of "Dakota" to the page, in effect repositioning the work as printed text, many of the media-specific components will be lost and, with them, the distinct historical tension that emerges between Pound's and Young-Hae Chang Heavy Industries' respective writing projects. At best, Young-Hae Chang Heavy Industries' text, although humorous to read, would suggest a mere pastiche of Pound's high modernist classic, where much of its literary value is confined to its persistent vulgarization of Pound's cultural ambitions to assume an epic voice convincing enough to restore a sense of purpose and unity within modern culture. While many of Pound's later politico-ideological visions continue to inspire criticism, any pretense to an epic voice or oral tradition in his writing is respectfully dealt with in the poem by Pound himself, as one of the more prominent motifs informing his literary project. Pound's search for sociocultural continuity between the classical and the modern plays out on a number of levels, including the disparate modes of reproduction associated with each period. Such conflicts echo loudly in Young-Hae Chang Heavy Industries' example of a Flash piece relating to the print tradition. Young-Hae Chang Heavy Industries poises itself to ask a question somewhat similar to Pound's: How do new media formats ultimately relate to prior ones?

The screen thus formally decries one of the most important aspects of literary value we tend to attribute to culturally revered works of written prose: a mimicry of the voice in the process of telling a good story. Many of Pound's poetic themes seem prompted by the tensions produced by print culture's intrusion into the oral traditions in the arts. Young-Hae Chang Heavy Industries, by contrast, is not specifically concerned with historico-material shifts in cultural production as symptoms of social fissure or rupture. To maintain this particular tension throughout his project, Pound must inevitably prioritize an indirect, somewhat contentious model of integration between production modes and cultural content. Pound's notion of physical presentation, although "fully materialised," as McGann suggests, enacts its historical emergence in terms of highly dynamic, erratic, even violent shifts in production methods and technologies. If, as McGann argues, Pound locates his *Cantos* project between the bibliographic periods of the nineteenth-century renaissance in print and his own contemporary present, the historical horizon subsequently constructed is one of revolutionary change, a progression once again ultimately evocative of an Odyssean journey to the very limits of knowledge itself: "A second time? why? man of ill star, / Facing the sunless dead and this joyless region." The answer for Pound is the same one that Odysseus might have given to Tiresias, had his reasons for traveling so far from his familiar seas been similarly queried: to learn how best to anticipate the future, to know which direction to take, both literally and figuratively, with respect to one's life.

Young-Hae Chang Heavy Industries' "Dakota" concerns itself, story-wise, with similar moments of transition in an individual's life, complete with naïve, class-derived posturing and drunken personal reflection on misspent youth in an ethnically mixed (indigenous and white), economically challenged landscape in the Midwest.

WE DRANK – AND / INSULTED – EACH / ØTHER'S – MØTHERS. –
BEER – IN – ØNE – HAND, – BØURBØN – IN – ØTHER, –
WE – DRANK – AGAIN, – THEN – ATE – SOME – HAM – AND –
CHEESE – SANDWICHES. –
THEN – I – SPØKE – A – GASSY – SPEECH – ABØUT – DYING –
YØUNG.

Three youths, bitter and filled with self-loathing, complain about missed opportunities, the depressed state of their lives: "FEEL-ING – LIKE – HELL, – SØRRY / FØR – ØURSELVES – LØST – SØULS – ØF – LØST – YØUTH, – GETTING – ØLD – FAST." Tiresias soon appears to the narrator in the form of Elvis (who else?) and, as with Odysseus, confirms that our contemporary protagonist will survive, despite already losing friends to gang violence while feeling irrevocably confined to an unforgiving cultural and economic landscape:

THEN /
SAID: – "HEY LØØK, /
TØUGH GUY, – TAKE IT /
EASY. – THERE'S /
A LØT – ØF RØAD /
AHEAD

Clearly "Dakota's" narrative structure carries forward many of the two previous epics' themes of historico-ideological transition, reflected symptomatically by a corresponding shift in the interactive relation-ship between modes of production and cultural expression. The first "written" song of Western culture reprises its narrative voice to accom-modate the rise of new literacies and the social structures informing them; the "man of ill star" confronts the nether reaches a third time, complementing yet another significant technological change in cul-tural reproduction.

Yale literary critic Jessica Pressman categorizes "Dakota" as an important example of what she calls "digital modernism." Pressman uses the term, however, primarily to describe attempts in contemporary electronic writing practices to acquire a kind of ready-made literary prestige through historical references to past canonical examples of modernist work. Further analysis might show that Young-Hae Chang Heavy Industries' creative transcription of Pound's epic work carries the poem's aesthetic and historical objectives much more adeptly and in a somewhat less self-serving capacity.

"Dakota's" particular use of Pound is no doubt partially motivated by the poet's special status as a defining figure in the annals of high modernism, and certainly the cultural capital associated with such a position presents an important, in fact necessary, target for later literary responses to this tradition. Pound's relationship to late nineteenth-century print culture displays much of the same motivation. However, the type of encounter "Dakota" seeks to replicate is in itself emblematic of Pound's earlier intertextual experiments, which in turn provide a much more layered and complex interpretive context for the work as both a technological artifact and a literary achievement. "Dakota" cannot be fully appreciated without contemplating its relationship to print via the screen. Watching the simple lines of text move forward, which provokes a uniquely literary experience of the screen, we stand momentarily struck as viewers, caught straddling two cultural worlds as much as two modes of media and two genres of art, possessing neither yet indebted to both. Thus does "Dakota's" relationship to modernist poetry echo Pound's earlier relationship to late nineteenth-century book culture.

Here again McGann's historical summaries raise valuable points. Pound's uniquely observant attention to the physical presentation of the first two volumes of the *Cantos*—*A Draft of XVI Cantos* (1925) and *A Draft of the Cantos 17–27* (1928)—inspired incredibly "lavish and expensive production values" personally supervised by the poet at two different presses: William Bird's Three Mountains Press in Paris and J. Curwen and Sons in England. Both presses produced fascinating facsimiles of medieval-style calligraphy, emphasizing a highly decorative, premodern appeal to ornamentation in both page and font (McGann 79). McGann historicizes these allusions to premodern culture collectively as a deliberate reference to the Arts and Crafts movement that dominated London's literary scene over the last decades of the nineteenth century. To view this level of print ornamentation in 1925 inevitably recalls, for McGann, a particular set of bibliographic references to modernism's founding cultural forebears.

Considered by literary historians a movement as much in printing technology as in aesthetics, the Arts and Crafts revisionary work of the late nineteenth century exemplified a particular concept of integration between visual composition and narrative content. Presses like William Morris's Kelmscott offer a distinctly paratextual approach to the practice of bookmaking derived, in part, from Morris's own fascination with late medieval culture and illuminated manuscript production. For Morris, the illuminated manuscript presented a unique unity in concept, design, and linguistic signification, where the author/visual artist confronted the entire page as a literary, visual, and communal practice. Hence, far from superficially prioritizing style over content in the literary arts, this historico-materialist poetics of the page openly eschewed the fetishization of graphic embellishment in a work for a much more politicized understanding of bookmaking as a mode of economic and social autonomy for the author as cultural producer.

Standard literary histories of such movements tend to overlook most of the more politically centered motivations behind Morris's embrace of the fully designed page. Central to his aesthetics remains a particular vision of the literary arts as the practical integration of labor, technology, aesthetics, and language. For pedagogical purposes, this emphasis on the material and practice-oriented aspects of writing comprises an important lineage in and of itself within modern aesthetics; Morris's and Pound's respective considerations of technology as a constitutive element of authorship may provide one of the most fundamental links between any grammatology of the page and current formalist experiments in electronic writing for a screen. What must continue to be emphasized in these histories is the consistent "writerly" focus on the work as a material, constructed object, the properties of which must inevitably contribute to the project's wider aesthetic aims. Interestingly, the first book to emerge from Morris's attempt to combine a labor-oriented politics with literary practice was his own translation of the *Odyssey*, published by Reeves and Turner in 1887.

Upon his arrival in London twenty years after Morris's experiments, Pound wasted little time in forming close associations with the city's more radical presses of the fin de siècle. McGann writes, "In 1910 a writer's allegiance to poetic experiment and innovation had to display some clear line of connection to the recent traditions" (19). Of course by this time, the actual movements centered around the presses were hardly as influential as they had been as the nineteenth century drew to a close. The "Yellow Nineties" were firmly over; Morris and Wilde were dead, the latter much reduced in cultural stature following his notorious trial. The first breath of twentieth-century British writing appeared particularly keen on reassessing many of the experiments of the prior decade as a kind of symptomatic collective whimsy typical of a long reign's final days. This historical tendency alone shows us that Pound's interests in London's recent literary past obviously extended beyond paternalism. The aestheticist movement, with its combination of pre-Raphaelite indulgences in the decorative arts and progressive socialist politics, presented Pound with a uniquely vibrant, formidable set of writing practices. In these works, Pound grasped a broad range of expressive possibilities derived specifically from new levels of engagement with advanced printing technologies and bookmaking skills.

Similar points, I believe, can be brought up with respect to Young-Hae Chang Heavy Industries' inspired reversioning of Pound's work some eighty years after the original publication of Cantos I and II. Pound's unique concept of the book as an aesthetic object parallels Young-Hae Chang Heavy Industries' vision of the screen as both a projection device and a new kind of media paradigm. The narrative structure informing "Dakota's" reversioning of the *Cantos* is derived as much from traditional cinema as it is from Pound's metric structures. Using a fairly simple Flash animation sequence, Young-Hae Chang Heavy Industries convincingly mimics the common spooling effect of a celluloid reel being projected on a wide screen. Hence, for viewers, the initial interpretive impulse inevitably suggests the pace and flow of conventional cinema. The first thirty seconds consists of quick screen flashes in progressively lighter greyscale tones, followed by the poets' signature countdown done, too, in the style of traditional movie reel introductions. At the thirty-second mark, the title flashes in high black-on-white contrast against the background, filling the screen and thus extending the cinema motif formally into the narrative per se. There is little ambiguity in what the form and template are meant to suggest: we are watching a film, or rather, the subtitles of a film, blown up large and presented at a pace just under frantic in a minimalist, modern style, complete with a mid-century jazz soundtrack. The text's font is consistent with this aesthetic mode, revealing its story in a simple, utilitarian, sans serif script called Monaco – evocative, perhaps, of both writers' ongoing penchant for the industrial and the ready-made in their work. On the choice of font, Voge remarks that the intent is "to communicate arbitrariness. It was an arbitrary decision. But it's true that it's quite pretty. And Monaco is also a very nice name. Monaco. It's a principality. All our work is set in Monaco. It's a wonderful place to be set" (see Voge and Polon). Irreverent as the tone may seem, Voge's comments on the effect of "arbitrariness" are both accurate and ironically poignant. The font's design does recall a specific geohistorical context, though the actual setting is closer to Cupertino, California, the location of the Apple corporation, and not the Mediterranean principality. Designed specifically for the Macintosh OS X by Susan Kare and Kris Holmes, it is representative of the second generation of Mac fonts, following the original group of bitmap graphics that took advantage of the Macintosh screen's originally unique capacity to display proportional typefaces. This interface attribute was one of the more significant features that Apple used to differentiate its vision of personal computing from its rival Microsoft, beginning the long-standing bisection of the home computer market into its major brand-oriented phyla: Microsoft programmers and Apple designers/artists. The first generation of proportional typefaces was supposedly named after what Steve Jobs termed "world-class" cities, for example, Chicago (the system's primary font), New York, Geneva, London, San Francisco, Toronto, and Venice (see Kare). By contrast, Monaco's monospaced format and decidedly non-urban branding do lend the font a certain arbitrariness. The similarity between the numeral zero and the letter O made it functionally necessary to strike through the former in order to signify their distinction. Accordingly, the font's overall aesthetic appeal derives from its apparent simplicity in structure and stark minimalism in design. As an exemplary piece of Flash art, "Dakota" remains poised deliberately on the edge of two cultural eras of the moving image, one defined by the art of film and one by software. Each era, of course, represents a specific type of screen, characterized, as Wassan has shown, first and foremost by physical size, and "Dakota" acquires its powerful aesthetic presence by evoking both simultaneously. Here the cinematic elements of celluloid combine effectively with the vector graphic techniques of Flash animation to signal both continuity and rupture in the moving image, much as Pound suggested with respect to the page in the first two pressings of his *Cantos* project.

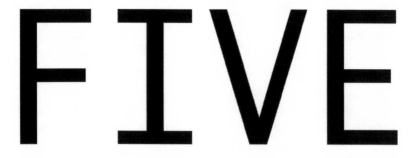

6.2. Still from "Dakota."

Both "Dakota" and *The Cantos* acquire a unique cultural poignancy by foregrounding the medium in which they are composed as an intricate part of their structural integrity. Pound's aesthetic objectives comprised nothing less than an extended interrogation of the page as an important constitutive element, not just of his project, but of the practice of writing in general. The pressing of the book, the physical imprinting of type upon page better signified the actual poetic work in process than simply committing thoughts to paper. Likewise, an updated grammatology confronts us in the work of Young-Hae Chang Heavy Industries, some eighty years later. As screen-based poets facing a plethora of new multimedia publishing formats, Voge and Chang have managed to bring to digital culture many of modernism's most significant concerns about history and its representation. For these writers, the screen itself, as both a space of composition and a physical mode of interface, demonstrates easily the same flexibility and creative potential that an experimental modernist like Pound saw in the printed page.

For contemporary poets like Voge and Chang who, as we've seen, maintain a sense of historical materialism in their practice despite the inherent spatiotemporal flattening of current electronic media network technologies, the screen formally advances many of the more pictographic-centered "linguistic impulses" McCaffery links to print's ongoing argument with the human voice as the de facto metaphysical source of meaning in language. Yet, as most literary artists partial to either inclination – the phonetic or pictographic – increasingly realize, the transition to programmable digital media carries with it a fundamental shift in the relationships, tensions, and conflicts defined by and through print's inherently complex rapport with verbal meaning. Pound's extensive bibliographic reconstruction of the epic voice of Western tradition helps contextualize and make concrete specific motifs, techniques, and devices that tend otherwise to forfeit their aesthetic attributes for a trans-historical sense of cultural edict or mores, yet enduring works of accepted literary mastery hold fast to forms that emphasize a general respect for a single "authorial" voice speaking through characters and complex narrative overlays to a willingly passive audience (of all ears). Perhaps the most accurate indication of print's conservatism is that writers who continue to work in a more visually oriented, verbally disjunctive relationship to meaning still bear the moniker of "experimental" or "avant-garde" a century after their publication. The same, of course, cannot be said of Young-Hae Chang Heavy Industries' impressionistic renderings of cinematic forms or genres in Flash. The mercurial nature of the software itself, with its capacity to project as video, animation, photographic slide show, text interface, or screen application ensures against any exclusive attachment to a single concept of communication. The success of Flash, in fact, derives from its profound capacity to mimic nearly all forms of cultural expression equally well – its capacity, in other words, to be fully reproducible, adaptable to any size of screen.

Perhaps nowhere is the screen's structural antipathy to the traditional literary conceit of verbal reference more apparent in recent literary history than in the topical, somewhat controversial poetic experiment by Jim Carpenter and Stephen McLaughlin, two highly accomplished artists in programmable media, known throughout electronic literary networks for some of the earliest screen-based creations in writing, such as the poetry generator "Erica T. Carter." Deceptively entitled *Issue 1*, Carpenter and McLaughlin's collaborative project appeared online in the fall of 2008 in the guise of a typical debut issue of a new poetry journal: a massive tome (available only in PDF format) that purports to have collected over 4,000 worthy works by still worthier poets.

A slightly more nuanced eye, however, will uncover that none of the works were actually written by their supposed authors; rather, they were generated by software and prepared by the editors as a kind of facsimile of a print journal, with all its formal elements firmly intact. The contributors are, for the most part, actual working contemporary poets, yet their inclusion in the project was mandated not by any usual submission process, but rather more likely by a mechanized procedure. Various authors have suggested that the names were drawn primarily from the blogging content-management software Blogspot, using the qualifying tag "poet" as its only selection criterion. The issue was first announced for download from a Blogspot site titled, with a nod to Beckett, ForGodot. So what do we have here? the electronic markup of a journal in progress? a practical joke? a postmodern, self-referential critique of the poetry-journal format as pastiche? or perhaps a kind of digital snapshot of a print-based literary genre reconceived for screen as nothing less than another template or motif to be sampled and re-versioned like any other literary form?

Just how significant the project is as a new screen work is still in the process of being assessed, yet one might note here that for many of the "official contributors," the piece has amounted to nothing less than a kind of literary libel. Numerous authors, upon learning of their inclusion in the work, immediately demanded that the editors "cease and desist," instructing them to either remove their contributions and good names, or face charges of copyright infringement. As one disgruntled writer complained in a blog post the very next day, "For the record: I did not write this poem, did not authorize the use of my name in association with this poem, and I have never heard of these people or their bizarre project. Could I lift a 3,785 page 'online anthology,' I would drop it on their heads."[3] Other contributors, though not as graphic in their comments, were decidedly more litigiously inclined:

> Call me "dour and humorless" if you like, but my sense of humor is really not the issue. If someone published an article containing false information about me, I would want it removed from the Web; it is no different for them to claim I wrote a certain poem when I did not. It is my basic right to protect my name and reputation, and I find it really tasteless that some people would laugh this off as some kind of avant-garde experiment. If my name is to be used in some sort of artistic "experiment," it should be with my permission. To do it without my permission is unethical as well as illegal. This "anthology" should be taken down immediately. Anyone know a good lawyer who can write a cease-and-desist letter?[4]

6.3. Cover image for *Issue 1*.

Even the well-known experimental poet, literary theorist, and anthologist Ron Silliman condemned the work as offensive to reputations. To see such an event as a marked threat to so many authors, as questioning their respective authenticities as professionals, seems indication enough that the screen is capable of challenging even the most progressive views of what is and what isn't deemed "literary" in the arts.

Bereft of color, illustration, and even the most rudimentary features of graphic design, *Issue 1* makes even Young-Hae Chang Heavy Industries' stark black-and-white flashes of Monaco text seem almost baroque in comparison; yet to call the file anything but a screen work is to imagine a false context where such a tome might conceivably be printed, bound, and distributed. Clearly *Issue 1*, as a project, is partially predicated on its nonprintability, establishing a very different relationship to the content it features with respect to publication, distribution, and consumption. As with Young-Hae Chang Heavy Industries' "Dakota," historical references to past media formats help constitute the aesthetic argument, but ultimately the screen provides a different kind of portal into the possibilities of writing as a programmable practice. Contemporary writers who remain hostile to these developments – or at least to their unsolicited participation in them – have a right to their anxiety, for what fears they have over losing control of established poetry formats and distribution networks are well founded. For many writers, projects like *Issue 1* signify first and foremost a challenge to professional relationships to the literary medium itself. Seeing how easily thousands of names can be associated with an equal number of originally produced works suggests a model of poetry practice that inherently calls into question the level of individual autonomy and control writers often seek with respect to individual writing projects. The sheer size and scope of Carpenter and McLaughlin's collaboration, an elephantine creation of almost 4,000 pages, assembled and placed into mass distribution and available to hundreds of millions of potential viewers within seconds indeed has much to say regarding how traditional print genres are being currently affected by electronic media. However complex these arguments are, the project's less-receptive participants obviously preferred a concise explanation from the editors of their intention over any philosophical discussion. Two days after the initial publication, McLaughlin offered the following statement:

> Indulge me in an obscure analogy. Let's say I sit down and write the most vile, nasty, over-the-line-type-of-toxic-racist missive I can think of. Better yet, rearrange some Google vomit into an original composition and save myself a few minutes. If I were to distribute this speech,

it would be considered a hate crime. I could, however, shape this text into letterforms—say, large 120pt letters composed of 10pt type. If I were to spell something like "racism is bollocks" out of such illegal text, the mode of reading would be altered. The formerly despicable statement would be neutralized. This is an approximation of my original expectations regarding the reception of this magazine. I expected its size, format, and (to my eye) clearly algorithmically generated content to make our intentions clear.[5]

Reluctantly apologetic in tone, McLaughlin's response registers primarily his own surprise at the level of personal and public offense provoked by his and Carpenter's project. To his disbelief, a fairly conventional, humanist concept of authorship as a fixed, individual cognitive identity appears still to dominate poetry practices in the twenty-first century. Here the very notion of procedurally generated meaning seems problematic at best, perhaps even too prohibitively obscure to consider critically.

How different poets' respective understandings of the screen appear to be: for Rappleye, it signifies a mode of presentation no different than the printed page; however, for McLaughlin, a much more complex set of textual operations is in process. N. Katherine Hayles, a media theorist and literary critic, provides a promising set of theoretical frameworks in support of McLaughlin's understanding of the screen work as a dynamic system of interplay between human end-users and digital computer networks. At its most developed stage, where both the domestic and professional work environments demand sophisticated networking functionality, a historically unprecedented relationship Hayles calls a "dynamic heterarchy" emerges, in which "the human and the computer are increasingly bound together in complex physical, psychological, economic, and social formations" (47). Such intense levels of cooperation between screen and mind inevitably foster increasingly detailed queries into the very nature of cognition, and Hayles recognizes that one of the most valuable outcomes of current human-computer formations is the possibility of constructing a functional artificial intelligence. "Like humans," she writes, "intelligent machines also have multiple layers of processes, from ones and zeros to sophisticated acts of reasoning and inference" (55). *Issue 1* may not necessarily constitute an example of "sophisticated . . . reasoning and inference," yet it respectfully invokes several key points of convergence between alternate modes of language use – some human, some silicon. This ultimately cybernetic model of poetry, for McLaughlin, clearly puts forth serious political, as well as intellectual, challenges to traditional concepts of readerly-writerly relationships; indeed, the notion of a more or less interactive cognitive dynamic between poem and poet provokes a radically different interpretive relationship to text in general.

Despite Rappleye's offense at his personal association with a generated text, we are, in fact, invited by McLaughlin (and Hayles) to consider the work grammatologically, that is, as a visio-spatial composition, not as letters so much as "letterforms," where the medium itself remains the primary object of analysis. The poem attributed to Rappleye, "Bonnie Winds and Fair Twists," demonstrates both its functions as a generated text and as lyrical verse primarily through its repetitive structure and open-ended phrasing:

Adored
Like a bird
Like a bonnie wind

To depart left and permission
To perceive velvet and hubbub
To leave forgiving for a right
To leave a privilege of bushes
To stir a growing scope[6]

The opening stanza, a tercet dominated by two rather unremarkable similes, introduces the work as an example of poetic adoration. Only the lack of figurative language creates any sense of tension or ambiguity in interpretation. After all, not all birds are adorable, and the figure's contextual association with "a bonnie wind" invokes a strangely fluid, unstable set of characteristics. As well, while the "bonnie wind" reference remains central, being the primary image in the title, any subsequent parallels between the bird and various "fair twists" unsettles the tone immediately. The following stanza completes the poem's shift into abstraction, its semantic integrity being entirely structural, while the imagery becomes increasingly vague and indistinct. Each line begins with a single infinitive verb form, offering a kind of extended anaphora punctuated by enjambment; yet the connotation is for the most part wholly ambiguous.

Critically comparing this work to Greg Rappleye's earlier oeuvre, one can see a few reasons for his initial discomfort with the attribution. A Midwest poet and creative writing teacher, author of three books of poetry and numerous contributions to literary journals, Rappleye displays a consistent penchant for descriptive narrative structures and an almost photographic realism in detail and theme. These are the opening lines from the poem "Terrible," published in one of his better-known books, A *Path between Houses* (2000):

> The man from room 8
> is washing and waxing his car.
> It's a black Ford, with flames
> stenciled on the doors,
> and the word Terrible
> inscribed in an elegant cursive
> on the pillars of the roof.
> I think I know his life. I lived it
> at Red's Motel, on a stinky bayou
> near Hopedale, Louisiana.
> We called it "Hopeless,"
> as in, "Maybe I'll call you,
> when I get back to Hopeless."[7]

One can hardly imagine a more divergent voice and structural style than that displayed by "Bonnie Winds and Fair Twists." Where Rappleye prefers to engage his readers with a personal, often reflective lyrical voice and situation-based themes, the *Issue 1* contribution demands a much more structurally attuned eye. Despite the work's ambiguous set of references, a semblance of meaning nevertheless emerges as different semantic contexts begin to materialize both within the poem and with respect to the poem's juxtaposition with other works featured in the publication. The semantic patterns are consistent enough to provoke a prominent set of visual and aural configurations that lend themselves to both instruction and critical reading. For example, verb phrases immediately incite a spatial and, consequently, thematic tension between the two stanzas. If it is a poem dedicated to a love interest, the object of adoration, the reader can only conclude a theme of absence or desertion, a psychological exchange of permission, rights (i.e., principles/order for "hubbub"), or chaos (i.e., growth – a "growing scope"). Of course, the semantic patterns become even more overt upon comparing the poem to other *Issue 1* "contributions." The repetitious similes that begin "Bonnie Winds and Fair Twists" also dominate a composition attributed to Ron Padgett, "Estimating Chalk":

> Like a merchant
> Like a patent
> Like a fable[8]

Jenny Davidson's supposed piece, "Stintless as Awe," structures its observations around infinitive verb phrases much like in the second stanza of Rappleye's work:

> To guess
> Telling rest
> Perched
>
> To notice descending
> A side
>
> To drop qualifying
> Like a heating
> In indigo
> To tell his enchanted grass
> Like a tune.[9]

Of course, such similarities serve primarily to demonstrate McLaughlin's point that the contents' origins are nonhuman, the fact of which remains, perhaps, the most important contextual determinant concerning the project's overall interpretation. Once the possibility of external subjective references is removed, the poems' respective meanings become newly dependent upon their spatial and semantic juxtaposition—a constructive model, one might add, that stimulates a uniquely vibrant process of interpretation. The rhetorical phrases, punctuated with obscure vocabularies, inevitably outline the periodical format itself as a semantic template. In this way, Carpenter and McLaughlin demonstrate a very different framework of literary interpretation than that historically associated with printed literary journals as venues of distribution for new poetry works—one where images of poems are placed side by side with images of poets in order to construct as accurately as possible the semblance of a new poetry periodical. The structural similitude is both inspiring and unnerving. Parallel to the internet's expanding functions as a powerful administrative apparatus, complete with its own set of sociopolitical objectives, the screen thus continues modern writing's intricate set of established relationships between signification and cognition, between media technology and cultural knowledge. Once again, we find ourselves standing with Pound gazing at the pages of Divus at the edge of new nether regions, contemplating the history of print technologies and their tendency to disquiet the status quo—at the beginning, in other words, of another odyssey.

NOTES

1. The text of the poem is available at UCLA Center for Digital Humanities, "Media Specific Analysis Project," ed. Jessica Pressman et al., http://dev.cdh.ucla.edu/~newmedia/platform/pdf/jessica/index.pdf.

2. Christian Wechel's Paris press opened officially in 1526 and operated in the French capital for two generations, until 1572 when his son moved it to Germany. During the sixteenth century, Wechel was quick to establish a reputation among Northern Europe's scholarly communities for his extremely capable production of classical Greek texts—which were still in the process of being reintegrated into the West following the Fall of Constantinople in 1453. Catholic imperialism at the time remained extremely wary of this increasingly steady flow of orthodox and classical ideas into its political culture; hence, it was not long before Wechel, one of the more accomplished sources of humanist writing, experienced his own religious persecution in 1534 for publishing a work by Erasmus. At this time, Erasmus's ongoing correspondence with Martin Luther had effectively branded the Christian philosopher a bona fide Lutheran in the eyes of conservative Catholics. Just how severe religious restrictions on Wechel's press were is open to much debate. It is no longer generally accepted that the Sorbonne forced him into poverty and then ordered the removal of the press from France. As suggested above, most likely the move to Germany was initiated by his son some decades later. See Ditchfield, http://www.gutenberg.org/etext/8485.

3. Greg Rappleye, blog post, *Poetry Foundation: Harriet* (4 Oct. 2008), http://www.poetryfoundation.org/harriet/2008/10/3785_page_pirated_poetry_antho.html.

4. Danny Pitt Stoller, blog post, *Poetry Foundation: Harriet* (4 Oct. 2008), http://www.poetryfoundation.org/harriet/2008/10/3785_page_pirated_poetry_antho.html.

5. McLaughlin, "Issue 1 Polite Clarification," http://www.forgodot.com/labels/issue%201.html.

6. Greg Rappleye, "Bonnie Winds and Fair Twists," in Carter.

7. Greg Rappleye, "Terrible," in *A Path between Houses* (Madison: University of Wisconsin Press, 2000), 18.

8. Ron Padgett, "Estimating Chalk," in Carter.

9. Jenny Davidson, "Stintless as Awe," in Carter.

REFERENCES

Carpenter, Jim, and Stephen McLaughlin. *Issue 1*. 2008. Rpt., Erica T. Carter, *Issue 1: Fall 2008*. Web. http://www.goodreads.com/book/show/4932117-issue-one. Accessed 15 Nov. 2011.

Carter, Erica T. *Issue 1: Fall 2008*. Web. http://www.goodreads.com/book/show/4932117-issue-one. Accessed 15 Nov. 2011.

Ditchfield, P. H. "Books Fatal to Their Authors." *Project Gutenberg* (1 July 2005). Web. Accessed 12 July 2008.

Goldsmith, Kenneth. "3,785 Page Pirated Poetry Anthology." *Harriet: News and Community* (n.d.). Web. Accessed 10 Oct. 2008.

Hayles, N. Katherine. *Electronic Literature: New Horizons for the Literary*. Notre Dame, IN: University Press of Notre Dame.

Kare, Susan. "The Original Macintosh: World Class Cities." *Folklore.org* (Aug. 1983). Web. Accessed 24 July 2008.

McCaffery, Steve. *North of Intention: Critical Writings 1973–1986*. New York: Roof, 1986.

———. *Prior to Meaning: The Protosemantic and Poetics*. Evanston, IL: Northwestern University Press, 2001.

McGann, Jerome. *Black Riders: The Visible Language of Modernism*.

Princeton, NJ: Princeton University Press, 1993.

Pound, Ezra. *The Cantos*. 1934. New York: New Directions, 1996.

Pressman, Jessica. "The Strategy of Digital Modernism: Young-Hae Chang Heavy Industries' Dakota." *MFS: Modern Fiction Studies* 54.2 (2008): 302–326.

Voge, Marc, and Isabel Polon. "Back Stage: Young-Hae Chang and Marc Voge." *Yale Daily News* (17 Oct. 2008). Web. Accessed 12 July 2009.

Wassan, Haidee. "The Networked Screen: Moving Images, Materiality, and the Aesthetics of Size." In *Fluid Screens, Expanded Cinema*. Ed. Janine Marchessault and Susan Lord. Toronto: University of Toronto Press, 2007.

Watten, Barrett. *The Constructivist Moment*. Middletown, CT: Wesleyan University Press, 2003.

Wershler-Henry, Darren. *The Iron Whim*. 2005. Ithaca, NY: Cornell University Press, 2007.

Young-Hae Chang Heavy Industries. "Dakota." *Young-Hae Chang Heavy Industries Presents* (2002). Web. Accessed 1 Oct. 2008.

7

"Let the Rhythm Hit 'Em": Hip-Hop, Prosody, and Meaning

ALESSANDRO PORCO

Hip-hop emerged in the South Bronx during the mid-1970s, the confluence of individual ingenuity (Grandmaster Flash developing his Quick Mix theory), diasporic flow from the Caribbean (DJ Kool Herc's sound system, dance-hall toasting), African American vernacular traditions (signifyin', the dozens, ballads), popular American music (funk, soul, rock, disco), a local party and club circuit (Audubon Theatre, Harlem World, T-Connection), and economic and educational policies that transformed urban spaces into post-industrial wastelands.[1] Four elements constituted hip-hop culture: DJing, MCing, tagging, and breakdancing. Interactions between the four elements produced what Greg Dimitriadis describes as "multitiered event[s] . . . dependent on a whole series of artistic activities and competencies" (16). These events ranged from block parties—where, like in Ralph Ellison's *Invisible Man*, DJs siphoned power from streetlights into booming Jamaican sound systems, and this radical *détournement* of city energy enabled a sonic reclamation of public space as a positive, communal place for dance—to more intimate, antiphonal ciphers performed by MCs in local parks and, soon after, at shows in New York City venues, both uptown and downtown. Graffiti tags appeared across New York's cityscape, most notably on subway trains, as commuting traces of disillusioned African American and Latino youth. B-boy dance crews participated in simulated battle, their popping and uprocking expanding and expending the martial body's *physis*. With their sidekick MCs, pioneering hip-hop DJs, such as

Kool Herc, Grand Wizzard Theodore, Grandmaster Flash, and Afrika Bambaataa, provided the soundtrack for the scene: "I'd throw on the Pink Panther theme for everybody . . . , and then I would play 'Honky Tonk Woman' by the Rolling Stones and just keep that beat going. I'd play something from metal rock records like Grand Funk Railroad. . . . I'd throw on 'Sergeant Pepper's Lonely Hearts Club Band'–just that drum part" (Bambaataa qtd. in Perkins 9). The break-beats and wildstyle mixes of early DJ-centric hip-hop had a simple goal: make people dance.

In 1979, the release of the Sugarhill Gang's "Rapper's Delight" changed everything.[2] Hip-hop's first record–a modest hit reaching number 36 on the Billboard Hot 100 chart–initiated major shifts in the music's production, consumption, and overall aesthetic. Coincident with shifts from live event performance to recorded medium and from localized ontology (i.e., the South Bronx) to nationally circulating epistemology (i.e., other boroughs, especially Brooklyn, as well as Long Island's "Black Belt," Philadelphia, Detroit, Baltimore, Boston, Toronto, and eventually south central Los Angeles) is the MC's displacement of the DJ as principal in hip-hop performance. As part of a hip-hop pastoral narrative, this shift in artistic praxis is often articulated in elegiac terms, a fundamental loss of *spirit* or *essence* precipitated by increasing "culture industry" demands.[3] However, the loss also generated qualitative and quantitative gains that have since come to redefine hip-hop. Post–"Rapper's Delight," MC-centric hip-hop stimulated a fractal-like revolution in verse-flow[4]–the functions and values of rhythm, rhyme, and voice, as well as diction, rhetoric, imagery, thematics, and content all multiplied exponentially.

Since the early 1990s, an abundance of cultural and literary readings of hip-hop have examined MC verse-flow content, thematics, imagery, and diction in relation to social, economic, cultural, and political contexts of production and consumption. These readings–in the cultural studies tradition–have yielded enlightening results. The estimable Tricia Rose, for example, lauds "rap's language wizards" (3), whose verse-flows provide historically informed counterdiscourses of resistance from the margins. For Rose, hip-hop MCs perform a vatic role, offering "alternative interpretations of key social events" as well as introducing "black noise" into mainstream (white) American discourse (18). Studies by Russell Potter and Imani Perry emphasize hip-hop's contribution to, and extension of, the African American vernacular tradition. Rose and Perry, along with Gwendolyn Pough and Nancy Guevara, have written thoughtfully on foundational female contributions to hip-hop. Publications by Felicia M. Miyakawa and Anthony Pinn have examined at length hip-hop's various theological and spiritual positions. Ethnographic works by Greg Dimitriadis, Joseph G. Schloss, and Ali Colleen Neff show how the hip-hop aesthetic is "invest[ed] and reinvest[ed] with value and meaning in particular times and places for particular ends and purposes" by young people (Dimitriadis 11). In his exemplary study *The 'Hood Comes First*, Murray Forman traces hip-hop's dissemination in relation to space and place and examines how those categories are mapped in MC verse-flow content. Especially rewarding is Forman's lengthy close reading of Grandmaster Flash and the Furious Five's "The Message," where he discusses how the recording's lyrics are an "engaged social critique" of an "ostensible ghetto reality" (83, 87). In hip-hop studies, only Richard Shusterman's twenty-page interpretation of Stetsasonic's "Talkin' All That Jazz" is comparable in length and depth. Shusterman's reading has two expressed purposes: first, to situate hip-hop aesthetics within the American pragmatist tradition; and second, to illustrate hip-hop's "polysemic complexity, ambiguity, and intertextuality" (203).

But MCs communicate through far more than paraphraseable or signified content. Unfortunately, rhythm, rhyme, and voice – the sonic, proprioceptive, pneumatic, and kinesic materials of hip-hop *poiesis* – are often remaindered in discussions of hip-hop, as if such metacommunicative particulars do not participate in the distribution and redistribution of meaning(s) or "messages."[5] However, scholarship by H. Samy Alim, Adam Bradley, Adam Krims, Alexs Pate, and Robert Walser has started to draw significant attention to the poetics of hip-hop. Though voice and rhyme are beyond the purview of this chapter, extended prosodic analyses of three representative performances from a watershed moment in hip-hop history (1987–1988) demonstrate how rhythmic phrasings complement and complicate the production and reception of verse-flow meaning.[6] Lyrically, Rakim's "I Know You

Got Soul" (from *Paid in Full*) and MC Lyte's "Lyte as a Rock" (from *Lyte as a Rock*) are rich, variably contoured rhythmic plexuses,[7] while Ice Cube's verse-flow on "Straight Outta Compton" (from *Straight Outta Compton*) is purposively severe, telegraphed, and compressed by comparison. Rakim's prosody nimbly navigates community-building and "so-lo-ist" imperatives, and it locates Rakim at the interface of hip-hop's past and future, an interface significantly mediated by radio technology. On the other hand, MC Lyte asserts her gendered difference through a parodic performance of "anything you can do I can do better" hypermasculine prosody. Finally, Ice Cube's prosody effects a synonymy between gangsta aesthetics, ethics, and ontology, while at the same time self-reflexively acknowledging that synonymy's performativity.[8]

A comparative reading of Rakim, MC Lyte, and Ice Cube sets into relief the two-pronged discourse of mystification that enshrouds hip-hop verse-flow: verse-flow is either subjected to general, misapplied, and undertheorized laudations,[9] or misrepresented as composed in accordance with an end-stopped, end-rhymed, four-stress ballad meter.[10] The former—however inadvertent—is illustrative of the epistemic violence upon which racist ideologies are readily founded and through which the black subject is repeatedly denied difference, relation, agency, and depth.[11] The notion that rap is composed according to a ballad meter administers and regulates the nonmetric signifying, signifyin', and asignifying qualities that define an MC's rhythmic plexus. Instead, my reading emphasizes the dynamic relation between stress and syllable counts; enjambment, anacrusis, and caesura; the (a)symmetric correspondence between grammatical, phrasal (or breath), formal (i.e., the rhymed couplet), and musical measures (i.e., the 4/4 musical bar); reciprocating and nonreciprocating stress and beat positions; the dispersal and displacement of rhymes by way of prosody; the "informational" rhythms of verse-flow, to borrow Richard Cureton's phrase;[12] and "kinetic orality" (West 102) and "phrasal propulsion" (McCaffery 152).

Ultimately, a demystified hip-hop prosody reveals the heterogeneity of verse-flow praxis, resists the popular myth of black rhythmic exceptionalism, and insists on the musical beat and lyrical rhythm as mutually imbricated audio epistemes that operate over, across, and against each other to produce meaning(s).

RADIO, SOUL, AND SOLO: ON RAKIM

In 1987, the Wyandanch, Long Island, hip-hop duo Eric B. and Rakim—DJ and MC, respectively—released their debut album, *Paid in Full*. The album is an *ur*-text in the emergent hip-hop canon, in large part due to Rakim's pioneering verse-flow, characterized by dense rhyming and contoured, multidirectional prosody. Critics, scholars, and fellow MCs alike consistently speak in reverential tones of Rakim. Paul Gilroy, for example, describes him as "the most gifted rap poet of the eighties" (84). In a 1997 XXL feature on the now semi-reclusive Rakim, journalist Robert Marriott states emphatically that Rakim "*laid down hip-hop law*. There's before *Paid in Full* and after" (190). William Jelani Cobb echoes this sentiment: Rakim became "the man to whom [any] vast new talent would necessarily be compared" (143). Jeff Chang goes so far as to say that with Rakim "[r]ap had found its Coltrane" (258), adding that "I Know You Got Soul" is hip-hop's "Giant Steps." Chang's jazz analogy is intended to lift Rakim's performance to the status of art, imbuing it with the value of the timeless in contradistinction to the ephemerality of the popular.

"I Know You Got Soul's" opening twelve bars are below. Stressed or strong syllables are indicated by accent marks. Unstressed or weak syllables remain unmarked. The left margin of the transcription coincides with the downbeat of the 4/4 musical bar, while the right margin delimits the end of the 4/4 bar. In other words, each line on the page equals one bar in musical time. Indented lines indicate that the first syllable is deferred to the upbeat. Commas indicate strong pauses (end-stops, caesuras). The hyphens that interrupt "so-lo-ist" indicate phonopneumatic fissures—that is, a single breath is stuttered across phonemes. Finally, lines that end without commas are enjambed: the phrasal unit is performed uninterrupted across the musical bar's 4/4 limit. With due attention paid to the relation between stresses, as well as to the interaction between grammatical, phrasal, and musical units, such a transcription approximates the haeccity of a given performance

by foregrounding the integrity of its dramatics—or what Dennis Tedlock calls the "audible measure" of verbo-vocal performance (7):

It's
Béen a lóng tíme, I shóuldn't have léft yóu,   1
    Withoút a stróng rhýme to stép tó,
Thínk of hów mány wéak shóws you slépt thróugh,
    Tíme's úp, I'm sórry Í képt yóu,
Thínking of thís, you keép repéating you míss, the   5
Rhýmes from the mícrophóne só-ló-išt, and you
Sít by the rádio, hánd on the díal sóon,
    Ás you héar ít, púmp úp the vólúme,
Dánce with the spéaker tíll you héar it blów,
Then, plúg in the héadphóne 'cause hére it gó, it's a   10
Fóur létter wórd, when it's héard it cóntról,
Your bódy to dánce—you got it—sóul

Proximity between performer and audience is replaced by the
disembodied Rakim's voice speaking to "you," first through the radio,
and later through headphones. This listening "you" is simultaneously
intimate (particular) and impersonal (general): radio "comes to us ostensibly with person-to-person directness that is private and intimate,
while in more urgent fact, it is really a subliminal echo chamber of
magical power to touch remote and forgotten chords" of community
(McLuhan 302). In the early 1980s, radio—especially black radio—was
resistant to the idea of placing hip-hop on the regular playlist rota-
tion. It threatened to upset black radio's middle-class propriety and to
exacerbate intergenerational aesthetic and ethical differences.[13] Thus,
Rakim's rapping *through* the radio dramatizes something like a tactical takeover of the airwaves. His even-keeled and near-basso voice
provides a covert cover for his otherwise irruptive/disruptive call to
action: "pump up the volume, / Dance with the speaker till you hear it
blow." Rakim's rhythmic performance returns that apostrophic "you"
to a sensory world; that is to say, his vocal vibrations and inflections,
transmitted via radio's electromagnetic waves, incite an apocalyptic
return—"Time's up"—to the body.

Rakim's verse-flow is a variably contoured rhythmic plexus. Within
the 4/4 measure, Rakim's syllable count ranges from a minimum of
eight to a maximum of twelve per line; his stress count ranges from a

minimum of three to a maximum of seven. On only one occasion do consecutive measures share an equivalent stress count (lines 9 and 10 both include five stresses); at no point do consecutive measures share a syllable count. The fractal relation between syllable and stress counts is illustrative of Rakim's rhythmic difference: there's neither an absolute coordination between maximum syllable (twelve) and maximum strong stress counts (seven) nor a coordination between minimum syllable (eight) and minimum strong stress counts (three). For example, line 3 includes ten syllables, seven of which are stressed, the effect of which is a very compressed sonic and semantic unit; on the other hand, lines 5, 7, and 10 have a total of twelve syllables, only five of which are stressed, providing more room for his words to breathe. Or consider lines 2, 5, 7, 9, and 10, all of which include five stresses; however, those five stresses are dispersed among eight, twelve, twelve, ten, and twelve syllables, respectively, ensuring that each line is cognitively processed as both the same (stress) and different (syllables).

In lines 1–2 of "I Know You Got Soul," Rakim repeats a double-stress pattern (two consecutive stresses) four times, and this stress pattern corresponds with a double-rhyme scheme (each line has an internal and an end rhyme): "long time" (1) / "strong rhyme" (2); "left you" (1) / "step to" (2). Note also the alliterative parallelism: "long" / "left" and "strong" / "step." Rakim enacts just what he claims, a "strong rhyme," through the redoubling structure. The sonic force of the redoubling awakens "sleeping" listeners, whose aural senses have otherwise been lulled by radio's regularly scheduled programming of weak pop MCs or R&B. The double-stress pattern continues forward into lines 3 and 4, with "how man-," "weak shows," "slept through," and "time's up," before reaching the concluding triplet of consecutive stresses, "I kept you." Though the complementary double-rhyme scheme doesn't continue in lines 3–4, a supplementary parallelism appears across the two opening couplets: the first syllables of lines 1 and 3 fall on the downbeat, while the first syllables of lines 2 and 4 fall on the upbeat. Finally, the closure of the opening four lines is produced by virtue of a structural chiasm. Lines 1 and 4 are both interrupted with a caesura (after "time" and "up," respectively), while lines 2 and 3 are single, uninterrupted phrasal units. This closure is reflected in the semantic content too: Rakim's opening "return" narrative is complete.

There is a noticeable rhythmic decompression at lines 5 and 6. Rakim's redoublings give way to a looser patterning. In lines 1–4, on only one occasion does Rakim express two consecutive *weak* syllables; otherwise, single, unstressed syllables occupy the passing nodes between the ubiquitous double stresses that lead to the ultimate triple-stress unit that closes out Rakim's apology ("I'm sorry I kept you"). But, now, at lines 5 and 6, consecutive unstressed syllables occur four times. And while lines 1–4 are teleologically disposed to a line-final rhyme and stress, lines 5–6 are more ordered at their starts (i.e., the repeated stress pattern of SWWS), only to dissipate into turbulence at their ends.

The prosodic shift I've described from lines 1–4 to lines 5–6 coincides with a tonal and perspectival shift. Having created a commons of active listeners via the rhetoric of emphatic stress patterns and co-incident rhymes, the "microphone so-lo-ist" now proceeds to show off his verse-flow skills. Lines 5 and 6 are an interpolated time-space, where Rakim improvises, loosening his rhetoric. Notice, for example, two instances of enjambment ("the / Rhymes" and "and you / Sit"), which displace the end-rhyme teleology of lines 1–4. Internal rhyme supplants an end-rhyme schematic. Line 5 is also modulated by two caesuras. In terms of diction, three instances of polysyllabic words appear: "repeating," "microphone," and "so-lo-ist." Rakim indulges in a staccato articulation of "soloist" (so-lo-ist), with the break between each phoneme having the aural effect of micro-caesuras. Rakim's *tempo rubato* verse-flow, with its dispersed stresses, displaced rhymes, and phonopneumatic stutters, is an "invagination" within the time structure, thus effectively challenging the duration of those eight beats; like a jazz soloist, Rakim situates his verse-flow in "an internal pocket larger than the whole," "a taking part in without being part of, without having membership" in the musical measure (Derrida 55). As Rakim explains in the documentary *The MC: Why We Do It*, "When I was young I played saxophone. What I did was incorporate my rhyme style with like a sax solo. The way a sax player would play sporadically or using certain, um, styles or pauses." But by lines 7–8, the perspectival focus returns to the listening "you," and Rakim stabilizes his verse-flow with the return of the double-stress pattern: "dial soon," "hear it," "pump up," "volume"—all phrases that emphasize the dramatic and thematic action of the verse.

At line 9, Rakim declares his imperative: "Dance with the speaker till you hear it blow." The "speaker" punningly refers to both Rakim, with his radio voice addressing "you," and to the technology through which the sound is emitted. Technology and voice are conflated, though only momentarily. Sound technology (i.e., the speaker system) proves unable to contain the sonic and semantic excess of black expressivity (i.e., the rapping voice). This "excess" of voice is "soul." Soul's an inter- and inner text that readily translates across mediums as required: Rakim's "soul" enacts what Ralph Ellison describes as "nimbleness," a way of successfully navigating the contingencies of the moment, whatever they may be (e.g., the speaker blows). Rakim's encoded allusion to "soul" as a "four letter word" further plays on this idea of excess: Rakim knows very well that, as a general expletive and as a verb, "fuck"–the four-letter word he playfully sets up listeners to expect, the utterance of which would confirm a priori prejudices against hip-hop aesthetics and ethics–exceeds black middle-class radio's sense of discursive and behavioral propriety, to say nothing of FCC regulations. If bad language is black language, then Rakim "flips the script" by aligning blackness, hip-hop, and the *other* four-letter word: "soul." He figures the dancing *physis* as a black site and sight of soul *at the limits* of being and *in commons* within and beyond the five boroughs.[14]

A paragrammatic reading of lines 9–10 is also readily available, a reading that hinges on the double action of "blow." Rakim's "blow" means something like an interruption: "To shatter, destroy, or otherwise act upon by means of explosion . . . in technical use often *to blow*, like 'to blast'" (OED 24a); or, more specifically, "Of a fuse: to melt under an abnormally high electric current" (OED 19c). But "blow" is what a reed player does; the blowing of air is the primary source of sound in wind instruments, such as the saxophone. The verb's also a metonym for improvisatory chops (e.g., "That guy can really blow!") and rhythmic movement (e.g., "blow through the changes"). "Dance with the speaker till you hear it blow, / Then, plug in the headphone 'cause here it go": Rakim fashions a figure of himself as the jazz "solo-ist" who "blows." But what matters most, for our purposes, is that Rakim's blowing, which begins at line 11, is articulated as coincident with a shift from public radio to private headphones and from audible to silent consumption. In the case of the former (i.e., public and audible), Rakim's aesthetic imperative is embodied by the extroverted figure of the dancer; in the case of the latter (i.e., private and silent), Rakim's aesthetic imperative is embodied by the introverted figure of the jazz soloist. His rhythmic performance is poised at the interface between these two figures.

Turning to the prosody of the final four lines, what's clearly discernible is the relative simplicity. Remember, Rakim's job is to move the crowd, and to do so does not require pronounced rhythmic rhetoric (lines 1–4 and 7–8) or indulgent soloist interpolation (lines 5–6). The MC must become anonymous, placing his words in service of the occasion. Appropriately, then, Rakim's lines – especially 9 and 10 – are fairly innocuous, employing a *laissez-faire* rhythm ethic. Line 11's playful signifyin' on the "four-letter word" is stabilized by the strong gestalt of the rhythmic chiasm (SSWSW / WSWSS): the line begins and ends emphatically (with the double-stress pattern), though opens up considerably in its middle, with the reprieve of two unstressed syllables. At line 12, Rakim extricates himself altogether from the performance, allowing for the dancing audience to respond to his verse-flow's call: the listeners recognize Rakim's "soul" (*"you got it"*) by his acousmatic radio voice's effect on their bodies' synapses. They're dancing in private and in public, as individuals and in commons – this is the simultaneously explosive and implosive effect McLuhan ascribes to radio, where the individual and the collective are situated in "a single echo chamber" (299). Ultimately, Rakim's prosody, with its purposive spaciousness, opens up an imaginary floor for real dancing.

LYTE-SPEED AHEAD

In 1988, MC Lyte released her debut album, *Lyte as a Rock*. The Brooklyn-based MC Lyte is, like Rakim, widely revered. She's recognized as the first great female MC in hip-hop. "Her flow was unique," writes Gwendolyn D. Pough, adding that "while some might say that we had never heard a girl rap like that before, I would venture to say that we had never heard *anyone* rap like that before" (10; emphasis added). But where, exactly, might we locate the "unique" difference (female *and* black) of MC Lyte's prosody? How is MC Lyte's rhythmic performance on *Lyte as a Rock* a swerve away from previous efforts by women in hip-hop, such as Roxanne Shanté and Salt-N-Pepa? How does MC Lyte's rhythmic performance "bring wreck" (Pough 77) to the male-dominated sphere of MCing? While MC Lyte's rhythmic plexus is less rhetorical and dialogical than Rakim's, her enjambment, expressive accelerations, phrasal propulsion, and rhyme patterns perform a meeting *in extremis* of female difference and black hypermasculinity. Her "anything you can do I can do better" performance signifies on the braggadocio of MCs, in effect neutering the gendered coding of the MC as masculine.[15]

Here is the third verse of "Lyte as a Rock":

> I'm a
> Sláve I'm a sláve I'm a sláve to the rhythm,   1
> Déf rhymes ón the mícrophóne is whát Í'm gívin',
> Yés I ám a róck and yóu are júst a pébble,
> Mílk turn úp the báss and róck adjúst the lévels íf a
> Ráp can paínt a thóusand wórds then Í can paínt a míllion,   5
> Wáit, Lýte is cápablé of páintin' a bazíllion
> Ráps, so whén I sáy ít, thís is whát I méan,
> Aúdió Tó an allíance ón the scéne, and Í'd
> Líke to sáy "What's úp!" to rhy prodúcer Kíng of Chíll, Párty
> Péople are you réady, jám if you wíll,   10
> Néver únderéstimate Lýte the MC I am á
> Rápper whó is hére to make thíngs the wáy they're méant to bé the
> Wórld Últimate, I'm hére to táke the títle bút I
> Hád a líttle tróuble upón my arríval, bút I
> Gót rid of thóse whó, tríed to róck mé,   15
> Lýte is hére, nó one can stóp mé

Within the 4/4 measure, MC Lyte's syllable count ranges from a minimum of eight to a maximum of fifteen per line; her stress count ranges from a minimum of four to a maximum of eight. Her range of syllables is greater than Rakim's, while her range of stresses is comparable to Rakim's. This accounts for her more diffuse-sounding lines. Consecutive strong stresses are not prominent: over the course of sixteen lines, she includes eight instances of consecutive stresses; by comparison, Rakim includes nine instances of consecutive stresses in just the first four lines of "I Know You Got Soul." Furthermore, Rakim's lines tend to rise to a strong-stress resolution. MC Lyte, on the other hand, repeatedly produces lines that fall to a final unstressed syllable.

The verse begins with a clean symmetry: line 1's repeated falling triplet (SWW) follows the single falling duplet (SW). Each stressed "slave" corresponds with the first, second, and third beat of the musical measure; the first stressed syllable of "rhythm," too, falls directly on the fourth and final beat. The shift to the falling duplet at the end of line 1 foreshadows the falling duplets that soon dominate lines 2–5. However, lines 2 and 4 both include minor but valuable variations: three consecutive stresses and a falling triplet, respectively. These rhythmic variations set into relief, at least momentarily, the falling duplet expectations that are developed. In the case of line 2, MC Lyte introduces consecutive strong stresses in order to provide dramatic closure to the opening couplet, which carries with it a statement of agency and value: MC Lyte is announcing to the world that she has MC skills.

Despite their regularity, lines 3, 4, and 5 are rhythmically rich. For example, lines 3 and 4 are similarly structured. Each line includes two grammatical units (e.g., "Yes I am a rock"; "you are just a pebble") that are joined by the hypotactic "and." The two grammatical units, joined by "and," interact through call-and-response: "I" and "you" (pronominal), "rock" and "pebble" (imagistic), "turn up the bass" and "adjust the levels" (narrative action). The call-and-response establishes a weak-strong informational pattern, one that's set against the strong-weak falling pattern at the intonational level of the lyrical discourse. Furthermore, there is a subtle but felt expansion from line 3 to line 4, as the syllable-stress count increases. This corresponds with an increase in elocutionary speed. Lines 4 and 5 each contain a remarkable fourteen syllables and seven stresses. The parallelism cuts across two discrete couplets (lines 3–4 and lines 5–6). Finally, notice that line 5's "words," which is stressed, falls *inside* beats two and three. The syncopated "words" is the thematic key to the line. That is, as a female MC, MC Lyte's more than just a sexualized, domesticated, or inferior slave/object; and her superabundant "words" are superior to those of the male "masters."

It's this abundance of "words" through which MC Lyte asserts her female subjectivity. The dramatic prosody of lines 4–5 and 11–13 – characterized by enjambment, acceleration, and phrasal propulsion – establishes MC Lyte's value beyond the authorization of male producers and, implicitly, other black *and* male MCs. Lines 4–5 present a single, twenty-eight-syllable phrasal or breath unit (fourteen syllables per line), uninterrupted by caesuras. It's a virtuoso moment. MC Lyte transgresses the 4/4 limit of the hip-hop line. She renders the line's beginning and end inaudible, effacing the gestalt of the rhymed couplet. She raps as many words as possible, trying to approximate that hyperbolic "million," which would top the "thousand words" of other MCs. Her speedy onslaught of "words" is experienced synesthetically as a blur of emotive colors ("paint") – like graffiti on a moving subway – rather than as an exclusive bearer of signified content.

Lyte later trumps her own virtuosity: in lines 11–13, her single phrasal unit extends continuously, without interruption, over three musical measures. It totals thirty-three syllables and sixteen strong stresses. In order to squeeze this excess of syllables/stresses into each 4/4 bar, MC Lyte accelerates her articulation of the words. Her mouth becomes a percussive machine. She performs each syllable as if a sixteenth note, creating a double-time signature on top of the regular 4/4 time signature. In expending her gendered and racialized body so as to engage in a caustic, mechanized hyperspeed, MC Lyte parodies the valuation of speed as a symbol of masculinity. This acceleration, which demands nonstop phrasal units extending over and across 4/4 bars, is intimately related to the concept of phrasal propulsion. *Phrasal propulsion* is "the *force* of language in its passage," explains Steve McCaffery, who theorizes the protosemantic concept in his book *Prior to Meaning* (152). In the absence of caesuras, MC Lyte's grammatical units are asyndetic, joining and then dissipating into a single, non-integrative phrasal unit, which in its serial effect and accelerated distribution disturbs the equilibrium of signified meaning(s): "the words," as McCaffery suggests, "neither arrest attention nor inhabit time long enough to insist on comprehension, but rather fill out a space whose positionality or situation is measured as a temporal shift. Kineticized this way, meaning registers plurally as evaporative effects" (154).

These "evaporative effects" are not simply effects of language; they are the result of short-term memory's cognitive limits, which, as Reuven Tsur explains, help determine a rhythmical performance: "The content span of short-term memory is limited to seven monosyllabic words plus or minus two. . . . In order to render a verse line perceptible as a rhythmic whole, the reciter must manipulate his vocal resources [grouping and over-articulation] in such a way that the verse line can be completed before its beginning fades out in short-term memory" (15). Lines 4–5 of "Lyte as a Rock" include twenty-eight syllables, while the phrasal unit that extends across lines 11–13 includes thirty-three syllables. MC Lyte's rhythmic performance is four and five times greater than what short-term memory can register. Due to the virtuosity of its quantity and its continuous quality, MC Lyte's performance ceases to even be classifiable as rhythmic, in much the same way as her words cease to be signifiers of content—that is, they become colors. Correspondingly, MC Lyte's very being "evaporates," thus rendering obsolete the slave-master dialectic with which the recording begins.

Two last points about MC Lyte's performance. First, the shift initiated by phrasal propulsion sends hip-hop's usually even-numbered structure (couplets and quatrains) into disequilibrium. The phrasal unit that extends from line 4 to line 5 causes the verse's opening quatrain to be enveloped by the cinquain and, by extension, the amputated second quatrain to be cognitively perceived as a tercet. A similar ambiguity appears at lines 12 and 13. The "slavish" symmetry, then, of even numbers is replaced by simultaneously superimposed odd-number asymmetry. Second, rhyme is another device whereby MC Lyte's masculinist braggadocio and femininity meet *in extremis*. Her polysyllabic rhymes are accumulations of euphonic wealth: "just a pebble" / "adjust the levels"; "paint a million" / "paintin' a bazillion"; "King of Chill" / "if you will"; "title but I" / "arrival, but I"; "rock me" / "stop me." Her verseflow is also marked by feminine rhymes: "rhythm" / "givin'"; "pebble" / "levels"; "million" / "bazillion"; "title" / "arrival." Ultimately, it is the confluence of MC Lyte's enjambment, acceleration, phrasal propulsion, asymmetrical structure, and masculine and feminine rhymes that confirms MC Lyte as an innovator. MC Lyte's light-speed prosody locates her in the free space of physics, where she may be heard and seen but, paradoxically, neither her words nor her body (one and the same) may be objectified or instrumentalized.

"STRAIGHT OUTTA COMPTON'S" GANGSTA RHYTHM ETHIC

In 1988, Rakim was the undisputed "leader" of New York ("So keep starin' soon ya suddenly see a star / You better follow it 'cause it's the

R" ["Follow the Leader"]), and MC Lyte had created a space for female MCs within the male-dominated MC community. That year, on the other side of the country, in south central Los Angeles, Ice Cube and his fellow N.W.A. crewmates (including Dr. Dre, MC Ren, the late Eazy-E, and DJ Yella) released *Straight Outta Compton*, the seminal gangsta rap album, which includes the infamous recordings "Straight Outta Compton," "Fuck tha Police," and "Gangsta Gangsta." Gangsta rap emerged as a carefully calculated response to south central Los Angeles's post-industrial collapse, which was characterized by increased unemployment and incarceration rates for working-class black youth. With its street hustlin' epistemology, capitalist imperatives, and violent imagery, gangsta rap simultaneously reflected and refracted the logic of Reagan era America in which the rich get richer and the poor get poorer (Quinn 52). But what made gangsta rap so popular–and innovative–was the synchronization of gangsta ethics, aesthetics, and ontology. That is to say, while gangsta rap participates in a playful signifyin' tradition, at the same time it also depends upon the uncanny trope of tropelessness or authenticity, so as to effect an affective homology between hustlin' and rappin'. Eithne Quinn comments on this very thing in a short discussion of Eazy-E's prosody: "The credibility of Eazy's . . . lyrical flow seems to inhere precisely in its lack of artifice and skill, which . . . announce that he is only about business. The rap is simply a hustle so his gangsta ethic is authentic" (72). Eazy-E's crew mate Ice Cube's verse-flow on "Straight Outta Compton" performs the hustle Quinn reads as naturalized in Eazy-E. This rhythmic "lack" identifies Ice Cube as gangsta rather than MC–an identification with mutually imbricated psychogeographic and generic implications.

Ice Cube's verse-flow on "Straight Outta Compton" begins with these lines:

> Straíght outta
> Cómpton, crázy mótherfúcker námed Íce Cúbe,   1
>   Fróm the gáng cálled Níggaz Wíth Áttitúdes,
>   Whén I'm cálled óff, I gót a sáwed óff,
>   Squéeze the trígger, and bódies are haúled óff,
>   Yóu tóo bóy if ya fúck wíth me,   5
>   The pólice are gónna háve to cóme and gét mé,
> Óff yo áss, thát's how I'm góin' oút,
>   For the púnk mótherfúckers thát's shówin' oút,

Níggaz stárt to múmble, they wánna rúmble,
Míx 'ém and coók 'ém in a pót líke gúmbó,   10
  Góin' óff on the mótherfúcker líke thát,
  Wíth a gát, thát's poínted át yó'
Aśs, so gíve it úp smóoth,
Aín't nó téllin' whén I'm dówn for a jáck móve,
  Hére's a múrder ráp to kéep you dáncin',   15
  With a críme récord líke Chárles Mánson

Ice Cube's "murder rap" is an extended threat: should anyone im-
pede his pursuit of the American dream, he promises to respond with
unequivocal force: "Squeeze the trigger, and bodies are hauled off."
Part character, part caricature, Ice Cube names and claims his pathology ("crazy motherfucker named Ice Cube"). Ice Cube even indulges
the popular historical association of cannibalism and blackness ("Mix
'em and cook 'em in a pot like gumbo"), in the process rendering
Compton a premodern aporia within the postmodern American imaginary. That slippage (premodern versus postmodern) is inscribed in Ice
Cube's grammatical tense. His verse-flow is in the subjunctive: "When
I'm called off," "if ya fuck with me," "The police are gonna have to,"
"that's how I'm goin' out," "they wanna rumble," "Ain't no tellin' when
I'm down for a jack move." In other words, what this "murder rap" lacks
is action – or, put simply, a murder. Ice Cube is simply "showin' out"
in his verse-flow, marking his territory. The only instance of the present indicative is in the final two lines of the excerpt, when Ice Cube
reflexively remarks on his own "rap" "record." In doing so, he draws
attention to the mediated condition of a gangsta epistemology (i.e.,
street knowledge). It also suggests how gangsta rap violently intrudes
into hip-hop's dominant context of consumption and use: dancing in
the club. But perhaps the most salient feature of Ice Cube's verse-flow
is the evocation of Compton, Los Angeles, as the psychogeographic
locus of the gangsta rap and as an ostensible, transcoded "ghetto" space.
As Murray Forman observes, in his excellent close reading of "Straight
Outta Compton":

> The general lyrical content . . . sheds little light on the city or its social
> byways and does not demonstrate any particular concern with the local-
> ity's economics and their impact on everyday life. . . . Without detailed
> spatial descriptions of landmarks and environment, Compton does

not emerge as a clearly realized urban space in the N.W.A. track even though it is the group's hometown. The California city is instead interpolated as a bounded civic space that provides both specificity and scale for the communication of a West Coast rap presence. (194–195)

It's the continual slippage or – to borrow from hip-hop parlance – "flipping" between and across the mediated and unmediated, the present indicative and subjunctive moods, and the particular (Compton) and the ostensible (ghetto) that contributes to what Eithne Quinn refers to as gangsta rap's "double vision" (15). This double vision is audibly amplified by Ice Cube's prosody.

Ice Cube's rhythmic plexus is far less modulated than Rakim's or MC Lyte's, but that's not to say that it is any less innovative. Ice Cube performs a smaller, more repetitive range of syllables and stresses across the musical measure. He maintains a steady balance between eight (minimum) and eleven syllables (maximum). In this excerpt, he averages 10.375 syllables per line. Line 6 ("The police are gonna have to come and get me") and line 13 ("Ass, so give it up smooth"), with twelve and six syllables, respectively, are anomalies that deviate only slightly from the standard eight- to eleven-syllable range. Ice Cube's stress count is equally consistent: lines have a range of 5–7 stresses, with the exceptions of lines 10 and 13, which include eight and four, respectively – minimal deviations from the average of six stresses per line. Ice Cube forces a high volume of stresses into his reduced syllable counts, producing a compressed rhythmic plexus that is like a monolithic structure.

How else does Ice Cube's prosody render geographic and generic difference? First, every line but one is end-stopped. Line 12 is enjambed in a grammatical sense but not in terms of the phrasal unit. It concludes with "yo," a single syllable Ice Cube extends in duration, for dramatic effect, before completing his phrasal/grammatical unit with the accented first syllable of line 13 ("Ass"). In performing "yo" in such a sustained manner, especially in contrast with the line's earlier staccato accenting of "gat," "that's," and "at," and by stressing "Ass" on the subsequent downbeat, Ice Cube audibly telegraphs one line's end and the next line's start, in effect muting the enjambment's transgressivity. Second, nearly every line is a discrete grammatical unit; only on one occasion does the end-stopped line interrupt a discrete grammatical unit, at lines 6–7 ("The police are gonna have to come and get me, / Off yo ass") – the semantic sense is momentarily suspended. Third, Ice Cube repeatedly defers line beginnings: ten of the sixteen lines do not begin on the downbeat. In combination with consistent end-stopped prosody, this momentary deferral at the start of lines does two things: it doubly accentuates the discrete nature of each line, as now both beginnings and ends are marked by distinct, conjoined silences – in those silences, gangsta rap's *eros* and *thanatos* are voiced. The deferral also ostensibly transforms the 4-beat measure to a 3- or 3½-beat measure (approximately). This further compresses Ice Cube's phrasal units.

Not surprisingly, the *telos* of Ice Cube's prosody is unremarkable. Unlike Rakim and MC Lyte, who present multiple trajectories, Ice Cube prefers moving toward double- and triple-stress line ends, which are accompanied by single or double rhymes. His verse-flow displays an excess of purposiveness. It is, quite literally, "straight" (i.e., direct, no-nonsense) outta Compton. It "lacks" the New York–based prosody's commuting circumlocutions, as symbolized by the city's famed subway system. (Los Angeles County's Metropolitan Transportation Authority didn't open its Blue Line into Compton until 1990.) At the same time, Ice Cube prefers blocks of consecutive strong stresses. Lines 5, 7, and 10 include instances of four consecutive stresses; lines 2, 12, and 14 include instances of three consecutive stresses; and a superabundance of double stresses is scattered throughout. Collectively, these stress blocks contribute to a rhythmic plexus that lacks a modulated strong-weak spaciousness through which expressive potentialities of rhythm are assessed and accessed. Instead, spaciousness is replaced by an agoraphobic intensity, a "showin' out" of power in the face of the powerlessness that plagued young black men in Ice Cube's late 1980s Los Angeles. In combination, Ice Cube's telegraphed prosody and block stresses map Compton as an aptotic territory, proving that indeed there can be verse-flow without (or, at least, with very little) modulation, despite Swinburne's claim to the contrary over a hundred years earlier.

But the gangsta rhythm ethic described above is not always "straight." To read gangsta rap as such is to overdetermine its meaning and make it available to conservative critiques of black pathology in need of containment and moral fine-tuning. Instead, at two key junctures, disequilibrium is produced by Ice Cube's introduction of figural disruptions into gangsta discourse. In "Taking the Side of the Figural," Lyotard describes the figural as the "sensible"–that is, it's of the senses (36). The figural is a three-dimensional or tactile way of being, as opposed to discourse's sense-less two-dimensionality, which imprisons the subject and meaning. The figural expresses, whereas discourse signifies. Accordingly, the figural is the locus of art: positioned "at the edge of and within discourse," figural "movement and force" cause "the table of significations to erupt through a quake which produces meaning" (39). Two formal manifestations of the deforming figural are metaphor and rhythm. In the case of the former, Lyotard writes, "Espouse the undulations of *metaphor*, which is the fulfillment of desire, then we will see how exteriority, force, formed space can be present in interiority, in close signification" (39; emphasis added); in the case of the latter, Lyotard writes, "Art wants the figure; 'beauty' is figural, non-related, and *rhythmic*" (37; emphasis added). Through the corresponding "undulations" of metaphoric language (notably, similes and puns) and modulated rhythmics, Ice Cube's "straight" homology becomes an indirect heterology; his gangsta discourse splits "into two sides" and leaves them in the "disequilibrium of which ethical life speaks" (36).

In the first figural instance, at line 10, Ice Cube engages the association of cannibalism and blackness: "Mix 'em and cook 'em in a pot like gumbo." The conceit radically departs from the matter-of-fact tone that characterizes the verse-flow until then; thus the line possesses informational prominence within the couplet and the overall verse structure. For a moment, Compton's contemporaneity ("sawed-off" technology) and geography (urban Los Angeles) are displaced and metaphorized as an anterior, primal stomping ground on which capitalism's consumptive appetite is played out in more embodied, fleshy terms.

In the second instance, at lines 15 and 16, the figural is even more stated. The rhymed couplet is pun-filled and, as noted earlier, is the first instance of the present indicative mood in the verse-flow, two qualities which make the couplet the most prominent in the entire excerpt. Ice Cube's "murder rap" alludes to both his recording (rap) and criminal activity (a "rap" sheet); "crime record" functions in a similar manner. The puns self-reflexively draw explicit attention to the mediated nature of the gangsta genre. They also indicate that Ice Cube is acutely aware of how hip-hop is "used" in clubs as dance music. Accordingly, the figural interruption into the gangsta discourse is coincident with an apostrophic turn: like Rakim, he's addressing an audience, whether real or imagined, that is partaking in a rhythmic action, dancing, which is a sign of the figural. So, on the one hand, "Straight Outta Compton's" lyrics clearly indicate that dancing – in and of itself – is an inadequate mode of action in the face of post-industrial south central Los Angeles's collapse; and Rakim's "soul" is a metaphysical concept that cannot compete with Ice Cube's "sawed off." Therefore, Ice Cube's allusion to dancing is an instance of signifyin' on New York City's "good times" party raps. The wonderfully macabre semantic rhyme of "dancin'" and "Manson" supports just such a reading, while psychogeographically re-accenting New York dance-based raps with a distinctly West Coast sign: the Manson murders. On the other hand, Ice Cube is also "dead" serious about "Straight Outta Compton's" classification as a "dance" record, as its funk-propelled, guitar- and horn-dominated soundscape indicates. His prosody affirms this, too. Lines 15 and 16 are singular in their feminine endings; they are audibly recognizable as the most modulated, in terms of strong-weak stress relations. At this moment, Ice Cube upsets any notion of gangsta essentialism through aesthetic apostasy: the thickness and compression of gangsta discourse and rhythmics are momentarily refused.

* * *

The three case studies – Rakim, MC Lyte, Ice Cube – indicate that hip-hop verse-flow is *not* composed in strict accordance with an abstract four-stress metric. Furthermore, the phrasal units, articulated both within and across the musical measure's 4/4 temporal limit, are neither end-stopped nor end rhymed at all times. Such descriptions of hip-hop prosody are indicative of a lamentable regression of listening, as only a few lines from the three excerpts actually accord with such a neat analysis. Rakim, MC Lyte, and Ice Cube produce complex rhythmic plexuses that reflect and inflect divergent thematic, generic, geographic, and gendered imperatives. Rakim's rhythmic performance oscillates between communal and soloist phrasings, thus establishing a rapport between hip-hop and jazz aesthetics (rap had found its Coltrane, after all) but also rendering Rakim as a vocal medium between hip-hop's old and new school contexts of use. MC Lyte's accelerated kinesic performance intrudes upon the commonly gendered coding of the MC as masculine. Her performance proposes a dissolution of gender as an a priori qualitative signifier. Finally, Ice Cube's rhythmic performance affirms *and* denies the realness of the gangsta hustle – figural irruptions (puns, similes, modulated stress patterns) within an otherwise compressed rhythmic plexus suggest the plasticity of the "real," the gangsta, and Compton. In each case, prosodic technique is the primary means through which the MC re-accents hip-hop, and quantitative analysis of such technique doesn't compromise the racialized haeccity – that is, the symbolic "blackness" – of hip-hop verse-flow but rather adduces the singularity of each MC's performance.

Implied in any prosodic analysis is that hip-hop is – despite the Poetry Foundation's claim to the contrary – a mode of poetry, one of many in postmodern America, including L=A=N=G=U=A=G=E poetry, new formalism, elliptical poetry, flarf, talk poetry, new brutalism, Oulipo, slam, etc. Hip-hop scholars from Tricia Rose to Bakari Kitwana and from Russell A. Potter to William Jelani Cobb have all, at one time or another, referred to hip-hop MCs as poets and, correspondingly, to verse-flow as poetry, though "poetry" is applied more to confer upon hip-hop a sense of prestige than to spur formal explication. Of course, a discourse of *poiesis* is embedded in hip-hop: Rakim, KRS-One, Big Daddy Kane, Q-Tip, Prince Poetry, Raekwon, Ghostface Killah, Canibus, and MF Doom are just a few of the many rappers who self-identify as poets, although they do so for various reasons. Take, for example, the Wu-Tang Clan's Raekwon, who self-identifies as a "slang-poet." Raekwon's cryptophonic idiolect on *Only Built 4 Cuban Linx . . .* (1995) – the album title is code for code – contests two contemporaneous phenomena: first, the moral panic over hip-hop subject matter initiated by both black and white conservative critics (i.e., if one does not know exactly what Raekwon's saying, one cannot critique his supposed pathologies); second, the success of the ghetto action film cycle of the 1990s, which made hip-hop's image-based lyrics obsolescent and necessitated his swerve to linguistic opacity – that is, to poetry.

But teaching hip-hop *as poetry* is a tricky endeavor. Too often, hip-hop is treated as a stepping-stone to the canonized, Arnoldian "touchstones" of English, American, and African American poetry.

One of the most egregious instances of this is the Cumbria (England) Tourist Board's rap version of Wordsworth's "I Wandered Lonely as a Cloud," which was meant to regenerate interest in the Lake District, Wordsworth's "Dove" cottage therein, and Wordsworth's poetry overall. Translation, as John Guillory reminds us, is "a powerful institutional buttress of imaginary cultural continuities" (43). However, such translative gestures distort both the tenor (Wordsworth) and the vehicle (hip-hop). A rhythm-based pedagogy imbues hip-hop lyrics with a historicity that makes such "imaginary cultural continuities" untenable. Likewise, a rhythm-based approach to hip-hop exposes the obsolescence of a racially circumscribed metric theory, which sublates, regulates, and homogenizes the cognitive experience of an otherwise manifold rhythmic plexus. A traditional foot-based parsing of hip-hop prosody (i.e., iamb, trochee, dactyl) would only suggest that hip-hop metrics are pathologically deviant, thus positing metrics as a formal index of the behavioral. On the other hand, a rhythm-based approach replaces a discourse of behavioral deviance with that of aesthetic purposiveness. A rhythm-based approach to hip-hop verse-flow is also useful as a means of contesting the open-closed formal binary that was the defining trope of late twentieth-century poetry. Hip-hop prosody is both closed and open: it's a double affirmative. Hip-hop's simultaneous yet unsynthesized audio epistemes – the beat and the lyric – produce a formal threshold of regularly irregular and irregularly regular intensities and sonorities. This is what poet-critic Alice Fulton describes as "fractal poetics."[16]

When teaching hip-hop in a poetry classroom, it's essential that hip-hop poetics be treated as an autochthonous phenomenon. For instance, at the State University of New York at Buffalo, in the winter semester of 2008, I created an "Introduction to Poetry" survey course. Each week of the term was dedicated to poems illustrative of a single poetic genre or mode (e.g., ode, elegy, pastoral). At the end of the term, I devoted an entire week – three one-hour classes – to hip-hop, allowing ample time for discussion of the genre's history and shifting sociopolitical contexts as well as close readings of representative recordings. By situating hip-hop at the end of the "Introduction to Poetry" course, students were better equipped to recognize how an MC uses metaphor, symbolism, rhymes, rhythm, tone, and voice. At the same time, students then retroactively recognized how hip-hop recordings include innovative takes on the ode (e.g., Ghostface Killah, "All That I Got Is You") or pastoral (e.g., Notorious B.I.G., "Things Done Changed").

Finally, close listening challenges the myth of black rhythmic exceptionalism. In America, this discourse emerged at the end of the nineteenth century: "At [that] moment," explains Ronald Radano in *Lying Up a Nation*, "the intellectual concepts of primitivism and African origins aligning with 'descent' intersected with the dynamic figurations of displaced Negroes in motion . . . a seminal body of figurations through which rhythm gained both its primal ferocity and its signature urban-based danger, which together identify fundamental elements of black musical modernism" (272). Rhythm came to signify the essential difference of blackness in America, while at the same time "betray[ing] its grounding in a cross-racial common soil" (276). As renowned Afro-musicologist Kofi Agawu has shown, this cross-racial "invention" of African rhythm dates to the eleventh century: "Christian physician and theologian Ibn Butlan, in a tract entitled 'On How to Buy Slaves and How to Detect Bodily Defects,' claimed that 'if a black were to fall from the sky to the earth, he would fall in rhythm'" (380). This myth persists: from the discourse around black athletes – who are supposedly more rhythmically attuned than white athletes and therefore able to occupy almost post-human, byzantine folds within the sporting habitus – to the 1999 anthology *"This Is How We Flow": Rhythm in Black Cultures*, edited by Angela Nelson, which repeatedly naturalizes a singular "black" rhythm in music and literature through either holistic, behavioral, or systolic conceits. This "invention" of black rhythm often denies to black aesthetic production "a critical element" (Agawu 386). But the response to this "invention" should not be to deny the function and value of rhythm altogether. That's been the modus operandi for cultural critics like Stanley Crouch and John Mc-Whorter, for example. Rhythm is not truth, argues McWhorter, in his polemic *All about the Beat: Why Hip-Hop Can't Save Black America*. McWhorter's claim doesn't radically negate the tautology (rhythm is truth or truth is rhythm) so much as reify the dubious terms up for debate. A more poetics-based pedagogical approach illustrates that, in hip-hop verse-flow, rhythm is a signifying, signifyin', and asignifying multiplex of communicative and metacommunicative elements; and prosodic analysis is an Agawu-inspired "political critique" insofar as it reveals the ideological forces of truth's naturalized artifice, while also drawing attention to the aesthetic successes of hip-hop performers.

NOTES

Thanks to Damien Keane, Bruce Jackson, Greg Dimitriadis, and David McGimpsey for their guidance. The chapter's title is borrowed from a Rakim recording of the same name.

1. See Jeff Chang's exhaustive cultural history, *Can't Stop Won't Stop*, which was published to much acclaim – rightly so – in 2005. Nelson George's *Hip-Hop America* also provides some excellent historical coverage.

2. For a more detailed description of this shift toward MC-centric hip-hop, see Chang 130–134; Forman 106–119; and Dimitriadis 15–34.

3. This shift has also been represented as the bifurcation of "hip-hop" and "rap" – the former embodying the original or pure spirit of a vanguard cultural practice (or what in hip-hop parlance is referred to as "keeping it real"), the latter signifying culture-industry imperatives, aesthetic compromise, and the deracination and depoliticization of a movement. See Adorno's *The Culture Industry: Selected Essays on Mass Culture*.

4. I use the compound term "verse-flow" to refer to hip-hop's lyrical production. "Flow" is the term most commonly used to refer to hip-hop lyrics. The addition of "verse" intimates an affiliation with poetry, but also refers to the common sixteen- or twelve-bar musical structure that MCs perform over.

5. See Gilroy's *The Black Atlantic* for discussion of "black metacommunication" (75).

6. The period 1987–1988 is a watershed moment because it marked the arrival of hip-hop's "golden age" – most notably, artists like Eric B. and Rakim, MC Lyte, N.W.A., Boogie Down Productions, and Public Enemy. In addition, as Murray Forman has demonstrated, the late 1980s also saw rap music's dissemination across multiple formats, for example, *Yo! MTV Raps* premiered on MTV.

7. Earl L. Stewart defines a "rhythmic plexus" as "an interconnected network of musical events. . . . Some events merge with other events" (11).

8. Literary and cultural scholars of hip-hop have much to learn from their musicological peers, who remain thoroughly invested in formalism. Adam Krims provides the most exhaustive – and exhilarating – analysis of how sampling, beats, and timbre produce "symbolic" identities. This chapter is offered as a prosody-based companion study to Krims's musicology; I supplement his "speech" and "percussive-effusive" classifications of verse-flow while also introducing prosody's nonsymbolic (signifyin', asignifying) values into the hermeneutic process.

9. Here is a short list of such terms: poetic, unique, original, powerful, idiosyncratic, sublime, energetic, soulful, syncopated, polyrhythmic, effortless, complex, sharp, and stylin'.

10. See Aviram; Bradley; Gioia; DJ Renegade; and Shetley – each uses the four-stress metric scheme when discussing hip-hop lyrical performance. Tracie Morris only implicitly suggests this

four-stress ballad meter when comparing early hip-hop and popular song. In addition, Burt emphasizes that hip-hop is composed in strict rhymed couplets, like Pope's neoclassical heroic couplets. However, the work of Alim; Bradley; and Krims does much to undercut Burt's commentary.

11. For a discussion of relation, see Glissant.

12. See Cureton's *Rhythmic Phrasing in English Verse*. Put simply, Cureton argues that rhythm is multidimensional, with weak (W) and strong (S) stress patterns extending beyond the syllable and into both sentence and narrative levels of lyrical discourse.

13. See Amiri Baraka's *Blues People* and *Black Music* for a discussion of similar tensions throughout the African American expressive tradition.

14. See Nancy 77–78.

15. My analysis is also offered as an adversarial response to Nelson George, who claims, "there are no women who have contributed to rap's artistic growth" (184). I see MC Lyte as an innovator.

16. "Fractal poetics is composed of the disenfranchised details, the dark matter of Tradition: its blind spots, recondite spaces, and recursive fields" – in other words, the "dub" side (Fulton 69).

REFERENCES

Adorno, Theodor W. *The Culture Industry: Selected Essays on Mass Culture.* New York: Routledge, 1991.

Agawu, Kofi. "The Invention of 'African Rhythm.'" *Journal of the American Musicological Society* 48 (1995): 380–395.

Alim, H. Samy. *Roc the Mic Right: The Language of Hip Hop Culture.* New York: Routledge, 2006.

Aviram, Ammitai. *Telling Rhythm: Body and Meaning in Poetry.* Ann Arbor: University of Michigan Press, 1994.

Baraka, Amiri. *Black Music.* New York: Morrow, 1967.

——. *Blues People: Negro Music in White America.* New York: Morrow, 1963.

Bradley, Adam. *Book of Rhymes: The Poetics of Hip-Hop.* New York: Perseus, 2009.

Burt, Stephen. "Original Gangsta: How the Poems of Eighteenth Century Poet Alexander Pope Prefigured Modern Hip-Hop Rivalries." *Poetry Foundation* (n.d.). Web. Accessed 25 July 2008.

Chang, Jeff. *Can't Stop Won't Stop: A History of the Hip-Hop Generation.* New York: St. Martin's, 2005.

Cobb, William Jelani. *To the Break of Dawn: A Freestyle on the Hip Hop Aesthetic.* New York: New York University Press, 2007.

Cureton, Richard. *Rhythmic Phrasing in English Verse.* New York: Longman, 1992.

Derrida, Jacques. "The Law of Genre." In *On Narrative.* Ed. W. J. T. Mitchell. Chicago: University of Chicago Press, 1980. 51–77.

Dimitriadis, Greg. *Performing Identity / Performing Culture: Hip-Hop as Text, Pedagogy, and Lived Practice.* New York: Lang, 2001.

DJ Renegade. "The Metrics of Rap." In *An Exaltation of Forms: Contemporary Poets Celebrate the Diversity of Their Art.* Ed. Annie Finch and Katherine Varnes. Ann Arbor: University of Michigan Press, 2002. 272–278.

Ellison, Ralph, and Albert Murray.

Trading Twelves: The Selected Letters of Ralph Ellison and Albert Murray. New York: Modern Library, 2000.

Eric B. and Rakim. *Paid in Full.* Island / Def Jam, 1987. CD.

Forman, Murray. *The 'Hood Comes First: Race, Space, and Place in Rap and Hip-Hop.* Middletown, CT: Wesleyan University Press, 2002.

Fulton, Alice. *Feeling as a Foreign Language.* St. Paul, MN: Graywolf, 1999.

Gates, Henry Louis, Jr. *The Signifying Monkey: A Theory of African-American Literary Criticism.* New York: Oxford University Press, 1988.

George, Nelson. *Hip-Hop America.* New York: Penguin, 2005.

Gilroy, Paul. *The Black Atlantic: Modernity and Double Consciousness.* Cambridge, MA: Harvard University Press, 1993.

Gioia, Dana. *Disappearing Ink: Poetry at the End of Print Culture.* St. Paul, MN: Graywolf, 1994.

Glissant, Édouard. *Poetics of Relation.* Trans. Betsy Wing. Ann Arbor: University of Michigan Press, 2000.

Guevara, Nancy. "Women Writin' Rappin' Breakin'." In *Droppin' Science: Critical Essays on Rap Music and Hip-Hop Culture.* Ed. William Eric Perkins. Philadelphia: Temple University Press, 1996. 49–62.

Guillory, John. *Cultural Capital: The Problem of Literary Canon Formation.* Chicago: University of Chicago Press, 1993.

Krims, Adam. *Rap Music and the Poetics of Identity.* New York: Cambridge University Press, 2000.

Lyotard, Jean-François. *The Lyotard Reader and Guide.* Ed. Keith Crome and James Williams. New York: Columbia University Press, 2006.

Marriott, Robert. "Allah's on Me." In *And It Don't Stop! The Best American Hip-Hop Journalism of the Last 25 Years.* Ed. Raquel Cepeda. New York: Faber and Faber, 2004.

McCaffery, Steve. *Prior to Meaning: The Protosemantic and Poetics.* Evanston, IL: Northwestern University Press, 2001.

McLuhan, Marshall. *Understanding Media.* 1964. Cambridge, MA: MIT Press, 1994.

MC Lyte. *Lyte as a Rock.* Atlantic, 1988. CD.

The MC: Why We Do It. Dir. Peter Spirer. Image Entertainment, 2004. DVD.

McWhorter, John. *All About the Beat: Why Hip-Hop Can't Save Black America.* New York: Gotham, 2008.

Miyakawa, Felicia M. *Five Percenter Rap: God Hop's Music, Message, and Black Muslim Mission.* Bloomington: Indiana University Press, 2005.

Morris, Tracie. "Hip-Hop Rhyme Formations: Open Your Ears." In *An Exaltation of Forms: Contemporary Poets Celebrate the Diversity of Their Art.* Ed. Annie Finch and Katherine Varnes. Ann Arbor: University of Michigan Press, 2002. 223–227.

Nancy, Jean-Luc. *The Inoperative Community.* Trans. Peter Connor et al. Minneapolis: University of Minnesota Press, 1991.

Neff, Ali Colleen. *Let the World Listen Right: The Mississippi Delta Hip-Hop Story.* Jackson: University Press of Mississippi, 2009.

Nelson, Angela M. S., ed. *"This Is How We Flow": Rhythm in Black Cultures.* Columbia: University of South Carolina Press, 1999.

N.W.A. *Straight Outta Compton.* 1988. Priority Records, 2007. CD.

Pate, Alexs. *In the Heart of the Beat: The Poetry of Rap.* Toronto: Scarecrow, 2010.

Perkins, William Eric. "The Rap Attack: An Introduction." In *Droppin' Science: Critical Essays on Rap Music* and *Hip-Hop Culture*. Ed. William Eric Perkins. Philadelphia: Temple University Press, 1996. 1–48.

Perry, Imani. *Prophets of the Hood: Politics and Poetics in Hip Hop*. Durham, NC: Duke University Press, 2004.

Pinn, Anthony, ed. *Noise and Spirit: The Religious and Spiritual Sensibilities of Rap Music*. New York: New York University Press, 2003.

Potter, Russell. *Spectacular Vernaculars: Hip-Hop and the Politics of Postmodernism*. Albany: State University of New York Press, 1995.

Pough, Gwendolyn D. *Check It while I Wreck It: Black Womanhood, Hip-Hop Culture, and the Public Sphere*. Boston: Northeastern University Press, 2004.

Quinn, Eithne. *Nuthin' but a "G" Thang: The Culture and Commerce of Gangsta Rap*. New York: Columbia University Press, 2005.

Radano, Ronald. *Lying Up a Nation: Race and Black Music*. Chicago: University of Chicago Press, 2003.

Rose, Tricia. *Black Noise: Rap Music and Contemporary Culture in America*. Hanover, NH: University Press of New England, 1994.

Schloss, Joseph G. *Making Beats: The Art of Sample-Based Hip-Hop*. Middletown, CT: Wesleyan University Press, 2004.

Shetley, Vernon. *After the Death of Poetry: Poet and Audience in Contemporary America*. Durham, NC: Duke University Press, 1993.

Shusterman, Richard. *Pragmatist Aesthetics: Living Beauty, Rethinking Art*. Cambridge, MA: Blackwell, 1992.

Stewart, Earl L. *African American Music: An Introduction*. New York: Schirmer, 1998.

Tedlock, Dennis. *The Spoken Word and the Work of Interpretation*. Philadelphia: University of Pennsylvania Press, 1983.

Tsur, Reuven. *Poetic Rhythm: Structure and Performance: An Empirical Study in Cognitive Poetics*. Berne, Switzerland: Lang, 1998.

Walser, Robert. "Rhythm, Rhyme, and Rhetoric in the Music of Public Enemy." In *Critical Essays in Musicology*. Ed. Allan F. Moore. London: Ashgate, 2007. 363–386.

West, Cornel. *The Cornel West Reader*. New York: Basic Civitas, 1999. 87–118.

8 Thinking Inside the Box: A Short View of the Immorality and Profaneness of Television Studies

C. W. MARSHALL AND TIFFANY POTTER

There is a widespread sense that popular media are consumed by people with inadequate education and no ideas of their own: "the young, the ignorant, and the idle." Social conservatives argue for the "danger" of media that engage in "scandal" and "smuttiness" that "in effect degrade human nature." Given, however, that the first quotation is from Samuel Johnson's 1750 discussion of the new genre of the English novel, and the second from Jeremy Collier's 1698 attack on popular theatrical productions,[1] modern objections to television's supposed frivolousness seem rather benign. Every new art form seems to struggle first with early perceptions of its failure to live up to the standards of existing forms, and then with arguments that excessive attention to such forms will contribute to the lowering of intellectual and social standards.

As J. Paul Hunter notes of the early novel, "[L]iterary protectionists had, early on, begun to worry about competition from the popular culture that novels represented" (26). That protectionism continues with a vengeance in many academic institutions. This chapter will argue that television occupies a similar place in the twentieth and twenty-first centuries: a narrative experience shared by people of all classes and domestic geographies (and often international ones too, in the case of American television). Janet Wasko is right when she asserts that television is "a storyteller, if not THE storyteller for [our] society. . . . television inevitably is a fund of values, ideals, morals, and ethical standards. In other words, television is an ideological source that cannot be overlooked in modern societies" (3). Less convincing, however, is her repetition of old arguments that offer justification of the medium as a stepping-stone to ostensibly real literature: "Despite disparaging comments about television's impact on print culture, some would point out that TV may serve as a catalyst for reading, as viewers may follow up on TV programs by getting books on the same subjects or reading authors whose work was adapted for the programs" (4). This perspective on television ("The more you know . . .") denies television's centrality as cultural discourse, rendering it secondary to print even in the introduction to a book titled A *Companion to Television*. Our interest in this chapter is not to pursue the reductive question "Is television literature?" It is, rather, to establish that methodologies of literary studies can be used to illuminate televisual narrative, and thus that television is a mode that contributes powerfully to the long history of the description and recreation of culture for audience consumption.

THE FRANKFURT SCHOOL AND TELEVISION STUDIES

Beyond the overly inclusive definition of "academic research on television," *television studies* is a somewhat slippery term, not least because of its high level of what has been called disciplinary hybridity. More than most fields of scholarly investigation, television studies flourishes in an environment of multidisciplinarity: departments of English, communications, film studies, theater, sociology, psychology, business, ethnography, women's studies, African American studies, and cultural studies, for example, might all house faculty members who study television. The handful of formal departments of television studies house scholars trained in very different traditional disciplines, united by the social and artistic phenomenon they study. Television is thus conceptualized along distinct and at times conflicting polarities: audience and reception (sociological studies of the impact of television on families and children, for example); ownership (including the economics of mass media and its relationship to ideology); distribution (television as cultural product, including issues of regulation of media); and cultural documentation (including analyses of specific programs under rubrics such as race or gender studies, or discussions of the cultural implications of television programs or genres as reflections and mediations of contemporary life).

One of the earliest approaches to the study of television originated, ironically, in the 1930s, long before the first program ever hit the airwaves. Members of the Frankfurt School in many ways began the systematic critical approach to studies of mass communication and culture with their study of what they termed "culture industries" and their work in the reproduction of contemporary societies. The Frankfurt School was the first to argue that since mass culture and communications stand at the center of leisure activity, they are critical agents of socialization, and so warrant intensive investigation and analysis. Given the era of the initial thinking, it is unsurprising that the Frankfurt School exhibits Marxist leanings in its original framework, reading mass communication as a device used to integrate the working class into capitalist societies. Students of the Frankfurt approach are generally more interested in problems of production and audience than in the content of cultural media, though textual analysis is still present as a secondary approach.

While the Frankfurt School was hugely influential in early television studies, only one of the prominent members of the school actually wrote on television per se, and even then, T. W. Adorno's "How to Look at Television" carries on the Frankfurt School's significant distinctions between high and low culture, with low culture such as television warranting only occasional consideration in a comparative context with more-established narrative modes. Still, later generations of scholars building on (and regularly challenging) the Frankfurt approach have long acknowledged the importance of television as part of contemporary cultural phenomena. Despite the Frankfurt School's waning influence in modern studies of television, its importance lies in its early recognition of media culture as a complex, multidimensional phenomenon, requiring a combination of social-science-based communication theory and textual analysis.

Over the course of the 1970s and 1980s, television studies evolved in such a way that three primary critical threads emerged: the less formal journalistic approach, which reviews recent television programs; the literary-critical approach, which studies television productions in the same way that literary and dramatic criticism examines novels and plays; and the social scientific approach, which examines the production, circulation, and function of television in contemporary society. Andrew Lockett argues that it makes sense to consider television studies in the same breath as the nearly universally recognized scholarly discipline of cultural studies, which he defines concisely as "the study of *popular* culture, particularly *contemporary* culture from a *critical-theoretical* perspective" in a way that is especially concerned with "subjectivity and power–how human subjects are formed and experience their lives in cultural and social space." Lockett's claim that "Cultural Studies and Television Studies are the proverbial twins separated at birth" (24)[2] seems an indication of the pervasive reach of television. This reach in turn authorizes the need for discursive modes of narrative analysis that are geared toward television specifically. Scholars working within the disciplinary focus of gender and race studies have yielded productive studies of television, as they consider television as a source of simplified representations of women and raced communities and, more important, as a creator of norms, codes, and ideologies of power around these groups. This approach, then, encompasses the production and content of television, as well as its communication and reception.

Much television criticism has engaged the problem of representation, and one might think that postmodern thinking–where boundaries between reality and unreality become permeable, where the artificial becomes more real than the real, and where perceived reality is read as an effect produced by the models and codes that precede it in experience and media–would be particularly useful. As Doug Kellner argues, some of the more sociologically situated postmodern thinkers, like Jean Baudrillard, "assert that television is pure noise and a black hole where all meaning and messages are absorbed in the whirlpool and kaleidoscope of the incessant dissemination of images and information to the point of total saturation, where meaning is dissolved and only the fascination of discrete images glow and flicker in a mediascape within which no image any longer has any discernible effects" (42). Baudrillard's indictment is characteristically exaggerated, but it is useful as a marker of something of a break between the social sciences and literary branches of television studies.[3] If one accepts television as mere noise, where any actual content dissolves, it's nearly impossible to accept it as functionally literary. But it is also essential to note that just as readers approach traditional text in different ways (from the disciplinary differences of scholars to the casual perception of the beach reader, often of the same narrative), audiences watch television in different ways too. Some, to be sure, do let it wash over them, without any critical engagement. This in itself is no different for some readers of books. The existence of heterogeneous responses to a work demands a scholarly response.

And so once again the question of high and low culture arises. As Horace Newcomb explains, "Philosophically, scholars in this movement [of television studies] often felt the works they wished to examine were more indicative of larger cultural preferences, expressive of a more 'democratic' relationship between works and audiences than the 'elite' works selected, archived, and taught as the traditional canon of humanistically valued forms of expression" ("Development" 20). The social relevance of a television program that reaches several million people per screening versus that of a novel that reaches several thousand over the course of its life seems difficult to challenge. This sense of a division between the elite and the democratic within narrative media can also be refocused, however, within television studies. Certainly it is tempting to articulate a canon of television studies in what is now widely termed "quality television," since studies of *The Sopranos*, *The Wire*, and *The West Wing* are fairly easy to sell to doubters as "important" cultural documents. Like most literary disciplines, however, television studies strives to resist the constraints of canon, recognizing that genres like science fiction and animated comedy in fact use their presumptive frivolousness to create a space for often razor-edged engagements of their cultures of production. Ronald D. Moore's reimagined *Battlestar Galactica*, Matt Groening's *The Simpsons*, and Trey Parker and Matt Stone's *South Park* are themselves sites of scholarly analysis as they use the comic or the alien to create space for social criticism, explicit political commentary, and critiques of contemporary ideology. As Julie D'Acci has pointed out, television is not just a technology, but is (like literature, we note) "a social institution with varied relationships to the countries in which it is produced and/or consumed, and to the economic, religious and ideological frameworks of those countries" (qtd. in Miller 91).

SOME PARAMETERS OF TELEVISION NARRATIVE

Television itself is not a literary genre. It is instead a medium (or mode) providing narratives of a variety of genres. As a medium, it can adapt preexisting genres (television westerns developed in the 1950s building directly on cinema's serial westerns); it can provide new audiences for genres (the televising of sports allows financial and geographic boundaries to be dissolved in athletic fandom); and it can enable the viability of some genres that could not or did not flourish outside of the medium (game shows, in which contestants win prizes provided by corporate sponsors, do particularly well, since the product is presented to the audience visually, and the distinction between advertising and program is irretrievably blurred). But in providing a literary analysis of television, it makes sense to think in terms of a unified whole because of the nature of the demands placed on the television audience.

Television requires commitment. In the traditional model of television consumption, the viewer is expected to set aside a single time, on a set day of the week, to invest in the television experience. Unlike the cinema, where the spectator chooses which screening to attend, or a novel, where each reader's reading pace and habits condition the rate and pace at which the narrative is absorbed, television imposes shapes and tempos on its audience. It changes and dictates behavior. This in turn affects network decisions about scheduling, as the following example makes clear (much of this discussion is focused on the North American television experience, since its global impact has been the greatest).

Between 1982 and 2004, NBC has experienced ratings dominance on Thursday nights in North America with its usual combination of four thirty-minute situation comedies and an hour-long drama broadcast between 8:00 PM and 11:00 PM.[4] The marketing strategy asserts that the viewer benefits from consuming a variety of programs with a unified time commitment. When successful, the combination of popular narratives generates particular results. Advertising revenues skyrocket as the viewership habituates itself to the investment of time within specific constraints. Once established, the network can juxtapose narratives, with less successful or newer shows placed at the half-hour following an established ratings hit. A program's success is determined at least in part by its place in the week's lineup, and there are many examples of narratively aggressive programming losing audience share because of an irregular broadcast schedule, as with Joss Whedon's *Firefly* (Fox, 2002), or because of changing days and time slots, as with Paul Attanasio's *Homicide: Life on the Street* (NBC, 1993–1999), based on David Simon's book.

In such cases, a show's popularity is effectively severed from its literary value or dramatic interest. Narrative experiments will often lack the supportive infrastructure that would allow a program to extend over many seasons: a narrative's longevity is tied not to creative aspirations, but to its ability to attract a consistent audience and thus consistent advertising. Successful shows are therefore in most cases directed toward establishing a large popular following, whereas experiments of form are both costly and unlikely to receive the support needed for popular success, as with Steven Bochco's combination of police drama and musical theater, *Cop Rock* (ABC, 1990), which was canceled after eleven episodes. Successful experiments in narrative form can still occasionally emerge, however: *24* (Fox, 2001–2010) purported to present a story in real time, with each one-hour weekly episode representing the next hour in Jack Bauer's day. By blocking time so rigidly (with the appearance of a 1:1 correspondence, as each season became a single, event-filled day in the main character's life), the creators constructed a perception of verisimilitude out of the conventional structure of the hour-long scripted drama.

Since unusual or intellectually demanding television narratives are unlikely to generate sufficient revenues for a major North American network, innovation is likely to originate outside of network television. Although changes in the technology of watching television have changed this situation in the twenty-first century, for the bulk of the medium's programming in North America this still holds true. In the United Kingdom, a different model exists, which favors shorter-run programs that are able to gauge success by measures other than length of run. There, programs produced by the BBC do not need corporate sponsorship, since they are funded in the greatest part by television licensing fees, collected by the government through a bizarre enforcement system.[5] This allows a greater range of experimentation, and it is perhaps unsurprising that many British sitcoms have been adapted for North American markets only after their commercial merits have been established in a parallel market.

Different markets establish different measures of success. In North America, the success of the animated comedy *The Simpsons* (Fox, 1989–) can be seen as the primary cause for the establishment of Fox as the fourth major network, since it provided a challenge to the complacent network schedules at ABC, NBC, and CBS through its engagement with popular culture and its use of animation in a show primarily targeted at adults and not children. The record for the longest-running animated series only pertains to one cultural market, however: in Japan, *Sazae-san* (Fuji, 1969–), broadcast Sunday nights at 6:30–7:00 PM, has produced more than 2,000 episodes.

The model of television production and its prevalence in society has two major social consequences. First, television becomes an assumed point of cultural literacy and cultural connectivity: for example, Americans are expected to know the theme song of *Gilligan's Island* (CBS, 1964–1967), memorized from repeated viewings of the show in syndication (reruns). Second, the commercial impulse toward homogeneous (and homogenized) narratives is reinforced by community and government watchdog groups, such as the Parents Television Council, which advocate censorship in the interests of protecting children from televised representations of sex, violence, and profanity. This effort has been met with aggressive challenges from the medium itself. The *South Park* episode "It Hits the Fan" (episode 66; initially broadcast 20 June 2001) uses the word "shit" 162 times, each tracked with a counter appearing on-screen, within a narrative concerning the use of the word in an episode of a police TV show.

There are three other variables that need to be remembered when approaching a television program as literature. First, television is a collaborative medium. Even when a series creator is identified as the principal creative impulse (drawing on auteur theory as developed for interpreting cinema), the efforts of many individuals may be examined as providing a unique contribution to the combined whole. This is true of many genres and media, but it must be remembered when a given television narrative is being examined. Second, television benefits from mass distribution. The viewer does not make a decision to invest financially in a particular narrative, but has already decided to bring the medium into the home. Since it is perceived to be a utility (on par with the telephone and electricity), television is a remarkably easy medium to consume. Even the most financially restricted families generally have access to over forty channels in the United States and Canada, and many programs produced for television can be watched free online within hours of their original broadcast through network websites, authorized collector sites such as Hulu, and myriad unauthorized online reproductions. The decision for most is not whether to watch, but what to watch. Third, the economics of television production means that the consumer does not pay for individual programs. Television production is funded almost exclusively by advertising. No matter how much autonomy viewers believe they exert in their choice of television viewing, the economics insists that the audience itself is the commodity being sold. Television networks sell access to a particular audience (which is conceived in terms of a likely demographic) to advertisers. In exchange for the ability to broadcast commercials during a particular program, advertisers pay the networks, which in turn invest in programs designed to capture that demographic. In a related model, specialty music channels such as MTV devote meaningful portions of their programming to short music videos of individual songs that are paid for and produced by the musicians or their labels as a form of self-promotion. This creates an inherent competitiveness among bands to create the slickest product, and allows the station to broadcast only those videos with the highest appeal. This in turn allows the station to package its audiences more specifically for sale to advertisers. Literary narrative in the medium of television is the means of providing the demographic to advertisers.

And this explains the single biggest defining feature for any narrative that originates on broadcast television. Unlike almost every other literary medium, television narrative is regulated by its length. Most programs produced for consumption in North America are timed precisely to twenty-two or forty-two minutes in length, and then broadcast over thirty minutes or an hour, with the remainder of the time filled with commercials. Most literary genres – theater, cinema, the novel, preliterate oral epic – are not governed so precisely by length. Even with those that are governed by length, such as the fourteen-line sonnet or the twenty-two-page American comic book or the contributions to this volume (which are restricted to a maximum length, though not by word total), the pace of consumption is determined by the reader. With television, however, every broadcast is governed by the requirement to allow advertising (and this requirement has increased over time: there are roughly twice as many commercials now as there were in the 1960s).[6]

THE FORM OF TELEVISION NARRATIVE

An awareness of the economic and formal pressures on television narrative is sobering, and exists in tension with the explicit goals of the artists and professionals who produce television programs, many of whom, we must assume, are sincere in their desire to entertain through their art. Despite these pressures, the narratives are indeed effective, in part because they are consumed and internalized within the comfortable space of the home, and in part because the spectator has mentally committed a given period of time to the consumption of television.

Reinforcing the comfort of repetition, television typically offers serial narratives. For the creators, this imposes limits in terms of preparation time, with new episodes required on a weekly basis. With some programs, filming might be only a few weeks ahead of the broadcast schedule (even less for a daily soap opera). But since the goal is to attract viewers week after week, a number of patterning devices exist, which link one episode to another. Obviously, the repetition of characters and situations from one episode to another offers a degree of familiarity. But even a show like *The Twilight Zone* (CBS, 1959–1964), in which new characters, actors, and narratives were offered each week, provided continuity through the introductions provided by series creator Rod Serling.

The analysis of the narratives of television can operate at any of a number of levels. There is literary interest in the narrative patterning of an individual episode, which itself is punctuated by regularly timed commercial breaks. For a program such as *The Muppet Show*

(1976–1981),[7] which used Jim Henson's distinctive puppets, familiar directly or indirectly to audiences from children's programming (*Sesame Street*, 1969–), in a musical-comedy variety show evoking vaudeville, the presence of a different guest star each episode served as the principal identifying feature. Individual scenes within the program, however, were framed by network commercial breaks, enabling a clear articulation between songs or sketches.

Narrative cohesion can also serve to link individual episodes into larger structural units. A short string of episodes might share common features, in what might be called a narrative arc. Even relatively unchallenging television narratives, such as the sitcom *The Brady Bunch* (ABC, 1969–1974), about a blended family with six children, could create a three-episode arc set during a family vacation in Hawaii, at the beginning of its fourth season (episodes 73–75; Sept.–Oct. 1972).

The economics of U.S. television production is more interested in the season,[8] however, since a network typically has contracts with actors that cover one year's worth of programming. Today, a standard television season represents twenty-two episodes, though there are many reasons for this number to be higher or lower; since some programs are canceled, there is need for "mid-season replacements," and for such programs the initial season might be shorter. The start of a new season will typically introduce cast changes, introducing new characters as the network hires different actors. An extreme example of a season as an integral narrative unit can be seen in the decision in *Dallas* (CBS, 1978–1991) to reintroduce in a cliffhanger a character who had been killed at the end of the previous season in a car crash, which meant that the entirety of season nine was a dream. The reintroduction of a popular actor at the start of a new season did not make up, however, for the narrative betrayal felt by the fans who had chosen to invest their time watching the thirty-one episodes over the course of the 1985–1986 year.[9]

An entire series may serve as one continuous narrative unit, able to be examined for its overall patterning. J. Michael Straczynski's science fiction series *Babylon 5* (1993–1998) was conceived as a five-year story, with each season representing one year. Occasionally, these layers overlap, and one of the most sophisticated narrative gestures in a comedy was seen in the final episode of *Newhart* (CBS, 1982–1990), "The Last Newhart" (8.24, episode 184; 21 May 1990). In the final scene, Dick Louden (played by Bob Newhart, the actor whose name was identified with the show) wakes up in bed next to his wife, except that she is no longer Joanna Louden (Mary Frann), his wife over the 184 episodes of the series, but Emily Hartley (Suzanne Pleshette), who had been the wife of Dr. Robert Hartley (also played by Bob Newhart) in *The Bob Newhart Show* (CBS, 1972–1978): the entire run of *Newhart* was subordinated to a dream in another comedy series, in a homage to the *Dallas* disaster and revealing the latent pun in the episode's title.

The manipulation of all of these levels can be seen in David Lynch's surreal *Twin Peaks* (1990–1991). Most of the thirty episodes each occupy a single day in the life of a small town in Washington state in which a high school student, Laura Palmer, has been murdered. Laura can be seen as a martyr for the series: her death before the series begins is what motivates FBI agent Dale Cooper's arrival in the first episode ("Pilot"/"Northwest Passage," episode 1.01; 8 April 1990). While her murder is apparently solved, the cliffhanger at the end of the second season, just before the series was canceled ("Episode 29"/"Beyond Life and Death," episode 2.22; 10 June 1991), put this into question. Similarly, the first season (with only eight episodes) ended with Agent Cooper being shot, his fate uncertain for the summer ("Episode 7"/"The Last Evening," episode 1.08; 23 May 1990); this necessarily created metatextual associations with the "Who Shot J.R.?" cliffhanger at the end of season three of *Dallas* (episode 54; 21 Mar. 1980), which (as the answer to the question was revealed in the following season) generated the highest-rated television episode in U.S. history at that time, with an estimated 83 million viewers.[10] *Twin Peaks* eschews linear narrative techniques, and instead juggles a large cast of mysterious, quirky, or upsetting characters who seem to be connected more by stream-of-consciousness than by the rigid patterning of episodes. By downplaying the divisions imposed on television narrative by the broadcast schedule, *Twin Peaks* garnered a cult following and demonstrated an increased sophistication in the TV representation of literary aesthetics.

Even in North America, however, not every channel is governed by the narrative patterns imposed by the commercial networks, though the same economic pressures exist. Public television (particularly the PBS network in the United States), which airs without commercials, is nevertheless not free of economic constraints: pledge drives replace advertising, centralizing the economy (as viewers send money directly to the station, rather than investing in advertised products and having the advertisers pay the station) but not fundamentally changing it. Because it asks for financial support from the viewers directly (not for individual programs, but for the type of programming offered by the network as a package), PBS produces shows that appeal to passionate niche markets with more narrow demographics than appeal to advertisers; corporate sponsorship remains, although it is not signaled with commercial interruptions, but with a general announcement as part of the program's title sequence.[11] Two particular types of show are associated with public broadcasting: children's programming, often with an explicit didactic function, and "high culture" art programs.

Until recently, children were not considered a separate demographic for marketers because they were not perceived to possess significant disposable income; perceptions on this have changed in recent decades. Gentle programming aimed at young children (whom advocacy groups believe would be unduly influenced by advertising) particularly finds a home on public television. *Mister Rogers' Neighborhood* (1968–2001) represents one of the most successful incarnations in North America, as Fred Rogers speaks directly to the camera, makes crafts or plays games with friends, sings songs, and encourages the use of imagination in the Neighborhood of Make-Believe. In the United Kingdom, *Blue Peter* (BBC, 1958–) has done much the same and for longer, but with a variety of presenters and a much greater range in its format. Educational children's programming has become an important part of the daily routine for many parents of young children, and is widely seen as an acceptable activity for children.

Television has always been devalued for its place outside of high culture (as the presence of this chapter in this book attests), but because of the medium's ability to penetrate into homes, the opportunity exists for large audiences to be gathered on a national scale for narratives that would not be able to attract sufficiently large audiences locally. Several programs exemplify this model. *Masterpiece* (PBS, 1971–; formerly *Masterpiece Theatre*) typically offers adaptations of novels and biographies, often presenting North American audiences with British-made series, including *I, Claudius, The Jewel in the Crown,* and *Upstairs, Down-*

stairs.[12] *Great Performances* (PBS, 1972–) presents concerts, ballets, and operas, as does *Live from Lincoln Center* (PBS, 1976–). By broadcasting other art forms, television provides access to entertainments that otherwise would be ephemeral and site-specific, but in itself this does not advance the medium as a means of providing new forms of literary narrative.

TECHNOLOGY AND TELEVISION TODAY

A number of advances in the technology of television have fundamentally changed how the medium is consumed. Some of these changes are at the level of delivery (and therefore correspond with a change in authorial practice) and others are at the point of reception (and therefore correspond to a change in reading practice). Both levels affect the way a television narrative is interpreted.

At the point of delivery, two major changes can be identified. The first is the proliferation of channels, which has created the possibility of the 500-channel universe. More channels becoming available to consumers as part of the provision of cable television to their homes[13] decreases the influence of network decisions that have traditionally catered to mainstream, middle-class demographics. The growth of demographic-specific specialty channels (focused on children's programming, comedy, pornography, food, home design, and even golf), funded by more closely targeted advertising, provides more choice to the viewer, but also almost automatically precludes large audiences. This has diminished the influence of the major networks and increased the total amount of television programming being produced, but the majority of the programming available will never achieve large cultural influence: the golf channel will never become fodder for water-cooler conversations.

Further, the option to pay directly for individual channels through subscriptions makes a different model of broadcasting possible. Originally, such channels offered movies and pay-per-view sporting events, but they have come to specialize in their own programming. In the United States, HBO (Home Box Office), AMC, and Showtime are associated with the most sophisticated fictional narratives on television. Without the constraints of corporate advertisers, these channels present more adult-oriented content, not just with swearing, nudity, and violence, but also with a developed literary sensibility. Programming on such subscription-based premium channels does not need to conform to hour or half-hour blocks, and can address topics deemed too sensitive for commercial television, such as drug use, homosexuality, political corruption, and the failings of the American school and penal systems, all of which were represented in a single series, David Simon's *The Wire* (HBO, 2002–2008). The change in the delivery system has fundamentally changed the nature of the television narrative.

At the point of consumption, the development of television-related technology has allowed viewers to begin to take control of the strictures previously imposed by commercial television. In the early 1980s, VCRs first allowed time shifting, permitting viewers to watch their favorite programs at a time they determined and not at the time imposed by networks. The devices also enabled viewers to watch two programs broadcast at the same time, by recording one while watching the other, again diminishing the imposition of network branding. More recently, digital video recorders have allowed viewers to edit commercials automatically, both shortening viewing time and asserting control over the viewing process. These developments allow viewers to subvert the traditional television funding model; no longer is the audience only a commodity sold to advertisers by the networks.

A parallel development is the widespread availability of complete television seasons or series on DVD (and related technologies). For someone willing to invest the purchase price, the only remaining benefit to watching broadcast television is not having to wait for the DVD release. Since the cultural impact of television leads to immediate social capital (evidenced in the ability to discuss a favorite show, for example), the direct purchase of television seasons has not eliminated the need for cable television (which also provides news, sports, and other time-sensitive programming).[14] Even this is being eroded, however, by downloadable programs, which are available through the internet on an episode-by-episode basis, often within hours of the initial television broadcast. These technologies enable new behaviors and fundamentally change the medium, and with that we should expect the narratives to change as well.

FOUR EXAMPLES

Television is a dynamic medium that has inserted itself into global media culture pervasively, and literary analysis yields meaningful insights that enhance the appreciation of television. Television can be analyzed with the tools of traditional cinema and other filmic narrative (with discussions of camera angles, editing, mise-en-scène, etc.): we take the value of such approaches to be self-evident and not needing independent demonstration. What separates the analysis of television from most other literary media is the legitimacy of examining the work at all its structural levels: it is meaningful to study an episode, a season, or a series as an enclosed unit, and it is possible to articulate changes in theme and character across these units. In what follows, short examples apply traditionally successful modes of literary analysis to a genre, a single episode, a season, and a series. This set of examples suggests a richness of such approaches that is not always available in the analysis of other literary forms: we almost never limit discussion to a single act of a play, a single stanza of a poem, or a single chapter of a novel.

Examining a Genre: Reality Television

Game shows, in which ordinary (non-actor) contestants compete for cash and prizes, offer a particular form of audience identification. The viewer cheers them on as they answer questions posed by the host or compete in other tests of skill or endurance. There is a sense of vicarious identification, so that when an individual wins a new car on *The Price Is Right* (CBS, 1972–), the viewer feels satisfaction, thinking, "I could have done that." Every episode offers a rags-to-riches story in miniature, and even when it is unsuccessful (and the contestant goes home with nothing), the opportunity for success always remains. The literary interest in the game-show narrative resides not in the individual story of a given contestant—it is rare for the identity of a contestant to enter the larger popular consciousness[15]—but in the shared wish-fulfillment fantasy offered by the program itself. Game shows function on a mythic scale, where the individual story is less important than the pattern extrapolated from repeated viewings of multiple programs.

A modern variation on the game show is the so-called reality show, such as *Survivor* (the U.S. incarnation of which airs on CBS, 2000–), which offers prizes to non-actor contestants who compete within an imposed set of rules. The principal distinction between these genres is only one of scale: what happens in a single episode of a game show is extended over a season for a reality show, with correspondingly larger prizes. Both of these models require few professionals in front of the camera, and consequently production is cheaper than many other forms of television.

Other types of reality television shows remove the game element and offer documentary-style stories: *Cops* (Fox, 1989–) employs a cinema verité style as actual police officers are recorded on video conducting investigations and arrests. The proposal for a show without writers held particular appeal during the 1988 Writers Guild of America strike, and the financial benefits quickly became apparent. Other models of reality television offer self-improvement (rewarding weight loss, providing fashion insights) or renovations (to homes, cars, and businesses), or showcase specialized artistic talent (e.g., *So You Think You Can Dance*, Fox, 2005–).

The audience appeal of such programming resides in the elevation of apparently ordinary individuals to celebrity status (an illusion created in large part simply by the fact that they are being televised), which permits both identification and schadenfreude. The perception of authenticity is, however, a conceit of the medium. All of these programs shape the narrative presented to the audience: when cameras have captured a certain amount of "reality," the selections made in what material is presented to an audience sculpt a story or series of stories in a replication of the authorial function. Further, producers structure potential narratives in advance, as strong, often volatile personalities are selected to represent the ordinary individual, and then the participants are placed in extreme situations. And, of course, in television's version of the observer effect in particle physics, the presence of the camera crews recording the events also affects the reality depicted. While the final edited version often downplays or eliminates the continual presence of the camera, there can be no doubt that as it is recording its immediacy heightens the potential for conflict. Reality television therefore offers a new means for sculpting literary narrative.[16]

Examining an Episode: South Park *and Race*

Two of the literary approaches most widely used in television scholar-ship are those of race studies and gender studies. And once again, such methodologies illuminate not just the one-hour dramas that are often assumed to represent "quality television," but also other forms of televisual narrative. Whether or not it stakes claim to realism, all televi-sion is a process of representation,[17] in which "commonsense" ideas of cultural truth are concurrently reflected and created by narratives for popular consumption.[18] In more formal terms, meaning is produced through practice.

South Park (Comedy Central, 1997–), a half-hour animated com-edy much decried for its at times shocking content, earned a Peabody Award for excellence in television in 2006. Because it has taken on ev-erything from the Middle East to disability, homosexuality to abortion, Scientology to pedophilia in the course of its run, the show has touched on several of the sorts of narratives that typify the conventionally liter-ary, even if it has done so in ways that have caused certain episodes to be banned from broadcast. Its frequent distastefulness, however, is part of what makes literary approaches to its discussion so useful: things are almost never as simple as they seem.

A seventh-season episode titled "Red Man's Greed" (7.07; 30 April 2003), for example, offers the opportunity for analysis of ideas of in-digeneity, race, and the constructed nature of cultural self-narrative. The basic narrative is simple and typically offensive:[19] Native Ameri-cans attempt to level the town of South Park to create a freeway from Denver to their casino; the townspeople resist, and bet their collective wealth of $10,000 at the casino in an attempt to gain enough money to buy back the rights to the town; they win, but then decide to "let it ride" and lose it all. There is a bulldozer standoff, and then passive resistance, to which the casino owners respond by rubbing naked Chi-nese men on blankets so that they can infect the protesters with severe acute respiratory syndrome (SARS). When Premise-Running-Thin, the son of Chief Runs-with-Premise, is saved from SARS by the "ancient white middle-class medicine" of chicken soup, Sprite, and DayQuil, the crisis is averted and the status quo restored. Taken at face value, this is merely an ugly depiction of multiple racial stereotypes, but in the same narrative moment, the episode interrogates the very ideas behind both racialized identity and the grand American national narrative.

The episode deconstructs the American creation myth by remapping power and race: when the blatant greed and violence of some early European Americans is located on Native Americans instead, it is the destructiveness of the act, rather than any moral, social, or religious rationalization, that must be recognized by viewers. By removing for an episode their culture's tacit equation of whiteness with economic and social power, writer-producers Trey Parker and Matt Stone assert its presence the rest of the time, with an indictment that extends across the entire television medium. The character Randy's gasping assertion to his son that after the SARS infection "only 98% of us will survive to fight on" affirms this–despite this momentary disruption, the majority will soon reassert itself, regardless of the economic resistance implied by the Indian casino venture.

Similarly, by having the indigenous characters constantly dressed in feathers and fringe, in casinos decorated with tomahawk slot machines, the episode emphasizes the constructedness of racialized identity and the various levels of self-consciousness involved in its performance. The Native Americans here perform a pastiche of their own cultural past (and that of indigenous nations from parts of America well outside Colorado) as a device to gain economic power by playing on the age-old assumption of the ease of tricking/stealing from an Indian. They fashion themselves as old-fashioned to tempt "stupid white people" into their casino, thus turning the conventional assumption of economic guilelessness into a device of economic empowerment. And as much as the Native Americans are the villains of the piece for their desire to eliminate one way of life in the service of another's economic agenda, the role reversal in the retelling of the 400-year-old narrative is so explicit that critical viewers are struck less by the obvious racial typification of indigeneity (performed consciously for profit in most of the episode) than by the relatively original critique of white entitlement and the absence of any substantive cultural identity in the "podunk, whitebread, redneck mountain town" of South Park.[20]

This acknowledgment of the constructed nature of social identity is affirmed in the "white middle-class" characters: they lack any sort of community identity at all (even their "shaman" is a white man in a trailer who has to appropriate a native tradition and wear a wolfskin headdress to attempt to convey any sense of spirituality). Their ancient medicine is DayQuil, a product that has existed only since 1974 (but that is regularly advertised on television). Their battle song is Pat Benatar's "Love Is a Battlefield" (1983). Even as it clearly commodifies indigeneity for its own narrative (and profit), the episode puts into play the idea of all identity as commodity, and thus identity as social construction as it also explicitly racializes the usually presumptive normativity of whiteness by having South Park residents appropriate the language of cultural difference. The language of the episode, then, is notable not as an attack on indigenous economic aspiration, nor as merely a mockery of conflicting social values; rather, it is a deconstruction of the whole idea of explicitly regulated, ostensibly natural ideas of racialized identity. It eschews the more conventional assimilationist approach to representing race (underplaying economic or cultural differences among ethnic groups) to take a more challenging approach to the ideas and implications behind difference in America. In this episode, as it so often is, *South Park* is a scourge of unthinking complacency and of the temptation to depend on generally facile and intellectually inadequate ideas of common knowledge.

Examining a Season: Buffy the Vampire Slayer
and the Destruction of Metaphor

At the end of season five in 2001, the main character of *Buffy the Vampire Slayer* (WB and UPN, 1997–2003) had been killed and the creator's contract with the network had expired. The announcement that the show would continue on a new network (UPN) elicited some surprise. Though fans were delighted the show was continuing, the sixth season was widely perceived as being unsuccessful. The failures can be explained in terms of a fundamental repositioning of the central conceits of the series. The presiding metaphor of the series had insisted on the literal representation of what most teenagers inwardly suspect: high school is hell.[21] The show is set in small-town California, where Buffy, a cheerleader, is the Chosen One, the defender of the world: only she, as the Slayer, can hold back the demonic forces infiltrating through the Hellmouth in her town. All teenage fears are realized through this supernatural device: teachers really are out to get you, bullies really are monstrous pack animals, and your boyfriend really does change once you sleep with him.

The high school metaphor was relocated to a university in seasons four and five, but season six abandoned the trope of delayed adolescence almost entirely. Buffy is resurrected by magic, but remains uncommunicative and unsympathetic for most of the season: rather than enabling an integration into adulthood, the plotline restricted the possibility of character development. As a series, *Buffy* had always emphasized the integrity of the season as a narrative unit, introducing a different "Big Bad" each season as the young superhero's principal opponent. In season six, however, Buffy's trauma and isolation provide the darkness, and the opposition is presented for the most part comically in the Trio, three nerdy guys whose lair is in the suburban basement of one of their parents' homes.

The failures of the season, however, can be ascribed primarily to the decision to remove the application of the conceptual metaphor.[22] Whereas in previous seasons, stories of sexual violence were generally presented within the coded frame of a vampire's penetrating bite, in this season, imagination is surrendered, and both the violent and the mundane become real. Buffy continues to be assaulted by vampires, of course, but this is kept separate from the attempted rape by a trusted ally, with whom she had self-destructive consensual sex earlier in the season. Spike's later attempt to rape Buffy ("Seeing Red"; episode 6.19) literally collapses the integrity of the supernatural world that had been so carefully established. Since Spike is a vampire, this plot decision seemed to contradict the conceit of the series' previous vampire narratives.

The show's wit and creative strength resided in the literalization of conventional cultural metaphors. To this was added a new metaphor equating the consuming nature of sexuality and desire with the consumption of the body through vampirism. When that metaphor was violently abandoned, the viewership was left without the means to apply its established interpretive tools. The creative intentions for the season never rehabilitated Buffy, and in the final arc Buffy's best friend, Willow, becomes evil, as an extension of the violent death of her girlfriend and a plotline associating excessive magic use with drug addiction: again, the literal and metaphoric abut jarringly. The season refused to restore Buffy's heroic status, and the world-ending destruction is averted by Xander, an ordinary friend, who reminds Willow of the virtues of her own natural ordinariness. His offer of unconditional love to her and his employment as a carpenter throughout the season inserted Christological associations that had not been part of any previous series narrative.

The sixth season of *Buffy* involved loss for the viewer. The coherence of the heroic narrative, inverted in this series by its reformation in the sort of blonde teenage girl whom cinema typically configures through victimhood, is undermined in several ways. The process is systemic, and it asserts the narrative unity and provides cohesion to the season even as it creates discomfort for the viewer. The resurrected Buffy is not a character we fully recognize or care about; she is not the hero she was before, and it becomes necessary to cast about for a new one. Alienated, she alienates the viewership, and as the metaphor that has driven the series is dissolved, the audience is confronted with something it does not necessarily like or want to see: a vision of sexual violence and addiction. Can I please have my metaphor back?

Examining a Series: ER and Gender

The NBC series ER (1994–2009) provides an example of ongoing-narrative quality television that addresses national audiences, without the exclusionary forces of cable's viewer-pay system. It was both critically acclaimed and popular, a top-thirty show for nearly its entire run, including nine seasons in the top five, and received over 120 Emmy nominations. The show was lauded for its representations of race, homosexuality, and disability in its fictional medical community, and also for its images of women in medicine. For all of its forward-looking work on gender, however, the show had a marked tendency to erase female characters from its narrative with much less fanfare and thus much less acknowledgment of their importance to the show (and its fictionalized recreation of American medicine) than was the case when major male characters departed.

Within the narrative, nearly all of the women were written out in circumstances that emphasized emotional, physical, or economic weakness or the secondariness of professional life for women as opposed to men. This pattern suggests that, much like the world it purports to represent, ER created a façade of gender equality, but ultimately reinforced conservative stereotypes of femininity. By writing women out in narrative lines of professional failure, parenting and custody issues, ailing parents, and the need to be near male partners, ER reproduces one of America's most popular anti-feminist rhetorical gestures, where "[a]nxiety-producing tropes [are] circulated in the popular media in a hegemonic effort to retract feminist gains" (Lotz 108). In service to the economic pressures that produce television narrative, ER walks a line common in network television: it attempts to appeal to all politics in all ways (and thus to all female consumers), assuming that viewers do not think critically about the larger implications of fictional narrative. When we apply the methodologies of literary criticism, however, we recognize the cultural significance of the way that television creates fictions as normative realities, exactly like other conventionally literary genres have always done. This creates "community standards" even as television purports only to observe and reflect them.

Given the length of the show's run, many characters came and went; this discussion will focus on the central characters of the show's first five seasons (1994–1999), when ER had the most public attention and thus the greatest potential social significance. In contrast with the treatment of female characters, when a male character on ER left the series, the departure was foregrounded within the narrative structures that pattern commercial television. This increases the drama: male characters depart heroically, nobly, or shockingly. Doug Ross (George Clooney) is forced out for violating hospital rules when he helped a mother to give her pain-wracked, dying child an overdose of morphine; he is depicted as a noble warrior, fighting injustice to protect innocent children ("The Storm Part 2"; episode 5.15). Mark Greene (Anthony Edwards) fights a protracted battle with a brain tumor and is written out in a highly promoted "very special episode" of ER shot on location in Hawaii ("On the Beach"; episode 8.21). Robert Romano (Paul Mc-Crane) is killed when a helicopter falls on him in the ambulance bay ("Freefall"; episode 10.8). John Carter (Noah Wyle) moves to Africa to work with Doctors without Borders ("The Show Must Go On"; episode 11.22). Male characters, it appears, can be drawn away from the high-stakes medicine of the emergency room only by force (after noble rebellion), by death, or to save the world.

The principal exception to this pattern is Peter Benton (Eriq La Salle), a driven African American physician who is written out after eight seasons when his character opts to move to a job with regularized hours so that he can have more time with his girlfriend and deaf son. What differentiates this departure from those written for female characters is that the show gives him a heroic plotline in his last episode in order to confirm his status as a brilliant surgeon: he saves the life of a six-year-old gunshot victim in a highly dramatic series of scenes ("I'll Be Home for Christmas"; episode 8.10). Benton's departure is given the tenor of noble sacrifice, as a great surgeon chooses surprisingly to take on a presumably less-demanding job in order to have more time with his disabled son.

Female characters, in contrast, are written out with no heroics and a clear implication that they are following natural feminized paths out of Chicago or out of medicine, in what amounts to little more than kitchen-sink theater. The first example of the departure of a major female character occurs when Susan Lewis (Sherry Stringfield) moves to Phoenix to be close to her niece, whose custody she has been forced to surrender to her incompetent sister ("Union Station"; episode 3.8). The departure is marked not by any work-related conflict or grand medical gestures, but rather by what the writers present as a naturally feminine desire to care for a child. The episode ends with Mark Greene professing his love and begging her to stay, giving her departure emotional heft primarily by locating its significance in the life of Greene. Susan Lewis returns to the show in season eight, and leaves again early in season twelve. In the first episode of that season, we discover that the affluent John Carter has been granted tenure over her (perhaps because he has personally donated a wing to the hospital). In the reaction scene between the two, Lewis locates her professional desire in the domestic: "This is my home. This is where I started. This is where I want to stay." Her final scene on the series shows her being comforted by her husband; her last line is "I really wanted this," conveying her ambition and the level of her failure ("Cañon City"; episode 12.1). It is not until four episodes later, however, that another doctor mentions casually that she has left to take a tenure-track job at another hospital ("Wake Up";

episode 12.5). Unlike the dramatic and heroic circumstances surrounding the exits of male characters, Lewis is dispatched after seven seasons as insufficiently economically productive, demoted from Chicago to Iowa City, without even becoming the focus of the last scene of the episode (which is about Carter). The departure of Anna Del Amico (Maria Bello) is nearly identical: after season four, her character simply does not return, and we are told in passing that Del Amico has moved to Philadelphia to be with her boyfriend ("Day for Knight," episode 5.1).

After a strong storyline on being a single woman facing HIV infection, Jeanie Boulet (Gloria Reuben) leaves to adopt a child and become a stay-at-home parent ("Peace of the Wild Things"; episode 6.6). Jing-Mei Chen (Ming-Na) departs in season one because she feels that she cannot cope with applied medicine ("House of Cards"; episode 1.21), and after her return to the series for six seasons, she leaves County General (and apparently medicine) first to care for and then to bury her father ("Twas the Night"; episode 11.9). And most notably, after six seasons, nurse Carol Hathaway (Julianna Margulies) decides over the course of a single episode ("Such Sweet Sorrow"; episode 6.21) to move herself and her infant twin girls across the country to pursue a relationship with the girls' biological father and her on-again, off-again lover, Doug Ross. The narrative emptiness of this episode is reinforced by the absence of Ross from the entire preceding year of the show; Hathaway leaves for an idea of domesticity rather than for a real man, though Clooney's philandering character does greet her warmly in their one very short scene together at the end of the episode.[23] In the world presented by ER, women are removed from the literary narrative and the working world for one of two reasons: professional failure (as with Lewis's second departure and Chen's first), or the domesticating opportunities offered by the love of a good man or the chance to care for a parent or child.

The single exception to this pattern is Kerry Weaver (Laura Innes), a surgeon and administrator for thirteen seasons. After dozens of plotlines, most notably her coming out as a lesbian and the custody battle over her child after her lover's death, she leaves the hospital to host a television program in Florida ("House Divided"; episode 13.13). The comparative triviality of this job, combined with the fact that an additional draw is a possible domestic relationship with the woman who offers it to her, affirms that even such a strong and at times powerful woman would really like to be valued for being telegenic and well-spoken rather than for her medical expertise. In her departing scene, a female character notes that she would never have become a doctor or a mother were it not for Weaver's example. There are no grand heroics in her departure, and her significance is located in her role as mentor and mother, rather than as surgeon and leader (and that in the very scene in which she walks away from the life for which she is praised).

This examination of the plots and characterization of the primary female characters demonstrates that ER is constructed as a foundationally reassuring conservative cultural narrative: doctors are human but basically good; more people survive miraculously than die unexpectedly; men truly are heroic; and women really just want to be caregivers, if only the economics of society would allow them to do so. As such, ER is typical of a mode of dramas that has established the significance of the shift since the 1980s toward television as a "feminine medium" (Newcomb, "Climate" 5): television is addressed through advertising (its raison d'être) to women, the culture's primary purchasers. The series ER locates women in the traditionally masculinized sites of highly educated professional work in order to attract the most desirable audience (conventionally imagined as white and affluent). Although the show depicts female characters in a way that purports to represent positively a generally depoliticized third-wave feminism (which assumes equality, often considers feminism in the past tense, and experiences the fruits of feminism, without activism), it actually puts forth a powerful counternarrative as it over and over again asserts that all that really matters to women are the domestic sphere and the Jane Austen–like pleasures of a life removed from the problems of work.

APPLICATIONS AND CONCLUSIONS

Television can be used as a medium through which to teach literary methodology and theory, or it can be taught by itself as an independent narrative mode. Depending on the nature of the course, different pedagogical agendas assert themselves. By definition, a robust theoretical approach should be open to any text, and television provides a largely shared point of cultural contact that allows classroom time to be spent in discussion and analysis rather than in recounting plot (either through watching specific episodes or through summary). Because students are saturated with experience of the medium, their perception may be that it is inherently easy to understand. Using devices of literary study to consider television can therefore provide students with a less intimidating path into modes of analysis that are often seen as exclusive and alienating. Television can thus move literary theory (in all its forms, including poststructuralism, postcolonialism, feminism, or Marxism) from the preserve of the exceptional student and make it meaningful to a larger audience. There is therefore perhaps a parallel to New Historicist literary approaches that recognize that literary texts emerge in dialogue with their culture of production. In using literary methodologies to address television, students are encouraged to consider not only a single episode (for example), but also that episode within its internal narrative universe, and the relationship between that (often fictional) universe and the program's culture of production.

As a subject to be examined in itself, television offers unique circumstances of production, marketing, and delivery, and these impose restrictions that shape the narrative product. Once these variables are understood by students, their analysis of a specific television show in the classroom becomes the foundation for further independent analysis, producing a more engaged and culturally critical viewership. Most viewers consume television daily, but lack the basic vocabulary for the economics of television and the ability to see themselves as a product being sold to advertisers. Television studies as a discipline and the use of television as a literary text in the classroom invite students both to recognize the continuity of cultural narrative across different media and to acknowledge previously unrecognized influences of that medium on their experiences. What must not be done is simply to incorporate television into one's teaching on the assumption that in doing so one instantly purchases a sense of relevance with students. At a minimum, the analytical skills taught must be applicable to other programs and forms of narrative: every student should be able to transfer the classroom discussion of an episode of *True Blood* (HBO, 2008–), for example, to larger questions of the politics of difference (enacted through metaphors of race and sexuality in the American South), the permeability of the body, and the larger history of vampire narrative (in the novel, cinema, and television at least). We believe that the examples in this chapter provide a toolbox for such approaches, using literary methodologies to enable extension from television to the larger cultural discourse that exists outside of the box.

Television is not literature; television is a delivery system for different modes of narrative. That said, it is clear that both long-standing and newer methodologies of literary analysis can be used to illuminate both elements of narrative and elements of the cultures of production, just as they can in studies of literature, where analysis is not limited only to textual content, but includes the history of the book as a medium, the dialogic relationship between narrative and culture, and myriad other possibilities. Television is certainly not "the same" as literature. That's a good thing. Television uses genre, form, narrative, character, image, and other devices that we are all culturally trained to associate with the literature classroom, but it uses them in ways that are mediated by its overriding profit motive and the demand for audience retention. The serial narratives of the nineteenth century (where chapters of novels would appear in print one at a time, before the work was itself completed) produced some of the same creative pressures as television does. Dickens needed to sell books to survive, and he was indeed at times paid by the word, but he ran little risk of cancellation.

This discussion has necessarily been limited and has only been able to examine a small selection of the ways in which television can be defined in terms of other literary narratives. More important, however, are the opportunities that the form presents. Television offers creative minds unparalleled access to huge audiences, and it is a medium that encourages the wide consumption of multiple narrative forms. Television presents viewers with a range and volume of narratives that would have been unimaginable to any previous generation. Becoming critical readers of television, understanding its production motives and developing a vocabulary whereby it can be discussed meaningfully, increases our ability to interpret what is arguably the most powerful imaginative force yet produced.

NOTES

1. See Johnson's *The Rambler* 4 (1750) and Jeremy Collier's *A Short View of the Immorality and Profaneness of the English Stage* (1698). With what could be reference to the language of HBO programs like *The Wire, The Sopranos,* and *Deadwood,* Collier adds delightfully, "Goats and monkeys, if they could speak, would express their brutality in language such as this."

2. He continues, "[B]oth Television Studies and Cultural Studies draw from literary textual traditions, from sociology and mass communication and from the diverse sources of contemporary theory—feminist theory, structuralism, poststructuralism, postcolonial studies, queer theory and Marxist critical thought" (Lockett 24).

3. Baudrillard's work is, of course, also influential in literary studies, but in this case his discussion of television addresses it as a cultural medium rather than considering the narrative content it transmits.

4. Shows broadcast at this time have included (at 8:00) *The Cosby Show, Friends, My Name Is Earl,* (at 9:00) *Cheers, Seinfeld, Will and Grace, The Office,* and (at 10:00) *Hill Street Blues, L.A. Law,* and ER.

5. Nick Lowe writes, "The institutional structures of television production in the UK challenge some overseas viewers' willing suspension of disbelief. . . . But the result is a system which has historically supported adventurous public-interest filmmaking across all channels, while British cinema has mostly failed to keep up" (154).

6. Some networks have experimented with "special episodes" of nonstandard length in an effort to keep viewers watching beyond the rigid half-

hour schedule. While this may yield short-term benefits, it is ultimately self-defeating in terms of creating larger narratives, because key episodes cannot be rebroadcast in reruns without significant editing.

7. *The Muppet Show* was presented in first-run syndication: it was not produced by a network, but sold to different networks and stations individually, syndicated in its initial broadcast.

8. In the United Kingdom, this is termed a "series," though North American usage reserves this term for the complete run of all episodes of a program.

9. The popularity of *Dallas* declined significantly over the course of the season: "Dallas has slumped from second place to No. 17 in the US ratings," proclaimed the supermarket tabloid *News of the World* in May 1986, immediately after the character's reappearance in the season finale. Fans' disappointment was evident even before the new season began, as this commentary (later proved accurate) in TV *Guide* demonstrates: "Speculation has been rampant, the favored theory suggesting that Bobby's tragic death last year was all just Pam's bad dream, from which she awakens only to discover Bobby blithely lathered in soap in her shower. Besides rendering the entire past season's episodes meaningless, what a cheat that approach would be for audiences" (30 Aug. 1986).

10. The only two-part episode of *The Simpsons* so far, "Who Shot Mr. Burns?," yoked the last episode of season six (episode 6.25; 21 May 1995) with the first of season seven (episode 7.01; 17 Sept. 1995), and drew heavily on the cultural impact of the *Dallas* cliffhanger.

11. This is a holdover from the 1950s; programming such as *The Colgate Comedy Hour* (NBC, 1950–1955) announced the sponsor in the title, but also had performers on the show promoting products directly, removing any distinction between the program and the advertising.

12. *Masterpiece* is interesting not as an example of "television as literature," but rather "literature as television," since it lays claim to the cultural status of other art forms.

13. Along with television ratings, A. C. Nielsen has tracked the average number of television channels receivable in an American household: 18.8 in 1985; 33.2 in 1990; 41.1 in 1995; 74.6 in 2000; 96.4 in 2005; 130.1 in 2008. Citing changes to the technologies of television delivery, Nielsen ended its tracking of available channels in 2010.

14. The earliest history of television associates it with the immediacy of live broadcasting, but today live television is seldom used for presenting scripted fiction. A notable exception is the late-night sketch comedy program *Saturday Night Live* (NBC, 1975–), which capitalizes on the risks associated with immediate broadcast. Live television is a powerful tool that effectively gives a global scale to local events, even allowing a transnational awareness that has since been replicated only through the internet. Millions can watch a sporting event and see the results simultaneously, and information about world events increases awareness to a nearly unimaginable degree. See also the work of Marriott, who discusses the impact of television on the events of 9/11 and the galvanizing of American consciousness in response to the terrorist attacks.

15. Arguably, the success of Ken Jennings on *Jeopardy* (current syndicated series, 1984–), who won seventy-four successive games in 2004, is an exception to this, but as his example demonstrates, for a contestant to enter popular awareness requires truly unparalleled success: the previous *Jeopardy* record had been eight games, though before 2003 the number of successive victories had been capped at five.

16. The term "reality television" for the contrived situations described here should always be imagined within quotation marks, but television news, which might be thought to represent unmediated reality, employs exactly the same techniques in its presentation of events. For every short news segment, hours of recorded information are discarded, and the process of editing is consciously hidden from the viewer. Events are sculpted into a specific narrative of conflict, trauma, or human interest in order to cultivate and maintain viewer interest in exactly the same way as fictional narratives are manipulated.

17. On representation and the construction of common sense, see Stuart Hall.

18. Rebecca Tsosie, for example, has argued that members of the Supreme Court get their "truths" about indigenous people directly from popular culture: "Where does Rehnquist get his 'truth' about the Lakota people? . . . The stories told by non-Indians in film, art, literature, and history transform the 'Indian' into part of the story of white America" (322). The consciousness exhibited by *South Park* of such links among television and larger issues is clear, and it creates both indigenous and white cultures as such overessentialized commodities that the ridiculousness of any larger legal or social use of the televisual is explicit.

19. As is often true of *South Park*, some viewers found the episode to be offensive. For a conscientiously collect-

ed overview of the controversies raised by the series, see http://en.wikipedia.org/wiki/South_Park_controversies. All *South Park* episodes can be viewed free online at southparkstudios.com.

20. As it is described in the opening song of *South Park: Bigger, Longer, & Uncut* (1999).

21. The pervasive use of a single metaphor in this way is not unique to *Buffy*. *M*A*S*H* (CBS, 1972–1983), for example, was set during the Korean War, and was therefore at some remove from the immediate concerns of the America in which it was broadcast; this allowed much more direct satirical criticism of the war in Vietnam, which was contemporary with the series. A similar device patterns *Battlestar Galactica* (Space, 2003–2009) and its presentation of the ongoing war in Iraq; see Potter and Marshall.

22. On the last two seasons, see also Edwards, Rambo, and South.

23. Viewers will recall that this episode was anticipated much less for the departure of a central character than for that brief appearance by Clooney.

REFERENCES

Adorno, T. W. *The Culture Industry: Selected Essays on Mass Culture.* London: Routledge, 1991.

——. "How to Look at Television." *Quarterly of Film, Radio and Television* 8.3 (1954): 213–235.

Arthurs, Jane. "*Sex and the City* and Consumer Culture: Remediating Postfeminist Drama." *Feminist Media Studies* 3.1 (2003): 81–96.

Butler, Jeremy G. *Television: Critical Methods and Applications,* 3rd ed. Mahwah, NJ: Erlbaum, 2007.

Collier, Jeremy. *A Short View of the Immorality and Profaneness of the English Stage.* London, 1698.

Edwards, Lynne Y., Elizabeth L. Rambo, and J. B. South. *Buffy Goes Dark: Essays on the Final Two Seasons of "Buffy the Vampire Slayer" on Television.* Jefferson, NC: McFarland, 2008.

Fiske, John, and John Hartley. *Reading Television,* 2nd ed. New York: Routledge, 2003.

Hall, Stuart. "Cultural Identity and Cinematic Representation." In *Black British Cultural Studies: A Reader.* Ed. Houston A Baker Jr., Manthia Diawara, Ruth H. Lindeborg, and Stephen Best. Chicago: University of Chicago Press, 1996. 210–222.

——. "The Work of Representation." In *Representation: Cultural Representations and Signifying Practices.* Ed. Stuart Hall. London: Sage, 1997. 13–74.

Hunter, J. Paul. "The Novel and Social/Cultural History." In *The Cambridge Companion to the Eighteenth-Century Novel.* Ed. John Richetti. Cambridge: Cambridge University Press, 1996.

Johnson, Samuel. *The Rambler* (London) 4 (1750).

Kellner, Doug. "Critical Perspectives on Television from the Frankfurt School to Postmodernism." In *A Companion to Television.* Ed. Janet Wasko. Oxford: Blackwell, 2005. 29–47.

Kelso, Tony. "'And Now No Word from Our Sponsor': How HBO Puts the Risk Back into Television." In *It's Not TV: Watching HBO in the Post-Television Era.* Ed. Marc Leverette, Brian L. Ott, and Cara Louise Buckley. New York: Routledge, 2008. 46–64.

Leigh, Wendy. "Dallas Star Bobby Back in a Flash!" *News of the World* (May

1986). Rpt. *ultimatedallas.com* (n.d.). Web. Accessed 2 May 2011.

Lockett, Andrew. "Cultural Studies and Television." In *Television Studies*. Ed. Toby Miller. London: BFI Publishing, 2002. 24–27.

Lotz, Amanda. "Postfeminist Television Criticism: Rehabilitating Critical Terms and Identifying Postfeminist Attributes." *Feminist Media Studies* 1.1 (2001): 105–121.

Lowe, Nick. "The Screen of Orpheus." *Arion* 15.2 (Fall 2007): 149–156.

Marriott, Stephanie. *Live Television: Time, Space, and the Broadcast Event*. London: Sage, 2007.

Miller, Toby, ed. *Television Studies*. London: British Film Institute, 2002.

Newcomb, Horace. "The Development of Television Studies." In *A Companion to Television*. Ed. Janet Wasko. Oxford: Blackwell, 2005. 15–28.

——. "Television and the Present Climate of Criticism." In *Television: The Critical View*, 7th ed. Ed. Horace Newcomb. New York: Oxford University Press, 2008. 1–10.

Potter, Tiffany, and C. W. Marshall. *Cylons in America: Critical Studies in "Battlestar Galactica."* New York: Continuum, 2008.

Tsosie, Rebecca. "Reclaiming Native Stories: An Essay on Cultural Appropriation and Cultural Rights." *Arizona State Law Journal* 34 (2002): 299–358.

TV Guide. "Exploring the Mystery of Bobby's Return." TV Guide (30 Aug. 1986). Rpt. *ultimatedallas.com* (n.d.). Web. Accessed 2 May 2011.

Wasko, Janet. "Introduction." In *A Companion to Television*. Ed. Wasko Oxford: Blackwell, 2005. 1–12.

9   Middlebrow Lit and the End
                        of Postmodernism

CLINT BURNHAM

The death by suicide of American novelist David Foster Wallace in the fall of 2008 had a resonance that went beyond the eerie similarity between his great theme of sadness and the crippling depression from which he suffered. Wallace – the author of the mammoth *Infinite Jest*, over a thousand pages long, including over a hundred pages of footnotes – was arguably the last postmodernist, the last experimental fiction writer in American or Anglo American literature. I do not mean there were not others, that there are not others, but Wallace's death can be seen – *must be seen* – as the end of experimentalism.[1] Which is to say that twentieth-century literary modernism – running from the minimalism of Mansfield and the exuberance of Joyce and the vernacular of Hurston to the silences of Beckett and the plots of Barth and the verbosity of Gaddis and the punk of Acker – has finally come to a shuddering halt. And the second "proof" of this ending – the subject proper of this chapter – is how it has been coming for a while, how the decline since the 1970s of formal innovation in general, in the novel, in fiction, has come to be the status quo of what constitutes literature.

It might seem that I am flying the flag for postmodernism, for experimental writing, for formal innovation. But that is not quite it. Rather, it seems to me that if we take the Lionel Trilling moment – the early 1960s anecdote about how he was teaching Conrad's *Heart of Darkness* and noticed that students were no longer freaked out by "The horror, the horror" or "Mistah Kurtz, he dead" – as the beginning of a certain break with or within modernism, then perhaps the critical mass of middlebrow literature in college curricula indicates a similar moment today.

This chapter, then, is not so much – as many are in this collection – a proposition about how we need to teach certain heretofore neglected cultural forms. Rather, what I would like to do is to examine why it is that we teach (and also, why we should teach) a form that constitutes the silent majority of lit classes: the middlebrow novel. That is, I want to make the following argument: first of all (and this continues, perhaps, the preoccupations of this collection's introduction), not only is the category of literature itself fairly arbitrary and sometimes suspect, but this arbitrariness is performed in literary production itself, a claim I will support with examples from two American novels – Raymond Chandler's *The Big Sleep* (1939) and Richard Price's *Samaritan* (2003) – and then with a spirited defense of middlebrow or popular fiction by Stephen King. Second, in what makes up the bulk of this chapter, I will look at two other novels – Cormac McCarthy's *The Orchard Keeper* (1965) and Ian McEwan's *Saturday* (2005) – as a way of thinking about how middlebrow literature is constituted. McEwan's and McCarthy's books, I will argue, instantiate the great themes of this collection: the relationship between literature and an "outside," and the role of teaching in determining that relation.

Turning to Raymond Chandler and Richard Price, we can first remember that Chandler is notable for his positioning – not least in *The Simple Art of Murder* (first published in the *Atlantic Monthly* in December 1944) – of detective fiction between the popular and the highbrow. He accomplishes this matter of distinction partly on the basis of gender, disparaging particularly the "old ladies who jostle each other at the mystery shelf" (3). These are interlopers, for, as Nicola Humble argues in *The Feminine Middlebrow Novel*, "Detective fiction ranked high [in the middlebrow canon] as it was the preferred leisure reading of men, particularly intellectual ones" (13); "its ratiocinative elements [offered] the illusion of an active, intellectually engaged reader, rather than a passive abandonment, allowing the male reader to indulge in escapist reading without experiencing a feared loss of control" (53).

But it is in Chandler's mystery novel *The Big Sleep* that a constitutive anxiety about the instability of literary categories makes itself felt. The detective, Philip Marlowe, is investigating blackmail and has come across a pornography ring that uses a bookstore as a front:

> I let the door close softly behind me and walked on a thick blue rug that paved the floor from wall to wall. There were blue leather easy chairs with smoke stands beside them. A few sets of tooled leather bindings were set out on narrow polished tables, between book ends. There were more tooled bindings in glass cases on the walls. Nice-looking merchandise, the kind a rich promoter would buy by the yard and have somebody paste his bookplate in. At the back there was a grained wood partition with a door in the middle of it, shut. In the corner made by the partition and one wall a woman sat behind a small desk with a carved wooden lantern on it. (23)

Chandler's critique here, conveyed to us by the scopic gaze of a private eye, is concerned with how literature stands in for a kind of class consumption, the conspicuous consumption of Thorstein Veblen or Bourdieu. Books are little more than a high-status commodity – that you "buy by the yard" – and that decorate a room a little more satisfyingly than a "grained wood partition." They conceal, whether in the present location or the "rich promoter['s]" library, the real(ity) of capitalism: pornography and profit.

Sixty years later, we have Richard Price's novel *Samaritan* (2003). Ray Mitchell, a disaffected television writer, teaches African American youths as a charity project. He takes two of them to a New Jersey mall and is predictably appalled at the chain bookstore:

> But once Ray steered Nelson inside, he saw right off that this place was a bust, too, the literary equivalent of all the other shit in the mall: a sea of discount tables stacked with endless piles of crappy pop-up books, *Star Wars* spin-offs, Disney spin-offs, sandy-assed bikini calendars, topless firemen calendars, massage manuals, astrology manuals, Idiots and Dummies Guides to everything from beer to cancer. (300)

But Ray then finds "the only shelving in the store that seemed to hold books that were actually books. There were two smallish sections: Fiction and Literature, like a value judgment. Ray wondered who working here got to decide which book went where" (301). Here, then, we have a different relation between books, or literature, and the real(ity) of capitalism. Here is not so much the literature of neoliberalism (Don DeLillo, David Eggers) as neoliberalism on the cheap, on full display with the discounted commodities, the shoddy and overpriced books. No need for pretentious tooled leather (except for perhaps those blank notebooks that are so often on sale) or glued-in bookplates.

These two fictional accounts are not objective historical analyses of retail patterns or the commodification of literature; rather, what they display is how anxieties about these concerns find their way, almost inevitably, into the production of literature itself. Thus it is that Humble, in her first chapter, pays "attention to the representations of the act of reading in middlebrow fiction . . . [to] trace the ways in which this mode of writing both established itself as a distinctive literary form, and worked to remake its readers in its own terms" (9). Humble's argument is that when characters in the middlebrow novel wax nostalgic about their childhood reading as a period of "intense literary fantasizing" (54) and encounter library clerks who "encouraged a highly instrumental attitude toward literature" (40), these representations also do the work of *interpellating* readers to be aware of their literary consumption as a form of class consciousness.[2] We may think about what kind of reader Price interpellates–one nostalgically critical of the mall-ification of bookselling. And we will come to think of the reader interpellated by Cormac McCarthy's novels.

Which is to argue against the notion of middlebrow literature as a form of escapism or, to be more precise, to critique the notion of escapism itself. As the earlier quotation from Humble evinced, the middlebrow text was somewhere between active consumption (the male reader of detective stories) and "passive abandonment," which would entail a loss of control for the "escapist reader" (53). Somerset Maugham, in a talk cited by Humble, notes the objection that "to read for pleasure is nothing but what in recent years has come to be disparagingly known as escapism. It is" (Humble 23). Maugham goes on to argue that "all literature is escapist." This conclusion is shared by Chandler who, answering middlebrow stalwart Dorothy Sayers's distinction between "literature of escape" and "literature of expression," contends that "this is critics' jargon, a use of abstract words as if they had meaning. . . . All men who read escape from something else into what lies behind the printed page" (*Simple Art* 13). But Maugham and Chandler both are rather disingenuous, I think: if all literature (Maugham) or even all reading (Chandler) involve escape, what is

perhaps more interesting is what that escape entails: the passive abandonment and loss of control that Humble pinpointed.

Another factor connecting Chandler's and Price's scenes is that
both take place in a concrete institution: the bookstore. If that material space has now been replaced for many readers, students, and book
purchasers by the virtual space of Amazon, is that change any more
monumental than the change from Chandler's simulacrum to Price's
mall outlet? Reflecting on that historical gap, Lynette Hunter has written that while such megastores as "Waterstones, Borders or Chapters"
differ remarkably "from those small, often dark and frequently slightly
seedy bookshops described so well in George Orwell's *Keep the Aspi-
distra Flying*" (10), the explosion of genres that troubles Richard Price's
character is, Hunter argues, how the chains "control your sense of
being overwhelmed by their sheer enormity by categorizing books,
and creating physically small spaces for science fiction, or poetry, or
humour, or philosophy" (10).

We can also ask if the anxieties here discussed–anxieties over
categorization as well as commodification, over losing control as well
as over gender–affect how we teach middlebrow texts, or how we
think about why we teach such novels and not (or not so much) the
formidably formalist exercises of David Foster Wallace or Kathy Acker.

A comment made by Stephen King may help to complicate as
well as reaffirm some of these anxieties and questions. Accepting the
2003 National Book Award, he noted the gap "between the so-called
popular fiction and the so-called literary fiction," adding that "[t]his is
not criticism, it's just me pointing out a blind spot in the winnowing
process and in the very act of reading the fiction of one's own culture."
King's *ressentiment* is instructive. As with Chandler, this is a disavowal
of the critical faculty. Unlike Price, this is an affirmation of the popular
over the literary. As with Humble, the popular or middlebrow is seen as
constitutive of "one's own culture." And in some ways, prize giving–especially in today's celebrity-driven culture–is, like the bookstore itself,
an institutional apparatus that serves the marketing and sale of books
by acting as a gatekeeper or filter for readers/consumers.

I would like now to situate these concepts and debates in terms
of two literary (or, perhaps, middlebrow) texts. First, let us think of
McCarthy's work in relation to its incorporation into the middlebrow

canon via Oprah's book club. In contradistinction, think of how his novels function linguistically, as texts, in terms of their heteroglossic incorporation of nonstandard English and untranslated Spanish. That formal strategy is arguably constitutive of their status as literature (as has been argued by John Guillory, drawing on Balibar and Macherey), which status then stands in antagonism with the institutionalization of McCarthy's books accomplished by Oprah.[3] This is to say that McCarthy's works stand as a limit concept for the literary or for the middlebrow.

In my reading of Ian McEwan's *Saturday*, I find an antagonism again around reception, first as argued in various discussions of the book (for the most part online), and then as thematized in key scenes in the book that revolve around pedagogy. In both cases I try to mix popular criticism (the blogosphere) and the academic, finding both of them to be active sites of production. Or to put it more crudely: in both cases I start with extrinsic, popular criticism – which fixes the texts in the middlebrow – and then, with various Bakhtinian and Lacanian readings, I trouble those categories, those fixings.

CORMAC MCCARTHY AND THE NATIONAL CONSTITUTION OF THE MIDDLEBROW

Cormac McCarthy's novels can now be read as middlebrow, as we see with both the film adaptations of *All the Pretty Horses* (1992; film: 2000) and *No Country for Old Men* (2005; film: 2007) and the money shot, McCarthy's *The Road* (2006) being selected by Oprah's book club, the keeper of the middlebrow canon. Here, I would like to flesh out this argument – that filming a novel or its inclusion in a book club marks it as middlebrow. The formulator of middlebrow theory has been Pierre Bourdieu, in both the collectively written *Photography: A Middle-Brow Art* and *Distinction: A Social Critique of the Judgment of Taste*. In the latter Bourdieu offers a succinct definition via two characters from modernist literature, Djuna Barnes's Felix and James Joyce's Leopold Bloom:

> [Their] pure but empty goodwill which, for lack of the guidelines or
> principles needed to apply it, does not know which way to turn, exposes
> the petit bourgeois to cultural allodoxia, that is, all the mistaken identi-

fications and false recognitions which betray the gap between acknowl-
edgement and knowledge. Allodoxia, the heterodoxy experienced as if
it were orthodoxy that is engendered by this undifferentiated reverence,
in which avidity combines with anxiety, leads the petit bourgeois to take
light opera for "serious music," popularization for science, an "imita-
tion" for the genuine article, and to find in this at once worried and
over-assured false recognition the source of a satisfaction which still
owes something to the sense of distinction. This middle-brow culture
[*culture moyenne*] owes some of its charm, in the eyes of the middle
classes who are its main consumers, to the references to legitimate
culture it contains and which encourage and justify confusion of the
two–accessible versions of avant-garde experiments or accessible works
which pass for avant-garde experiments, film "adaptations" of classic
drama and literature, "popular arrangements" of classical music or "orchestral versions" of popular tunes, vocal interpretations of classics in a
style evocative of scout choruses or angelic choirs, in short, everything
that goes to make up "quality" weeklies and "quality" shows, which are
entirely organized to give the impression of bringing legitimate culture
within the reach of all, by combining two normally exclusive characteristics, immediate accessibility and the outward signs of cultural legitimacy. (323)

For Bourdieu, then, the middlebrow is characterized by a dumb-
ing-down that "cannot . . . admit to being what it is" (*Distinction* 323) – a
popularization – since it is marketed to an audience that has to fool
itself that it is getting the real goods. Key, too, for Bourdieu is that
middlebrow culture is relational, positional, or a matter of difference:
it's a mistake, he argues, "to locate in the works which enter into middle-brow culture at a given moment the properties conferred on them
by a particular form of consumption", for what is middlebrow culture
"is not its 'nature' but the very position of the petit bourgeois in social
space" (327). That is to say, middlebrow culture is made in reception,
in consumption, fully as much as it is in production. But just because
Bourdieu says that a film adaptation is middlebrow don't mean it's necessarily so. Let's look at a comment on the imdb.com message board
for *All the Pretty Horses* and glean a sense of the relation between film
and novel. "peters 159-1" wrote the following on 16 June 2006:

> After seeing Matt Damon carrying "The Rainmaker" I sat up and be-
> came a real fan of the actor. In that movie he impressed me greatly. I
> decided to see what was he doing next. I read where he was slated to star

in All the Pretty Hourses [*sic*] so I got a copy of the book to see what it
was all about. I liked what I read and was looking forward to see Matt
Damon in the effort. When I read where Billy Bob Thornton was to
direct I became ecstatic, I remembered his acting and directing in Sling
Blade. Later, I read where there was trouble with the length of All the
Pretty Horses that the producer threatened to cut the movie. Mr Thornton's version ran almost 4 hours, the released version to theaters was 117
minutes. Of course I went to see the movie and could see that it should
have been longer. Any movie buff could see that. What perplexes me
is how studios and produce[r]s can contract certain directors and then
butcher their completed work. Sergio Leone's Once Upon a Time in
America suffered a humiliation when the studio decided to cut his film
drastically; it lost it's [*sic*] meaning, and money. Later, the DVD restored
version, 225 minutes, came out and was instantly received by customers.
Thank God David O. Selznick stuck to his guns with Gone with the
Wind. And look at how much money that! made. Like some others I
hope that some one one day will be able to assemble the 4 hour version
of All the Pretty Horses so that those of us who love movies can at least
see what we've missed. I think we deserve to judge the movie for ourselves. Who knows, we might be missing a masterpiece.

This comment bears many of the hallmarks of middlebrow taste,
including seeing a film for its actors, not its director (see *Distinction*,
where Bourdieu argues not only that "[k]nowledge of directors is much
more closely linked to cultural capital than is mere cinema-going"
and "knowledge of actors varies mainly . . . with the number of films
seen" but the "least-educated regular cinema-goers knew as many actors' names as the most highly-educated"; 27–28) – but note, too, that
not only is Billy Bob Thornton both an actor and a director, but the
desire to see a Matt Damon movie leads peters 159-1 to read "All the
Pretty Hourses [*sic*]." Here we run into a stumbling block, a challenge
to our Eurocentric theory of the middlebrow. For peters 159-1 seems
to also be writing from a place of high culture, with an interest in the
director as an artist (I refer to the discussion of the movie's length).
Three observations are germane: first, note the quantifiable nature of
the complaint over Thornton having to cut his film: it all comes down
to numbers, to four hours versus 117 minutes. Second, note how directors' cuts have become a valuable commodity on the DVD market, yet
another way to sell yet another version of the film. Finally, peters 159-1
twice uses the phrase "I read where," a wonderful form of the vernacu-

lar that indicates how news about (some) directors' travails has become as much part of the American entertainment media as gossip about the stars.

I will now approach a Bakhtinian reading of McCarthy in a more extrinsic or performative way, and will argue that in McCarthy's great swath of novels from *The Orchard Keeper* to *Suttree* (1979)–the Appalachian series–and then from *Blood Meridian* (1985) to the border trilogy (*All the Pretty Horses, The Crossing* [1994], *Cities of the Plain* [1998]) and *No Country for Old Men*, we have two linguistic contradictions at work: the first between regional dialect and highfalutin literary language, the second between English and Spanish. Thus the Appalachian novels stage an *internal* contradiction (internal both to the English language and to the American nation-state), and the westerns an *external* one (appropriately, the latter works are set in motion with the Vietnam or foreign policy allegory of *Blood Meridian*).[4]

The linguistic thesis of the Appalachian novels is that there is no standard English: it is either the local, apparently uneducated, ono-matopoeic dialect or the cultural capital–signaling literariness. A brief list of these competing dialects in *The Orchard Keeper* should give a sense of not just McCarthy's talent as a writer, but, more crucially, the way in which these novels open a space between the two discourses. Indeed, McCarthy's dialect, too, splits: between the local pronunciations (*fellers* for fellows [24], *betcher* for bet you [23], *minners* for minnows, *jest* for just, *ast* for asked, and *yander* for yonder [all 70]) and words that possess specific regional meanings (*highbinders* or *highbounders* [14]; *needled*, meaning sexual intercourse at one point [21] and then the usual meaning of bothered [30]; and, most gloriously, *dope* or *dope box* or *orange dope*, meaning soda [96, 115, 116, 136, 137, 148]).[5] Standing in counterpoint to this regional dialect is McCarthy's biblical or archaic or highfalutin language–which relates thematically to the geologic and colonial history he continually weaves through his Appalachian novels–which includes *microcataclysm, muscadine, carboniferous, saurians* (all 11), *Mellungeons* (12), catacombic (13), *communicants* and *troglodytes* (150), *querulous harridans* (173), and *cloistral* (224). A passage that unashamedly indulges in such twenty-five-dollar words is the following description of Knoxville, Tennessee:

> He was still standing on the sidewalk and now he saw the city, steamed and weaving in heat, and rising above the new facings of glass and tile the bare outlandish buildings, towering columns of brick adorned with fantastic motley; arches, lintels, fluted and arabesque, flowered columns and crowstepped gables, baywindows over corbels carved in the shape of feet, heads of nameless animals, Pompeian figures . . . here and there, gargoyled and crocketed, wreathed dates commemorating the perpetration of the structure. (81)

I have two observations about McCarthy's use of language in these examples. First, the paragraph just quoted is from a passage in which the focalizer is the young boy John Wesley Rattner, and certainly we are not supposed to believe that he has such a lexicon of architectural terms at his disposal.[6] So we have here a contradiction, an antagonism, between the character through whose consciousness we are experiencing the novel and the language being used to form that experience.[7] This split is reproduced in the gap between the formal and archaic language, on the one hand, and the various kinds of dialect to be found in McCarthy's novels. These contradictions, as a structuring principle, are important for two reasons: first, they mitigate against a formal unity in the novel itself. If we see McCarthy's Appalachian novels – including of course the Joycean *Suttree* – as late modernist texts, the play of dialect and high language renders the texts asunder and keeps them from attaining any holism. Second, the contradictions can be seen as tangible examples of Bakhtin's principles of dialogism, which argue:

> Every language in the novel is a point of view, a socio-ideological conceptual system of real social groups and their embodied representatives. . . . any point of view on the world fundamental to the novel must be a concrete, socially embodied point of view, not an abstract, merely semantic position; it must, consequently, have its own language with which it is organically united. A novel is constructed not on abstract differences in meaning nor on merely narrative collisions, but on concrete social speech diversity. (411)

Which is to say that the novel instantiates a "concrete social speech diversity" in its antagonism of the dialect and the formal. This same speech diversity (and it is unfortunate that Bakhtin's phrase should now carry the anodyne whiff of political correctness) can be located in terms of McCarthy's career, too, for the linguistic argument of the western novels is that English is no longer the only national language of the United States: untranslated Spanish interpellates a reader able to navigate this American language as surely (and often unsurely) as his characters navigate Mexican mores and terrain. A different sort of work than the interpellation that Humble detected in the middlebrow novel, perhaps, in that the literary here is in the service of a national project, the project of a post-unilingual United States.[8]

The most sustained critical engagement with McCarthy utilizing Bakhtin may be Christine Chollier's essay "Autotextuality; or, Dialogic Imagination in Cormac McCarthy's Border Trilogy." There Chollier concentrates on the characterological aspect of the play of languages and discourses in McCarthy, seeing in particular the characters' borrowing of words and phrases from each other as an indication of Bakhtin's argument that "the character's consciousness and voice are likely to be inhabited by other voices" (Chollier 9).[9] Chollier also discusses at great length the multilinguistic wordplay going on with the use of Spanish in the novels. Thus the Mexican place names are particularly resonant: "In *All the Pretty Horses*, Alejandra meets John Grady in Zacatecas for the last time. The town of Zacatecas may not have been chosen only for geographical or historical reasons. Indeed, *Zacatecas* is another name for *sepultureros* (gravediggers), which marks the town as an appropriate place to inter one's love: Alejandra has agreed to come to Zacatecas to bury their relationship" (29). The pair of dialectics (regional-literary English, English-Spanish) in McCarthy's novels is thus also characterological as well as (auto)biographical. For just as *The Orchard Keeper*'s Marion Sylder and the titular Suttree are paradigmatically "this affluent son returned" (*Orchard Keeper* 29) to the hardscrabble South, so the Appalachian novels' dichotomy of dialect and literariness rewrites such a social contradiction (which is, again, possibly McCarthy's own history) via the novel's use of dialect in conversation and literariness in narration.

The Orchard Keeper is an Oedipal-Faulknerian tale of a dead father, lusting son, and prodigal son; the novel is concerned primarily with the young John Wesley Rattner, the bootlegger Marion Sylder, and Rattner's mountain hermit uncle Ather. Their relationship is based on a certain unknown contradiction or irony: Sylder killed Kenneth

Rattner, John Wesley's father. The irony or double irony is that neither knows this: Marion knows he killed Kenneth but not who he is or was, and John Wesley knows his father is dead (or absconded) but not who killed him. (For McCarthy in general, Sophoclean knowledge never comes to his characters.) The ideas of killing, capturing, and the relation of languages, then, all relate intrinsically, but also problematically, not only to the status of the novel as middlebrow, but to their place (the novel's place, middlebrow literature's place) in the classroom. For middlebrow literature is what is left when literature is taken out of the classroom: it is the text that is left, the literary text, the book.

If one way in which the novel *qua* novel relates to its reader is via interpellation, another, similar operation is its process of capturing the reader, a process figured thematically or metaphorically in the fiction. Thus *The Crossing* begins with attempts to capture a wolf and return it to Mexico (15–53), a return that is a sociolinguistic opening to the Spanish language. In *The Orchard Keeper*, Marion Sylder is trying to avoid capture by government agents (in the end, he is unsuccessful), and uncle Ather regales John Wesley and his friends with stories of his own hunting before being, in turn, captured by the Coke-swilling outsider. Arguably, this is the status of McCarthy's oeuvre itself as it is captured by the literary: "Increasingly [McCarthy's] novels are required reading in literature courses" (Owens xiv).

McCarthy's novels, then, in their capturing of animals, of characters, of readers, feature what in Lacanian terms might be considered the captation of the subject, that is to say, the immersion into the imaginary. Captation has to do with desire, with Lacan's thesis that desire is the desire of the other (176–177). This notion of desire occurs on two planes, first in terms of imaginary captation (seeing oneself in relation to the other), and then in speech, through the mediation of language, the symbolic relation of you and me. Marion and John Wesley are caught up in that mutual misrecognition: the son who admires a substitute father but does not recognize the killer of his father, and the murderer, the would-be or want-to-be father, who does not see or recognize the murder he has committed.

But the notion of captation goes further in the McCarthy canon: let us consider the body of the father, of Rattner Sr., which Marion, after killing him, has to dispose of in classic crime narrative fashion.

The body ends up in some mysterious concrete hole in the ground, a hole that is both the effect of modernity (a modernity that will capture both Marion and Ather through the agency of the agents, the local police force) and, as with McCarthy's archaic language, irredeemably atavistic or uterine (figured, too, by the caves into which boys in the novel at one point hunt or retreat, until they smoke themselves out–again, a moment of the imaginary: they have been captivated by their own backwoods stupidity). This body of the father can be seen as the fate of literature itself in McCarthy's canon, as in the child that is a product of incest in *Outer Dark* (1968); the lovers' lane victims that Lester Ballard stashes in caves in *Child of God* (1974); and the misfit's misfit, Gene Harrogate, in *Suttree* (1979), who, after a bout of watermelon-only miscegenation, determines to blow up Knoxville, Tennessee, from below. In McCarthy's writings, Lacan's captation is of literature itself.

So where are we? In a structural way, following Bourdieu's argument, we have seen that Cormac McCarthy's novels have come to be read or positioned as middlebrow. This is the effect not only of their Hollywoodization, but their embrace by Oprah. But looked at formally, the novels trouble this categorization. Their linguistic contradictions, their interpellation and captation of the reader, unsettle the middlebrow, engaging as they do with the nation and, indeed, with the relation between the book and the middlebrow.

IAN MCEWAN AND CULTURE AS BARRICADE

I will now turn to the work of Ian McEwan, and in particular his 2005 novel, *Saturday*, because I think it thematically and formally addresses these issues of what literature is and how confidently we can assume its constitution and effects. McEwan's body of work has, for instance, in its use of horror and violence and the Gothic, imported into the literary what are often seen as more properly the province of genre fiction: thus incest and murder in *The Cement Garden* (1978) and *The Comfort of Strangers* (1981), kidnapping in *The Child in Time* (1987), the cutting up of a body in *The Innocent* (1990), the suggestions of bestiality in *Black Dogs* (1992), and what critic Jennifer Szalai called the "lurid" matter of "treachery, cross-dressing, and mutual homicide" (87) in

Amsterdam (1998) all work both to elevate such topoi from mass culture to the middlebrow and to smooth the elitist edges of literary fiction. Too, his novels have since the 1990s featured the kind of factoid-heavy info-speak that we might associate more readily with Michael Crichton or Tom Clancy (think of the incredibly detailed accounts of spying apparatus in *The Innocent*–details that would never make it into the more psychological fictions of John le Carré, one might note–and the brain surgery in *Saturday*).[10] And make no mistake: it is this very turn to the turgid detail that has, for at least one critic, marked off McEwan's fiction as suspect. Eviscerating *Saturday*, John Banville wrote in the *New York Review of Books*:

> Perowne goes on to his squash game, which . . . is one in the series of discrete set pieces out of which the book is assembled. The hard-fought match between Perowne and his American-born rival is meant, we assume, to illustrate the competitive, indeed warlike, nature of the human male, and to show us that McEwan is not entirely Mr. Nice Guy. Here, as elsewhere, the author is wearyingly insistent on displaying his technical knowledge and his ability to put that knowledge into good, clean prose. This is the case especially in the medical scenes, of which there are many, too many.

If one aspect of McEwan's fiction is its borrowing from low culture (and I will talk about another form of borrowing below), a key locus of critical disagreement over McEwan's *Saturday* is the role of culture *qua* culture in the novel. Culture is foregrounded in two senses: first, the novel's central character, Henry Perowne, is a philistine who does not enjoy literature and does not get irony (but enjoys other high and middle cultural forms such as Bach and the blues); second, his daughter's recitation of Arnold's "Dover Beach" momentarily dissuades home invaders from rape and pillage. The character's imperviousness to irony is worth dwelling on momentarily, if only because, as McEwan himself has noted in an interview, it is ironic when you have a fictional character who does not like fiction. The novel takes place during an antiwar rally in London, and, driving to his squash game, Perowne hears on the radio an actress quoting from Shakespeare, and he cannot understand the irony of using a canonical speech against its context. Here, Banville's review is worth returning to:

For years Daisy has been trying to educate her father in matters literary, but to no avail. His ignorance of literature is frankly incredible.
Are we really to believe that an intelligent and attentive man such as
Henry Perowne, no matter how keen his scientific bent, would have
passed through the English education system without ever having heard
of Matthew Arnold, or that any Englishman over fifty would have no
acquaintance with the St. Crispin's Day speech from Henry V, if only
through Laurence Olivier's ranting of it in the wartime propaganda film
of the play? The awful possibility arises that Perowne's ignorance may
be intended as a running gag; if so, it is the only instance of humor in
the book, if humor is the word.

Banville's thundering is useful here for two things that it tells us
about how literature is received. First, he sees Perowne's philistinism,
or simply his ignorance, as implausible, but while a member of the
British upper-middle class may have heard of Matthew Arnold at some
point, this is not the same as being familiar enough with "Arnold" as a
signifier to realize that the Victorian poet is being referred to. That is,
when Perowne's father-in-law, the poet John Grammaticus, remarks,
"there came a point after Daisy recited Arnold for the second time
when I actually began to feel sorry for that fellow" (229), it is surely
likely that Perowne would miss the reference or that he might ask,
"Arnold who?" (230). And, well, that *is* funny, especially if we admit that
many readers would not have caught the reference from the fragments
of the poem that Daisy has recited. And, in this regard, Perowne, the
thug Baxter, and the reader are all in the same boat. (More on this
below.) But what is more telling about Banville's disbelief is how it
reveals him – or his persona as reviewer – to be as narrowly philistine
as Perowne. Banville, it seems, is so immersed in the world of books
that he doesn't realize that many people, yes, perhaps even educated
people, do not go around with the names of Victorian British poets at
their fingertips.

I will continue here in the vein of using critical commentary on
Saturday as a way of arguing two different things. First, that the novel
is radical in how it reveals culture to be effectively nothing more or
less than a class barricade. That is to say, the novel's use of cultural
material contradicts the liberal, pro-invasion views of Perowne. Or does
it? One could, of course, be in favor of the invasion of Iraq – whether
for reasons of Perowne's empathy for Saddam's victims or for more
realpolitik reasons of the Cheney-Rumsfeld ilk – and still see culture

in Bourdieu-esque terms, as a class barrier. It is a myopia of liberals/ leftists to believe that it is only we intellectuals who see culture "for what it really is." Second, that this use of culture in the novel mitigates against its status as a middlebrow novel. Again, as with McCarthy, I am less interested in slotting the novel into a category than in seeing how it makes us think about categories. The middlebrow text – in my view, a form of literary production which is a historic compromise that waters down the great innovative moments of high modernism: Woolf for McEwan, Faulkner for McCarthy – is in the service of the commodity text: a promiscuous hybridity of, again to be specific, generic fiction's codes and signals: Gothic or horror fiction for both authors and, in the later McCarthy, of course, the western.

Three comments found on Mark Sarvas's blog, *The Elegant Variation*, are useful to our purposes here (spelling, capitalization, and punctuation are per the originals):

> I cannot understand myself the hysterically enthusiastic reception for this work (a Da Vinci Code for middle-brow Brits). It is clunky and incredible. There is some merit in the idea of Perowne – an everyman hero removed from the high falutin' preoccupations of the chattering classes but nevertheless quietly doing breathtaking things. But he's a little too reasonable and his life is a little too perfect to make him come alive. The book is worth a read though even if it's not destined to become a classic. (marcus breslin, 16 May 2005)

> What Banville objects to is the formula of the fairy tale, and he erroneously sees that formula at work in the book. Sad academics have long beaten into their students the need for ambiguously negative endings, to differentiate themselves from the popular genre formulas with "happy endings." (Richard L. Pangburn, 1 June 2005)

> "Saturday" may err on the smug side but for me there's plenty of intelligence and insight and irony in the novel to ponder on and make it well worth the reading. Perowne the neural surgeon and his family were certainly no less interesting to me than the crumply art historians that appear in too many of Banville's books. Why should Banville think it incredulous that Perowne had never heard of the poet Arnold or had little appreciation of nineteenth century liturature? Surely most people would be in that boat, even brain surgeons. Neither did I think there was too much medical terminology in the novel. If Perowne is cast as a little too "straight" so be it. There must be as many "straight" people out there in real life as there are crumply art historians. (Anthony, 26 Oct. 2008)

The first comment (out of a total of twenty-two over a period of three and a half years) answers its own disbelief, of course: by calling *Saturday* "a Da Vinci Code for middle-brow Brits," marcus breslin explains the "hysterically enthusiastic reception" of the novel. A middlebrow novel allows those readers who wish to distinguish themselves from the run-of-the-mill *Da Vinci Code* readers to get their pleasure *and* their cultural capital. But perhaps I am misreading breslin: he did, after all, call the *readers*, the nationally identified readers, "middle-brow Brits."[11] So here is a question of subjectivity: Is the person middlebrow, or is the text he or she reads? Can or do middlebrow readers read literature or schlock? If we teach a middlebrow text does that make us, as academics, middlebrow, or does it make our students such?

Certainly this question of transference, if I can call it that, complicates any surety with which we would use the label. When I was teaching a Laurie R. King detective novel to a graduate class a couple of years ago, one student, a high school teacher, confessed that he felt embarrassed to be reading it in public in a coffee shop (thick novel, embossed cover, the whole nine yards). Like a status update on Facebook, the book that we carry signals who we are – or, rather, to be Lacanian, it functions in the imaginary realm as our image. And – why not? – we can indeed carry out a full tripartite Lacanian analysis of the role of the middlebrow text:[12] in the imaginary, the book signals who we would like others to think we are: literary but not too literary, not a pointy-headed academic; in terms of the symbolic, the text can only have that meaning in a system of literary difference, of signifiers, of being neither lowbrow trash nor highbrow obscurity; then, in terms of the real, the inaccessible raw stuff of life, the book is still a commodity, a manufactured object of paper and ink and glue which, if we can't make out the title or, from far off, even what the object is, has no meaning whatsoever.

But let us turn back to marcus breslin's comments from the blog for one last point of argument. How does breslin support his assertion that *Saturday* is middlebrow (or is for middlebrow readers)? First through difference: it is not *The Da Vinci Code*. Then through thematic qualities of the text: its use of an "everyman" character (Perowne is an upper-middle-class surgeon who owns a veritable mansion in central London but, still, not of the "chattering classes," not, again, an intellectual). But also, it seems, and this is actually breslin's first point, this is a text that has had a "hysterically enthusiastic reception." So part of the middlebrow text's qualities is that it is very popular, unduly popular, or popular with the wrong people. I think that this logic makes sense in some ways: the middlebrow text steals the popular audience from low culture, and the quality of writing from high culture.

Then we have Richard L. Pangburn's comment, which does similar differential work as breslin's. Pangburn astutely points out that Banville "objects to . . . the formula of the fairy tale," or thinks literary novels should have unhappy endings (a point George Orwell made in the 1940s with respect to modernism). As Banville put it: "Henry has everything, and as in all good fairy tales, he gets to keep it, after getting rid of the troll who had sought to challenge his right of ownership." Banville's and Pangburn's comments must be viewed dialectically, however. While certainly they are sneers, the sneers work in two different ways. First, comparing the novel to "all good fairy tales" seeks to deflate the literary pretensions of the novel. *Saturday*, Pangburn and Banville are saying, is just like a fairy tale: too unrealistic, suitable for children. Then, Banville reduces the novel's plot to merely "getting rid of the troll" (Baxter, the thug who invades the Perowne household) as a way of Henry Perowne "keeping" everything.[13] The problem here is that both commentators display their ignorance of what literary scholarship has argued since the 1960s (French structuralism) or even since earlier in the twentieth century (if we take the origins of Vladimir Propp's *Morphology of the Folktale* back to the Russian formalists). Narratives, the structuralists and formalists argue, be they high cultural or folk cultural, literature or fairy tales, have certain properties in general that have no connection to questions of value (thus, in the sixties, both Eco and Barthes wrote on the Bond novels). Then, as Pangburn's "sad academic" comment argues, Banville is tied to a normative view of the literary: it has to be a downer. So Pangburn's work here is both structural and has to do with content: it shows how Banville's critique of *Saturday* depends on the novel's similarity to folk culture (and, hence, difference from literary culture) and, too, how that critique is really based on a misperception of affect.

The third blogger, Anthony, takes on Banville's argument that it is unrealistic to expect a middle-class doctor not to recognize a Matthew

Arnold poem. I'm not exactly sure if misspelling "nineteenth" and "literature" proves Anthony's point or not, but we must take the generic conventions of blogs and online discourse in general into account here. Since this brings us back to my discussion of Banville above, let us look again at the scene where Daisy recites "Dover Beach" and the staging of reception.

It is important to keep in mind how McEwan has set up this scene: we already know of Daisy's literary education and that her grandfather Grammaticus

> had firm, old-fashioned views of the fundamentals, not all of which he thought should be too pleasurable. He believed in children learning by rote, and he was prepared to pay up. Shakespeare, Milton and the King James Bible – five pounds for every twenty lines memorised from passages he marked. . . . The summer of her sixteenth birthday, Daisy earned a teenage fortune at the chateau, chanting, even singing, parts of *Paradise Lost*, and Genesis and various gloomy musings of Hamlet. She recited Browning, Clough, Chesterton and Masefield. In one good week she earned forty-five pounds. Even now, six years on, she claims to be able to spout – her word – non-stop for more than two hours. (134)

Grammaticus (a name suggesting both the pedagogical [grammar school] and the syntactic [the order of grammar]), the superannuated poet, living in his cups in a French chateau – can there be any plainer portrait of the academic? the dirty old man as alcoholic? But somehow he is still an effective pedagogue (and we see, later in the novel, how effective indeed): able to use money to inculcate some old-fashioned learning. And is not the economic carrot that Grammaticus uses for his pedagogy a wonderful rejoinder to John Guillory's argument that high cultural texts are irrelevant under late capitalism? If, as Guillory argues in *Cultural Capital*, "the center of the system of social reproduction has moved elsewhere [from the curriculum of literature], into the domain of mass culture" (80), if middle-class students take business courses instead of Victorian poetry, then perhaps we should adopt Grammaticus's technique and simply pay students to learn – nay, to love – our field.

This pedagogical scene is an example of what Barthes, in S/Z, calls the hermeneutic code, or "all the units whose function it is to articulate in various ways a question, its response, and the variety of chance events which can either formulate the question or delay its answer; or even constitute an enigma and lead to its solution" (17). The *meaning* of the pedagogical scene, that is, at first appears to be filling in some of Grammaticus's character quirks and providing the background to Daisy's literary education. We are told Grammaticus's pedagogical method as part of the mini-narrative of Daisy having won a poetry prize, which alienated her from her grandfather (oh, those envious academics: "his protégé had struck out"; 135), an alienation to be ended or mended: "At dinner tonight the reconciliation will be sealed" (139).

But what appears to be a minor narratological moment in the plot will, of course, come to have the greatest import in the novel's climactic scene: Daisy's memorization has not only made her a great poet, but will actually save the day. Not only is literature useful after all, but the *teaching* of literature is as well. So let us turn to this climax. When Baxter and then his colleague Nigel ("Let's hear your dirtiest one. Something really filthy"; 220) bully Daisy into reading from her book, Baxter at first asks a question familiar to any writer: "All your own work, is it?" (219). This question is telling because of the general incredulity with which civilians greet an author – especially one encountered outside a literary setting (not at a bookstore signing or reading) as a family member or socially. The nonwriter is generally so intimidated or impressed or even nonplussed by such a sight that the first suspicion/disbelief has to do with originality. So McEwan is pointing to a social attitude that he exploits for his novel: as Lacan put it, the mistake turns out to be true.[14] That is, the philistine's "mistake," to think that poets don't write their own poems, turns out to be true in that Daisy presents Arnold's poem as her own.

Asked to read a poem from her book, Daisy at first is too frightened (the thugs have a knife to her mother's neck, Daisy is standing naked and pregnant). Her grandfather tells her, "Do one you used to say for me," and while at first she looks at him "blankly," "now she seems to understand" (220). If we are to think that Daisy understands Grammaticus to be telling her to just recite a poem she memorized, the question here surely is: Why does Grammaticus do this? Why is it necessary for the novel not just for a young woman to present a Victorian poem as her own (a reference to culture as a bulwark against anarchy, as Arnold saw it, but also to Adorno and Horkheimer, in the Odysseus section of *Dialectic of Enlightenment*), but for this idea to come from her grandfather?

Perhaps this is still a pedagogical scene. Perhaps, if Grammaticus is in the role of the teacher (as the "subject supposed to know" in Lacanese), then one student is Baxter (the "subject supposed *not* to know"). Baxter won't be able to tell the difference, so read him something you've memorized. Or: the canon is better than your modern piffle, so reach for the greats, "the sources of all good English verse and prose" (134). If this is another pedagogical scene, then the students would include Baxter (who has requested the reading), Henry Perowne (the one who focalizes), and the reader. Look at Perowne's reaction: "Henry has been through her book a few times, but there are certain poems he's read only once; this one he only half remembers. The lines surprise him – clearly, he hasn't been reading closely enough. They are unusually meditative, mellifluous and wilfully archaic. She's thrown herself back into another century" (220). This is not a bad response – both honest in its misprision and attentive to the text. The irony in "this one he only half remembers" is interesting: Perowne mistakes his *lack* of remembering the poem from Daisy's galleys (which he has seen) for *half* remembering. Much of Perowne's interpretation, then, becomes biographical as he "slip[s] through the words into the things they describe" (220). Thus "[h]e sees Daisy on a terrace . . . [s]he calls to her lover, surely the man who will one day father her child. . . . Perowne sees a . . . young man . . . standing at Daisy's side. . . . now they're having a child . . . when desert armies stand ready to fight" (220–221).

Part of my reading of this scene, indeed of the novel, then, is teasing out how much it is about the middlebrow reader, and how much that reading is a feature of the modern or postmodern classroom. Perowne's reading does two things: it embodies the typically middlebrow position of reading texts literally or biographically (think of Bourdieu's comments, in *Photography: A Middle-Brow Art*, where photo club members judge the quality of a photograph on the basis of the portrayed person or object; 78–79), and it projects onto the text his own anxieties. First, his sudden anxiety about his daughter's pregnancy – so the poem had better be about the *father* of her child (note, again, that this anxiety must still be filtered through middlebrow literalism; it cannot be transferred onto aesthetic concerns, such as the form of the poem) – and then his anxiety about the impending invasion of Iraq: "desert" armies is misread or misheard for "ignorant" armies.

There are also a lot of mistakes at work here. If the teaching of the middlebrow novel is a pedagogical mistake (we are abandoning the formally innovative tradition of modernism), it is a mistake which tells us something true about our place as teachers in the commodified present of literary production (as argued above, when I looked at moments in texts where the bookstore *qua* scene was presented). Then, the listeners (or at least two of them, Baxter and Perowne, and perhaps the book's readers as well) of Daisy's/Arnold's poem make the mistake of thinking it is hers. But, again, *that mistake is true* in that the poem is hers culturally, as cultural capital, in a way that it will never be Baxter's. "Dover Beach" *is* by Daisy because it is *for* Daisy. But will it be Perowne's? Will he now turn to literature? How does cultural capital work in the neoliberal present, when, as Guillory forcefully shows, traditional literature is no longer necessary as a social lubricant for the middle and upper classes? Finally, there are the mistakes in Perowne's reading, especially in the details of thinking the poem is about Daisy's pregnancy and the Iraq invasion. The second misreading is cleared up when Daisy reads the poem again, and in McEwan's clunker of a sentence: "Even in a world 'where ignorant armies clash by night,' Henry discovers on second hearing no mention of a desert" (222).

What, then, is the truth of Perowne's mistake, a mistake he clears up? Lacan's meaning was that for Freud, the subject's truth – his or her true anxieties or traumas – emerges in slips of the tongue, mistaken projections, and so on. And certainly there is a truth to Perowne's mishearing "ignorant" as "desert," a mishearing that even without the pressures of the Iraq war could follow naturally from the previous line in Arnold's poem: "And we are here as on a darkling *plain.*" Plain, desert, planes (the beginning of the novel describes Perowne looking out the window at a plane on fire flying across early morning London, evoking, of course, 9/11): the connection makes sense at the level of the signifiers – but only if, unlike Perowne (but like McEwan?), we do *not* "[slip] through the words into the things they describe" (220). Which is to say that Perowne's mistake is not only overdetermined, but also a form of reading, of interpretation, that mitigates against the novel's middlebrow status.

This is the crux of the matter, which turns out to be two cruxes: first, the way in which thinking the poem is Daisy's becomes an object lesson in how cultural capital works, and second, the way this also relates – to turn back to an argument made above – to affect. The way in which, that is, the poem calms down Baxter. How much, I ask, are these two moments related? How much is the affect related to the cognitive? (A brief note on other affect: Nigel, the other thug, is nowhere concerned with either who wrote the poem or what it is about: "The disgust with which Nigel listened to the poem a second time has only just faded from his face" [222]. Now *there* is a student we can all [mis] recognize!)

So "Baxter has broken his silence and is saying excitedly, 'You wrote that. You *wrote* that'" (222), and the next paragraph begins: "It's a statement, not a question." But that's wrong, isn't it? Grammatically correct (Baxter's utterances are in the form of a statement) but culturally incorrect. For this moment, this interchange, shows us the bulwark of cultural capital: Baxter's amazement that Daisy *"wrote"* the poem – the emphasis is McEwan's – is, before it is about being awestruck by the sublimeness of Arnold's verse, a phatic indicator that he is not used to being in the presence of an author, a writer. Baxter repeats: "And you wrote it" (222). And on the next page: "'How could you have thought of that? I mean, you just wrote it.' And then he says it again, several times over. 'You wrote it'" (223). This misrecognition is key, again, for McEwan is taking a common scene of the philistine's amazement at encountering a writer, and pointing out the truth of that misrecognition. A philistine, a middlebrow, will be surprised at an author having, as Baxter put it, "thought of that," at creativity or originality. But of course, all that Daisy thought of, prompted by her pedagogue, was to recite a poem by Arnold instead of one of her own. So the truth of Baxter's mistake is that she did not write it, in two senses: first, in the postmodern, intertextual sense that all literature refers to other texts, is not original, is a simulacra; and second, in the cultural capital sense that the ruling class uses literature and the awe it evokes to keep the masses in line.

CONCLUSIONS

When I began working on this chapter I thought the argument would be fairly simple: both McCarthy's and McEwan's novels fall into the category of the middlebrow. I would show this in two different ways: extrinsically with McCarthy, in terms of his works' status as filmed books, as Oprah-ized texts, and intrinsically with McEwan, in terms of his works' uneasiness with the literary, with poetry. But as I looked at critical responses to the texts and at their formal and thematic machinations, this certainty quickly dissolved. The dialogic tensions and contradictions in McCarthy's novels–the regional versus literary dialectic, the turn to Spanish–as well as the thematic concerns with captation, all problematized things. Then, with McEwan, the popular critical responses themselves, while telling us something about how the middlebrow is constructed, failed to account for the intricacies of the pedagogical scenes that are, in my reading, the crux of the novel. Indeed, both authors' works are finally viewed in the contemporary moment, a neoliberal moment where the commodification of literature is a done deal, where the blogosphere is an ethnographic site of critical praxis, and where the political, be it matters of nation and language or culture and class, cannot help but be represented both formally and thematically in the text (and, further, affected by those representations). And this neoliberal moment is also the moment of our classroom, for in that large undergraduate lecture hall, with laptops glowing, our students are simultaneously captured and let go, wired and tired, surfing and listening.

NOTES

1. The publication in 2011 of Wallace's last–uncompleted–novel, *The Pale King*, only reaffirms this statement. It is the *death* of the author, of Wallace, that made possible his final gasp of experimentation–an unfinished novel that is more Wallace-like because of his death.

2. With the term "interpellation," I am drawing strictly on the work of Althusser, and especially his argument in "Ideology and Ideological State Apparatuses," which is not only that "*all ideology hails or interpellates concrete individuals as concrete subjects,*" by the functioning of the category of the subject" (173; emphasis in original) but also that such ideology functions especially through cultural forms and the educational system or apparatus. I am arguing that this is Humble's meaning, in a sense, and I return often to the term

in this chapter as a way of determining exactly how novels and their taste-based categorizations (middlebrow or not) function to "hail" or "interpellate" the reader as a certain kind of subject.

3. While Guillory argues that literature sees the "triumph of a class-based sociolect over regional dialects" (77), his critical thesis draws as well on Bakhtin, acknowledging the "centrifugal" force of the novel *qua* genre, drawing other classes and readers and writers into literary production. Arguably it is this very debate for which McCarthy's work stands as a limit case.

4. In *Cormac McCarthy's Western Novels*, Barcley Owens devotes a chapter, "*Blood Meridian* and the Reassessment of Violence," to comparing the novel to atrocities committed by U.S. forces in the Vietnam War, to street violence in the United States, and to the changing depiction of violence in U.S. cinema (19–43).

5. It is worth noting that toward the end of *The Orchard Keeper*, when a government agent is waiting at a store to arrest uncle Ather, we are told, "Later in the afternoon the man came in again and drank a Coca-Cola" (199), indicating his outsider status to the community/region.

6. The term "focalizer" draws on Mieke Bal's *Narratology*, where she introduces this technical version of such terms as "point of view" or "perspective" to emphasize precisely the gap I am describing here, that is, to make "a distinction between those who see and those who speak" (146).

7. John Cant has linked this strategy of McCarthy to Faulkner, to the latter's tendency in *As I Lay Dying* "to render the complex thoughts and feelings of simple characters in a language they could not possess" (13).

8. In the compelling essay "'Blood

Is Blood': *All the Pretty Horses* in the Multicultural Literature Class," Timothy P. Caron compares his largely Anglo class in an L.A. college to the novel's characters, arguing that McCarthy's dystopian vision "runs contrary to the popular conception of a warm, fuzzy multiculturalism" (163).

9. Other critics have found elements of dialogism in McCarthy's work. Steven Frye, for example, has argued that the multiple monologues in *The Crossing* "resemble Melville's, as well as the dialogism M. M. Bakhtin finds in Dostoevsky" (52), but ultimately Frye sees McCarthy's vision as more affirmative than that of Dostoevsky: in *The Crossing*, "the notion of the one story mitigates the multiplicity of perspective." And David Holloway argues that an auction scene in *Child of God* can be seen as an act of popular will akin to Bakhtin's notion of the carnivalesque (128).

10. Here I am contradicting myself: damning McEwan by association with Clancy and Crichton, but then saying that the same formal aspect of his writing – detailed technological exegeses – is what differentiates it from an equally mass culture writer, le Carré. But I think that this demonstrates how much what constitutes high culture, or mass culture, or midcult, is not monolithic and, too, how one text can embody conflicting signals or codes. Surely what is remarkable about le Carré's fiction has been how it eschews the hardware for the software, avoids the James Bond machinery, and instead focuses on the more literary themes of betrayal and guilt. And to further twist the screw: in a *Boston Review* essay, Roger Boylan wrote: "*The Innocent* in some aspects – Berlin, espionage, Anglo-American tensions, the morally burdened central figure – could be de-

scribed as the novel that John le Carré failed to write."

11. Note the transnational nature of this text. *The Elegant Variation*, we are told on its home page, is "A Guardian Top Ten Literary Blog" but is written by L.A.-based Sarvas; then, we have an Irish writer's (Banville) review of a British novel, first published in a New York literary magazine. The blog contributors are less easy to fix: is breslin more or less likely to be a Brit if he slags the novel's would-be readers? Indeed, such a move on breslin's part might be seen as an example of Žižek's "interpassivity" (see his "The Interpassive Subject" and also *The Plague of Fantasies* 104–126) – the "subject supposed to be middle-brow." In this sense, too, the middlebrow reader is resented because he or she is "stealing my *jouissance*": if I am interpellated as a reader of popular fiction, of trash, then I am anxious because the middlebrow reader seems to be too learned. If I am a highbrow intellectual, then I am anxious because the middlebrow reader is encroaching on my territory. But to return to the transnational for a moment, this condition of the blog is surely commensurate, if not contemporaneous, with McEwan's novel. There a British doctor's views of the impending invasion of Iraq are swayed by having known an Iraqi patient; his son returns from playing music in the United States; his daughter and father-in-law are visiting from France; and, of course, his route to play squash with his American colleague is blocked by a political demonstration that is addressing the geopolitical situation.

12. A common problem in writing on middlebrow texts or culture is to confuse middlebrow with popular fiction or pulp fiction. But I am prepared to argue that Laurie R. King's detective novels (one series focuses on a female companion of Sherlock Holmes, the other on a lesbian detective in late twentieth-century San Francisco) are, with their level of historical detail and quality of writing, hardly the same type of trash as, say, a Janet Evanovich novel (with thanks to J., my research assistant in this area).

13. There may be a meta-internet pun at work in this blog comment, as "troll" is internet slang for someone who posts critical or obscene comments in such forums.

14. "[T]here is no error which does not present itself as truth. In short, error is the habitual incarnation of the truth." Lacan, *Seminar I*, 263 ("Truth Emerges from the Mistake").

REFERENCES

Althusser, Louis. "Ideology and Ideological State Apparatuses (Notes towards an Investigation)." In his *Lenin and Philosophy and Other Essays*. Trans. Ben Brewster. New York: Monthly Review Press, 1971. 127–186.

Bakhtin, Mikhail. *The Dialogic Imagination: Four Essays*. Trans. Caryl Emerson and Michael Holquist. Austin: University of Texas Press, 1985.

Bal, Mieke. *Narratology: Introduction to the Theory of Narrative*, 3rd ed. Toronto: University of Toronto Press, 2009.

Banville, John. "A Day in the Life" (Rev. of *Saturday*). *New York Review of Books* 52.9 (26 May 2005). Web. Accessed 10 Nov. 2008.

Barthes, Roland. *S/Z*. Trans. Richard Miller. New York: Hill and Wang, 1974.

Bourdieu, Pierre. *Distinction: A Social Critique of the Judgment of Taste*. Trans. Richard Nice. Cambridge, MA: Harvard University Press, 1984.

Bourdieu, Pierre, et al. *Photography: A Middle-Brow Art*. Trans. Shaun Whiteside. Stanford, CA: Stanford University Press, 1990.

Boylan, Roger. "Ian McEwan's Family Values." *Boston Review* (Jan.–Feb. 2006). Web. Accessed 10 Nov. 2008.

Cant, John. *Cormac McCarthy and the Myth of American Exceptionalism*. New York: Routledge, 2008.

Caron, Timothy P. "'Blood Is Blood': *All the Pretty Horses* in the Multicultural Literature Class." In *Cormac McCarthy: New Directions*. Ed. James D. Lilley. Albuquerque: University of New Mexico Press, 2002. 153–170.

Chandler, Raymond. *The Big Sleep*. 1939. New York: Vintage, 1992.

——. *The Simple Art of Murder*. 1944. New York: Ballantine, 1980.

Chollier, Christine. "Autotextuality; or, Dialogic Imagination in Cormac McCarthy's Border Trilogy." In *A Cormac McCarthy Companion: The Border Trilogy*. Ed. Edwin T. Arnold and Dianne C. Luce. Jackson: University Press of Mississippi, 2001. 3–36.

Frye, Steven. "Cormac McCarthy's 'World in Its Making': Romantic Naturalism in *The Crossing*." *Studies in American Naturalism* 2.1 (Summer 2007): 46–65.

Guillory, John. *Cultural Capital: The Problem of Literary Canon Formation*. Chicago: University of Chicago Press, 1993.

Holloway, David. *The Late Modernism of Cormac McCarthy*. Westport, CT: Greenwood, 2002.

Humble, Nicola. *The Feminine Middlebrow Novel, 1920s to 1950s: Class, Domesticity, and Bohemianism*. Oxford: Oxford University Press, 2001.

Hunter, Lynette. *Literary Value / Cultural Power: Verbal Arts in the Twenty-First Century*. Manchester, England: Manchester University Press, 2001.

King, Stephen. "National Book Award Acceptance Speech." *National Book Award* (n.d.). Web. Accessed 18 Dec. 2008.

Lacan, Jacques. *The Seminars of Jacques Lacan, bk. 1: Freud's Papers on Technique, 1953–1954*. Trans. John Forrester. New York: Norton, 1988.

McCarthy, Cormac. *The Crossing*. New York: Vintage, 1995.

——. *The Orchard Keeper*. 1965. New York: Vintage, 1993.

McEwan, Ian. *Saturday*. Toronto: Vintage, 2005.

Owens, Barcley. *Cormac McCarthy's Western Novels*. Tucson: University of Arizona Press, 2000.

peters 159-1. "Comments." *Internet Movie Database*. Web. Accessed 18 Dec. 2008.

Price, Richard. *Samaritan*. New York: Knopf, 2003.

Szalai, Jennifer. "Daytripper" (Rev. of *Saturday*). *Harper's Magazine* 310 (May 2005): 87–92.

Wallace, David Foster. *The Pale King*. New York: Little, Brown, 2011.

Žižek, Slavoj. "The Interpassive Subject." *Lacan Dot Com* (n.d.). Web. Accessed 11 Dec. 2008.

——. *The Plague of Fantasies*. New York: Verso, 1998.

PAUL BUDRA is the author of *"A Mirror for Magistrates" and the de casibus Tradition* (2000) and co-editor of the essay collections *Part Two: Reflections on the Sequel* (1998) and *Soldier Talk: The Vietnam War in Oral Narrative* (IUP, 2004). He has published on early modern literature, historical writing, and contemporary popular culture. He is an Associate Professor in the English Department at Simon Fraser University and Associate Dean of the Faculty of Arts and Social Sciences.

CLINT BURNHAM is the author of *The Jamesonian Unconscious* (1995), *The Benjamin Sonnets* (2007), and other works of criticism, fiction, and poetry. His latest book is *The Only Poetry That Matters: Reading the Kootenay School of Writing*. He is an Associate Professor in the English Department at Simon Fraser University.

DARREN JAMES HARKNESS completed his M.A. in 2008 in humanities computing, focusing on a theoretical study of the development of online identity in blogging. He currently works as a web developer and project manager for Athabasca University's e-lab, researching and implementing innovative uses of web-based technology to deliver quality online instruction and research. He has written books and articles on the Apache web server, social media, web design, and intranet development.

DANIEL KEYES has written articles and book chapters on film and television since completing his dissertation on daytime talk shows at York University in 1998. He is a co-editor of *Hinterland of Whiteness* (2012), with Luis Aguiar and Lawrence Berg, and serves as a reviewer of media studies publications for *PsycCritiques*. Keyes is an Associate Professor of English and cultural studies at the University of British Columbia, Okanagan, where he currently serves as the Director of Interdisciplinary Graduate Studies.

ANDREAS KITZMANN is an Associate Professor in the Department of Humanities at York University. He has written widely on the impact of communications technology on the construction and practice of identity, memory, and electronic communities, and on the influence of new media on narrative conventions. His publications include *Saved from Oblivion: The Place of Media, from Diaries to Web Cams* (2004), *Hypertext Handbook: The Straight Story* (2006), *Memory Work*, as co-editor with Conny Mithander and John Sundholm (2005), and *Memory and Migration: Multidisciplinary Approaches to Memory Studies*, co-edited with Julia Creet (2011).

PHILIP A. KLOBUCAR writes and teaches on internet research, electronic literature, and social media. Recent articles include "Between the Pixel and Word: Screen Semantics," *Hyperriz: New Media Cultures*; and "Lines of Sense: Aesthetics and Epistemology in the Poetics of Louis Zukofsky," *Talisman: Journal of Contemporary Poetry and Poetics*. His current book project is *From the Lamp to the Screen: Programmable Writing and the Aesthetics of Information*; he is an Assistant Professor of English at New Jersey Institute of Technology.

TANIS MACDONALD is the author of *Rue the Day* (2008) and two other books of poetry, as well as the editor of *Speaking of Power: The Poetry of Di Brandt* (2006). Her latest book is *The Daughter's Way: Canadian Women's Paternal Elegies*. She is an Associate Professor in the Department of English and Film Studies at Wilfrid Laurier University.

C. W. MARSHALL is an Associate Professor of Greek and Roman theater at the University of British Columbia, Vancouver. He is the author of *The Stagecraft and Performance of Roman Comedy* (2006) and has co-edited, with Tiffany Potter, volumes on *Battlestar Galactica* (2008) and *The Wire* (2009), and, with George Kovacs, *Classics and Comics* (2011).

ALESSANDRO PORCO is a Ph.D. candidate at the State University of New York, Buffalo; his dissertation focuses on hip-hop poetics. He is the editor of *Population Me: Essays on David McGimpsey* (2010) and the author of two poetry books, *Augustine in Carthage* (2008) and *The Jill Kelly Poems* (2005).

TIFFANY POTTER specializes in both eighteenth-century literature and popular culture studies at the University of British Columbia. Her most recent book is the edited collection *Popular Culture, Women and the Eighteenth Century* (2011); and, with C. W. Marshall, she is co-editor of volumes on *The Wire* (2009) and *Battlestar Galactica* (2008). Her research on eighteenth-century theater includes work on Elizabeth Cooper's 1735 comedy *The Rival Widows; or, Fair Libertine* (2007) and Robert Rogers's 1766 historical tragedy *Ponteach; or, The Savages of America* (2010).

KIRSTEN C. USZKALO is the author of *The Witch and Prophet in Print* (2012), the lead of the Witches in Early Modern England Project, and a co-editor of the journal *Preternature: Critical and Historical Studies on the Preternatural*. She has published on early modern literature and popular cultures as well as digital humanities. She is an adjunct professor at Simon Fraser University, a CIRCA scholar at the University of Alberta, and an e-lab scholar at Athabasca University.